Hidden Genocides

THE CENTER FOR THE STUDY OF
GENOCIDE, CONFLICT RESOLUTION
& HUMAN RIGHTS

Genocide, Political Violence, Human Rights Series

Edited by Alexander Laban Hinton, Stephen Eric Bronner, and Nela Navarro

Alan W. Clarke, *Rendition to Torture*

Lawrence Davidson, *Cultural Genocide*

Alexander Laban Hinton, ed., *Transitional Justice: Global
Mechanisms and Local Realities after Genocide and Mass Violence*

Walter Richmond, *The Circassian Genocide*

Irina Silber, *Everyday Revolutionaries: Gender, Violence,
and Disillusionment in Postwar El Salvador*

Samuel Totten and Rafiki Ubaldo, eds., *We Cannot Forget:
Interviews with Survivors of the 1994 Genocide in Rwanda*

Ronnie Yimsut, *Facing the Khmer Rouge: A Cambodian Journey*

Hidden Genocides

Power, Knowledge, Memory

EDITED BY

ALEXANDER LABAN HINTON, THOMAS LA POINTE,
AND DOUGLAS IRVIN-ERICKSON

RUTGERS UNIVERSITY PRESS

NEW BRUNSWICK, NEW JERSEY, AND LONDON

LIBRARY OF CONGRESS CATALOGING-IN-PUBLICATION DATA

Hidden genocides : power, knowledge, memory / edited by Alexander Laban Hinton, Thomas LaPointe, and Douglas Irvin-Erickson.
    pages cm. — (Genocide, political violence, human rights series)
    Includes bibliographical references and index.
    ISBN 978–0–8135–6162–2 (hardcover : alk. paper) — ISBN 978–0–8135–6163–9 (pbk. : alk. paper) — ISBN 978–0–8135–6164–6 (e-book)
    1. Genocide—History. I. Hinton, Alexander Laban. II. LaPointe, Thomas, 1962– III. Irvin-Erickson, Douglas, 1982–
    HV6322.7.H53 2014
    364.15′1—dc23   2013006016

A British Cataloging-in-Publication record for this book is available
from the British Library.

Visit our website: http://rutgerspress.rutgers.edu

Manufactured in the United States of America

CONTENTS

PART ONE
Genocide and Ways of Knowing

PART TWO
Power, Resistance, and Edges of the State

PART THREE
Forgetting, Remembering, and Hidden Genocides

ILLUSTRATIONS

ACKNOWLEDGMENTS

This volume developed out of an academic conference, "Forgotten Genocides: Memory, Silence, and Denial," held in 2011 in New Jersey, co-sponsored by the Center for Peace, Justice and Reconciliation at Bergen Community College and the Center for the Study of Genocide, Conflict Resolution, and Human Rights at Rutgers University. We are grateful to the many participants and audience members whose comments and contributions helped make the conference such a success.

We extend special thanks to Seta Nazarian Albrecht and Joseph L. Basralian for raising the resources that made the conference and this volume possible. For their work on promotional materials for the conference and with the media, we thank the Bergen Community College public relations team, Joe Cavaluzzi and Tom Deprenda.

We also thank David Eichenholtz and Chris O'Hearn for their organizational support, as well as Jade Adebo, Sara Bradsema, Stephen Bronner, and Yannek Smith. We are particularly grateful to Nela Navarro for the support, advice, and energy she devoted to this project.

We wish to express our appreciation to the Bergen Community College Foundation and the Rutgers Newark Alumni Association for their support of the conference that led to this book. Thanks also to Barbara Yeterian for allowing us to use her painting *Genocide Series #22* as the cover art for this volume.

Finally, we are grateful to Marlie Wasserman, Marilyn Campbell, Allyson Fields, Molan Goldstein, and the rest of the team at Rutgers University Press for providing guidance and support throughout the editorial process, and to the external reviewers of this volume for their insights and suggestions.

Hidden Genocides

Introduction

Hidden Genocides: Power, Knowledge, Memory

DOUGLAS IRVIN-ERICKSON, THOMAS LA POINTE, AND ALEXANDER LABAN HINTON

Is slavery genocide?

On one level, a critical genocide studies asks us to consider whether slavery in the United States is a case of hidden genocide. But this is just the tip of the iceberg. As we consider such questions, we must challenge our taken-for-granted assumptions and ask why given cases have been ignored, denied, or deliberately hidden. The Turkish campaign of denial of the Armenian genocide provides a vivid example of this issue, involving a long period of forgetting and then, as the Armenian diaspora mobilized, attempting to discredit, divert attention from, and deny the idea that a genocide had taken place.

The United States has its own contingent of genocide deniers. A state senator from Colorado was recently quoted as saying that calling the U.S. treatment of American Indians "genocide" would diminish those in other countries "who actually died at the hand of governments."[1] Another, also of Colorado, said legislation recognizing genocide in the United States was disingenuous because "we have not destroyed totally the Native American people."[2] On the same day, this second senator signed legislation recognizing a day of remembrance for the Armenian and Rwandan genocides. One wonders, does she think there are no longer any Armenians or Rwandans alive? Most likely, this lawmaker's inconsistencies were underscored by her own narrow interest in getting reelected, recognizing and denying genocides while calculating the votes garnered and lost by taking each position.

Currently, we see movements afoot to recognize hidden genocides, such as the genocides against the Circassians, Assyrians, native peoples in the Americas and Australia, and formerly colonized peoples from across the world. We are fortunate to have chapters in this volume that consider all of these cases. These movements involve struggles with political regimes whose interests lie in denying genocide, and clashes with social forces dedicated to preserving unproblematic historical narratives that claim a given genocide never occurred.

But we should also be asking, to what extent have we as a scholarly community—as people—forgotten genocides not out of purposeful neglect but because of our own traditions, canonizations, and biases? Why, for example, have scholars—including Raphael Lemkin, who invented the concept of genocide—failed to fully consider whether the European and American trade in African slaves was a form of genocide? Why have we often remembered the Rwandan genocide as perpetrated only by Hutus against only Tutsi victims, without considering the executions of moderate Hutus, or the series of genocides before and after, as part of the same historical process? These are difficult questions to ask. But we must ask them if we want our field to continue to grow.

Critical Genocide Studies and Hidden Genocides

Our volume shares much with René Lemarchand's recent volume, *Forgotten Genocides: Oblivion, Denial, and Memory*, and Don Bloxham and Dirk Moses's *Oxford Handbook of Genocide Studies*, though our volume is focused more directly on the aforementioned intersection of power, knowledge, and memory.[3] A central theme of Lemarchand's book is the pattern of denial, silence, myth making, and historical revisionism by which so many genocides become forgotten. From Lemarchand's volume, it is clear that what is remembered and what is not remembered is a political choice, producing a dominant narrative that reflects the victor's version of history while silencing dissenting voices. Building on a critical genocide studies approach, this volume seeks to contribute to this conversation by critically examining cases of genocide that have been "hidden" politically, socially, culturally, or historically in accordance with broader systems of political and social power. As such, the contributions to our volume pick up discussions on the various dynamics related to power, knowledge, and memory that have led to certain cases of genocide being denied, diminished, or ignored.

The term *critical genocide studies* appears to have been first used by A. Dirk Moses in his 2006 essay "Toward a Theory of Critical Genocide Studies."[4] Moses draws on critical theory to argue that genocide studies would do well to explore larger global and materialist dynamics—as illustrated by the work of Immanuel Wallerstein and Mark Levene—that are the focus of a "post-liberal" perspective. Central to Moses's approach is Max Horkheimer's insistence that theory must be holistic, historical, and able to reflect on its own role in the process of social reproduction. More recently, in his essay "Critical Genocide Studies," Alexander Hinton has taken a Foucauldian and Derridian approach to argue that the field of genocide studies is premised upon a number of assumptions and biases, including gatekeeping notions underpinned by a dilution metaphor, Holocaust-centric models of the genocidal process, and a canon of cases (see fig. I.1, discussed below).[5] For genocide studies to continue to flourish, the field needs to explore its presuppositions, decenter its biases, and shed light on the blind spots.

One way to approach the problem of hidden genocides is through discourse analysis. In *The Archaeology of Knowledge*, Michel Foucault invites us to imagine what human discourse might look like in physical form. It would not look like the great mythical book of history, he writes, but rather an archive, filled with lines of words that transcribe the thoughts of others in distant places with a system that establishes these statements as actual events and things.[6] "The archive is first the law of what can be said," Foucault writes. It does not preserve every utterance for future memory but structures them through a silent process to prevent everything ever said from accumulating endlessly in an amorphous mass. The archive thus produces meaning, with a "system that governs the appearance of statements as unique events" in order to conceal the processes by which the archive was constructed so that the meaning of the archive feels uncontrived, self-evident, or natural.[7] In such a way, human discourses are shaped by silent processes that establish laws over what beliefs or statements are to be included, actively shaping what people believe is the truth of history in line with greater systems of social and political power.

Take the Colorado state senators' denial of the Native American genocide as an example. The statement that Native Americans did not "actually" die at the hands of the U.S. government illuminates a discourse in the United States that the "American" treatment of Native Americans was benevolent by instinct, and their deaths were unfortunate happenstance. We might suggest that a significant thread prohibited from entering this discourse is that the U.S. government, for most of its existence, stated openly and frequently that its policy was to destroy Native American ways of life through forced integration, forced removal, and death. An 1881 report of the U.S. commissioner of Indian Affairs on the "Indian question" is indicative of the decades-long policy: "There is no one who has been a close observer of Indian history and the effect of contact of Indians with civilization who is not well satisfied that one of two things must eventually take place, to wit, either civilization or extermination of the Indian. Savage and civilized life cannot live and prosper on the same ground. One of the two must die."[8]

The question for a critical genocide studies is not whether the United States did or did not commit genocide, however. Rather, we should be asking why U.S. society at one time acknowledged and celebrated the attempt to exterminate Native Americans, only to deny it in later generations and hide it discursively in the interstices of history. What interests are served by denying something that was openly said in the past? And, what is at stake by remembering this hidden genocide?

The process of knowing and the process of knowing history through language are ongoing. Historical interpretation, we contend, is always grounded in the interests and biases of the present historical moment. We approach the problem of hidden genocides noticing that existing idioms of genocide emphasize images of killing fields, concentration camps, and mass death. When one sees genocide as mass killing rather than a cultural destruction, the "truth" of history shifts and the entire conquest of the Americas looks different, David Moshman writes.[9] In the United States, mass killings of Native peoples became less frequent, slowly replaced by policies of cultural integration. Therefore, when we understand genocide to be synonymous with mass killing, we lay the foundation for understanding genocide as a dwindling phenomenon connected to a distant past, if at all.[10] These predispositions are revealed in the assertions of the Colorado senators—that the United States did not commit genocide against Native Americans because there were still Native Americans alive, or because the U.S. government did not "actually" use violence.

The chapters in this volume were originally written for a conference on "Forgotten Genocides: Memory, Silence, and Denial," co-hosted in March 2011 by the Center for the Study of Genocide, Conflict Resolution, and Human Rights at Rutgers University and the Center for Peace, Justice, and Reconciliation at Bergen Community College. The conference dealt with issues of memory, representation, denial, truth, memorialization, generational transmission, state ideology and silencing, definition, and diaspora. Participants considered a wide range of cases of hidden genocides, employing a critical genocide studies approach to varying degrees. A major theme of the conference, which translates into the participants' essays, is that the ferocity of the excesses of mass murder and genocide have too frequently been matched by the denial of these atrocities. Or, perhaps worse yet, genocides have seemingly been hidden, lost in the interstices of history and human discourse.

The authors in this volume approach the problem of hidden genocides in a variety of ways. As Donna-Lee Frieze turns to Emmanuel Levinas, and Daniel Feierstein to Raphael Lemkin, Adam Jones establishes a productive historiography of hidden genocides through Thomas Kuhn's classic *Structure of Scientific Revolutions*. Realist approaches are very productive as well, as denying genocide is often in line with concrete political interests. For Hannibal Travis, ethnonational realpolitik and the privileging of present-day concerns played a significant role in hiding genocides against Greeks and Assyrians as the historical narrative of the Armenian genocide took shape. As scholars, we have a responsibility to trace the ways in which both genocide and the hiding of genocides manifest as social practices, as well as political and historical processes, using a variety of methodological tools at our disposal.

Genocide and Ways of Knowing

The book is organized into three parts around the interrelated themes of knowledge, power, and memory. All three of these themes are deeply intertwined, especially because states and political communities define themselves through imagined pasts and shape official and collective memories accordingly.[11] Oftentimes, governmental institutions dynamically shape these discursive, historical narratives in broader society in order to assert the legitimacy of the state.[12] In post-genocidal societies where current regimes are built on a past generation's genocides, this often entails hiding genocides from historical memory through the law, public memorials, or state education policy. To think critically about why and how genocides become hidden in such ways, we begin by examining the way scholars know genocide and create knowledge about the phenomenon.

When people think of genocide, certain cases remain exemplary, first and foremost the Holocaust. A perusal of book publications, course syllabi, and popular discourse suggests a canon of cases: the Armenian genocide, Bosnia-Herzegovina, Cambodia, the Holocaust, and Rwanda. Historically, however, there are many cases of genocide from antiquity to modernity that are rarely described as genocide, if they are remembered at all. In other situations, largely forgotten genocides, such as the Armenian and Ukrainian cases, suddenly emerge into the foreground. In a recent article in *Genocide Studies and Prevention*, Alexander Hinton writes that to date there has been a strong bias toward a canon that often follows roughly along the lines depicted in figure I.1 (though the chart is, of course, an ideal type).[13]

Much scholarship in the field of genocide studies, especially from the 1980s through the 1990s, has focused on the Twentieth-Century Core, with the Holocaust both foregrounded and backgrounded. Taking up this task and asking whether or not the Holocaust's place in the canon has helped us remember or forget other genocides, Dirk Moses in his contribution to this volume looks at a controversy that arose over competing gallery space devoted to genocide at the Canadian Museum for Human Rights in Winnipeg. Placing the debate into the context of Canadian anxieties over other hidden genocides, Moses highlights the degree to which memory is believed by many people to be a zero-sum game, where memorializing one genocide is seen as obscuring others.

Human history is filled with genocide. Like the Angel of History in Walter Benjamin's allegory, we oftentimes look helplessly at countless human catastrophes, unable to bring back the dead and make whole the broken.[14] But some of the leading work on the anthropology of violence would remind us that human beings are not fated to violence by their nature, nor are violence, war, and genocide unavoidable parts of our social existence.[15] A genocide studies that critically engages hidden genocides therefore isn't simply about compiling a list of atrocities and documenting every human victim in books of facts written for jaded

Prototype	Holocaust
The Triad	Holocaust
	Armenian Genocide
	Rwanda
Twentieth-Century Core	Holocaust
	Armenians
	Cambodia
	Rwanda
	Bosnia
	Darfur (twenty-first century)
	Indigenous peoples (taken as a whole)
The Second Circle	Bangladesh
	Kurdish case
	Guatemala
	Herero/Nimibian
	Kosovo
	Carthage
	Settler genocides
	Ukrainian/Soviet
The Periphery	Indonesia
	Specific cases of indigenous peoples
	Genocides of antiquity
	Assyrian and Greek cases
	East Timor
	Burundi
	Maoist China
	DRC
Forgotten Genocides	Multitude of more or less invisible/hidden/ forgotten cases

FIGURE I.I. The Genocide Studies Canon

idlers in the garden of knowledge, to borrow Benjamin's phrase. We should move beyond simply documenting human suffering and expose the historical processes by which genocides are orchestrated, then denied, and later hidden where they can be forgotten in the first place.

One reason why scholars are often implicated in the hiding of genocides may well be a "liberal" tendency among some genocide scholars to seek "progress" and,[16] as the U.N. Genocide Convention states, "to liberate mankind from such an odious scourge." A critical genocide studies does not demand that we give up this objective but instead that we think about its genealogy and framings and our potential conceptual biases and thereby find new ways to approach the problem. How does the "savage"/"barbaric" Other we construct in our analyses of genocidists also construct, through inversion, an image of ourselves as modern, developed, and civilized? What do we miss by such identifications? Our gaze may too easily be directed away from the relationship of genocide and modernity and toward explanations of genocide that smack of ethnic primordialism, stage theory, atavism, or biological and psychological reductionism (our "barbaric" or "sadistic" "nature"—think of *Lord of the Flies*).

For instance, consider how metanarratives of progress and civilization structure our thinking.[17] Oftentimes, our belief in progress directs our gaze away from regimes we consider liberal and open, and toward genocidal despots and authoritarian regimes (think of how the names of Hitler, Pol Pot, and Milosevic so easily connote genocide). The U.N. Genocide Convention codifies this language, stating that genocide is "condemned by the civilized world." Such language implies that genocide is carried out only by "barbarians" and "savages," an understanding condensed by symbols such as the shrunken head from Buchenwald that was exhibited at Nuremberg.

There is a tendency in Western societies to view the violence of liberal democracies as "legitimate" while the violence committed in the name of unfamiliar political ideologies is condemned.[18] While genocide is brutal and to be condemned, it is not something that only "savages" and "barbarians" do. All peoples have the capacity to be genocidists, and genocide is also something that is closely intertwined with modernity and even democracy.[19] The discipline's longstanding neglect of Native Americans, slaves, and indigenous peoples illustrates this point.[20] These biases in our thinking contribute to widely held beliefs inside and outside of the academy that genocide afflicts "weak" or "failed" states and is more common in dictatorships and totalitarian or authoritarian regimes. This implies that genocide is unlikely or even impossible in strong states or democracies. A critical genocide studies would suggest that part of the reason why we remember certain genocides is because it makes "us" feel quite civilized and humane by contrast.

To relate this issue of canonization to our volume, we might say that the "barbaric/civilized" binary at work in the canon has produced a discourse that imagines Germany as "descending" into "savagery" with the rise of the Nazi party. But, as Elisa von Joeden-Forgey's chapter in this volume helps us to see, this narrative overlooks the era before the rise of the Nazi party—a time presumed to be more "civilized" by contrast, but nonetheless a deeply genocidal era as the German Imperial state conducted brutal and extensive genocides throughout its colonial empire.[21]

As is true of all canons, there has been fluidity with some groups (for example, the beginnings of a shift of the Ottoman Assyrian and Greek genocides from the status of invisible/forgotten genocides to the Periphery or perhaps even the Second Circle). The model in figure I.1 is, of course, an ideal type, but it points toward some of the disciplinary biases that have emerged in the field. For example, while cutting against the grain in many ways and discussing the Periphery or even Forgotten Genocides at times, Adam Jones's introductory text still gives primacy to the Twentieth-Century Core.[22] A similar statement could be made about readers and edited volumes in the field (see Frank Chalk and Kurt Jonassohn for an early exception).[23]

Issues of definition and canonization are not value neutral but also link to issues of power and knowledge. Why, we must ask, is it that certain cases of genocide are forgotten? The literature on denial has grappled with this question. But we also need to consider why we focus on certain cases and topics and what sorts of inclusions and exclusions ensue. What is left invisible to us and what can we do to cast light on what has formerly been opaque? Given the inevitable politicization of our topic, how might we be influenced by given interests and agendas?

Like all silenced historical narratives, there is a certain amount of victor's justice involved, whereby the people on the underside of power are removed from the story. Foucault may have been wrong when he claimed that genocide was the "dream of modern power," for surely genocide predates the modern state.[24] But Foucault was correct to point out that the battle of genocide does not involve two sovereign powers following the ritualized behaviors of standard warfare but rather one side using military force and other instruments of the state to exterminate an imagined group. So who is the victor when one side uses military, social, economic, or political force to exterminate an imagined group? We usually speak of none.

In his contribution to this volume, Daniel Feierstein returns to the definition of genocide provided by Raphael Lemkin, arguing that genocide re-creates the social world in the image of the perpetrators. Lemkin defined genocide as a colonial practice: "a coordinated plan of different actions aiming at the destruction of essential foundations of the life of national groups, with the aim of annihilating the groups themselves." Genocide had two phases: "One, the destruction of the national pattern of the oppressed group; the other, the imposition of the national pattern of the oppressor." Importantly, Lemkin defined nations as "families of mind" whose collective identity was built through shared symbols, art, languages, beliefs, mythologies, and so forth. He did not conflate the definition of a nation with the social groupings of the nation-state but believed such groups could include any imaginable human group.[25] Genocide, Lemkin believed, was an attempt to destroy "families of mind" in order to restructure the human cosmos. Any human group—such as a religious group, an ethnic group, or even "card players" or "tax criminals"—could be targeted for genocide.[26]

Feierstein's chapter allows us to argue that the social paradigms that are a part of the genocidists' ideology become the paradigms by which future generations remember the genocide. We follow Feierstein's lead and argue that genocidal mechanisms conspire to invent a target group and mobilize populations toward exterminating this imagined threat. These manufactured differences between the victims and perpetrators are made "real" by the very act of genocide being committed. Genocide, therefore, can be said to be a process that somehow transforms an imaginary community into a "real" one by attempting to obliterate the members of the imagined group. Death here functions as a kind of reality effect that confirms the authenticity of the imagined perpetrator group through the negation and suppression of the imagined victim group.

When genocide is denied, the dehumanizing mechanisms in place during the actual genocide are transferred forward in history, ensuring that the genocide continues into perpetuity, long after the physical killing has been done. When we remember genocide, therefore, we often do so in the terms and metaphors invented by the perpetrators. For example, it was the European settlers in North America who invented the concept of an Indian and labeled these people as one coherent group opposed to the peoples of Europe. In historical memory, the social diversity among the native peoples of North America has collapsed into one single category of "Indian" over time so that categorical binaries that frame the genocide place the European citizenry of the United States in opposition to the Indians. This not only denies the historical actuality of North American societies before the advent of the United States, but it makes the category of "Indian" a real category—a category that hides the full scope of the cultural and physical destruction on the North American continent while concretizing the identity of what it means to be an "American." These binary identities, steeped in connotations of the savage versus the civilized, were concretized within the context of a colonial and settler society that explicitly sought to exterminate the entire group of people. The legacy of genocide thus lives on within the political institutions and laws of the U.S. government, which relegates Indians to reservations and deals with them through an exploitative treaty system.[27]

Power, Resistance, and Indigenous Peoples

The second part of this volume looks at the elements of power and resistance involved in historically hidden genocides. Using newly available primary sources in recently opened Russian archives, Walter Richmond's contribution to this volume is the first systematic and scholarly work to document the genocide of the Circassian people as the Russian state expanded into their traditional homeland in the nineteenth century. Caught in the crosshairs of the Great Game, the Circassians bore the deadly brunt of British, French, and Russian imperial geopolitics. But it was the interests of the Russian state that finally spelled their doom. Richmond reveals that top Russian military commanders explicitly stated that the Circassians could never be consolidated into Russia, and had to be expelled if Russia were to hold the Circassians' strategically important homeland. The Russian state embarked upon a purposeful attempt to destroy the Circassian people as a group and repopulate the territory with the more favorable Cossack settlers. Currently, the Russian government does not deny that this region of the North Caucasus was the Circassian ancestral home. Denying that the events constituted genocide, Russia currently dismisses Georgia's acknowledgment of a Circassian genocide as a political slight stemming from their defeat in the brief 2008 war and accuses Circassian activists in diaspora of attempting to incite a Circassian rebellion within Russia.[28]

Our approach to hidden genocides implicitly acknowledges that the practice of state building often involves genocide. As imperial Russia did with the nineteenth-century genocides it committed, the United States, Canada, and Australia couched the destruction of entire peoples in the language of benevolence and progress. Chris Mato Nunpa notes in his chapter that the U.S. and European genocide against the peoples of North America—which reached its most cruel heights in the nineteenth century—resulted in a 98.5 percent extermination rate of indigenous peoples. While the genocide is currently denied and hidden, this was not always the case, Mato Nunpa shows. In fact, historically speaking, the genocide in North America is not a hidden genocide. United States policy makers and military commanders openly stated that they sought to exterminate any native peoples who resisted being dispossessed of their lands, subordinate them to federal authority, and assimilate them into the colonizing culture, Mato Nunpa notes. It was later generations that hid the genocide, in part because—as Moses writes in his chapter on the Canadian Museum for Human Rights—a government that derives political legitimacy from claiming to uphold universal human rights historically cannot admit that it was founded through genocide.

Frieze's chapter approaches a similar situation regarding the so-called Stolen Generations, where Aboriginal children were taken from their parents by Australian states to be raised as Australians of European descent. This practice of forced removal of children remained an official Australian policy up until 1970, long after Australia voluntarily became a party to the Genocide Convention. Why did Australian policy makers not realize that the forcible removal of children to facilitate the destruction of the Aboriginal group constituted genocide? Frieze asks. Were they ignorant of international law? How could something so clearly defined as genocide under the U.N. Genocide Convention have been conducted as if it were a humanitarian project? To approach the question, Frieze employs Emmanuel Levinas's *Otherwise than Being, or Beyond Essence* to help explain how perpetrators of genocide could come to see their acts as a form of benevolence toward the victims.

Forgetting, Remembering, and Hiding Genocides

Certain cases of genocide are recognized, intentionally hidden, written out of history, forgotten, and then remembered in new ways. In her chapter, Krista Hegburg traces a series of paradoxes that emerge from the Holocaust reparations program in the Czech Republic, which promised Czech political justice for the Romani peoples who suffered at the hands of Slovaks and Germans. Hegburg demonstrates how historical memory of the Holocaust was (and is) mobilized to create a newly imagined Czechoslovakian legal order which, in turn, shapes the way the Holocaust is actively remembered.

Even scholars of genocide have been implicated in the "unremembering" of genocides, Hannibal Travis writes in this volume. Prior to the 1960s, Travis notes, the Greek, Assyrian, and Armenian genocides were considered together as part of a broader anti-Christian persecution within Turkey. But, as the Armenian genocide became centralized in the historical narrative, the genocides against the Assyrians and the Greeks slipped under the surface of scholarly and popular historical memory. Travis critically investigates the processes by which the legal and scholarly language of genocide worked to hide these other genocides, as the concept of genocide came with stricter and narrower definitions than the term "massacre," leading many scholars to regard the experience of the Greeks and Assyrians as something other than genocide.

But a genocide does not have to be written out of history in order to be a hidden genocide. In some cases, as Frieze shows us, state policy and law crystallizes around a version of historical memory that does not consider the genocide to be an atrocity at all. These hidden genocides are not recognized as genocide in the first place. In her chapter, Elisa von Joeden-Forgey asks us why some genocides are hidden, in the sense that they are remembered not as genocides but as acts of benevolence. She argues that the identity of victims of Imperial Germany's genocides in southwestern Africa were constructed through legal categories that undermined cosmopolitan and humanist values in society but served to maintain the legal and social protections of German citizens. Joeden-Forgey thus provides us with an example of how genocide comes to lie hidden in plain sight, where observers in everyday life don't recognize the killing of victims going on around them as bad, or even as killings.

How are cases of genocide revealed and known historically, especially when they are interpreted by many as benevolent and just? How do scholars come to know these cases? Adam Jones's chapter in this volume provides a useful conceptual tool to account for how the field of genocide studies establishes paradigms of inquiry that constantly shift, placing canonical cases into new contextual light and establishing new conceptual frameworks. Jones writes that the canonical cases of genocide—the Holocaust, the Rwandan genocide, and the Armenian genocide serve as prime examples—often function as "anchoring genocides," to which other avenues of scholarship are tethered.

If blood in the sand is doomed to fade into oblivion, should we grieve? Must we remember? Allowing genocides to remain hidden has exacted its toll. We need only look to Jones's chapter for proof. The wider disinterest in the 1972 killings in Rwanda, and in the Great Lakes region of Central Africa as a whole, set a pattern that played out in the 1994 genocide, Jones argues. The killings in the Democratic Republic of Congo that followed the 1994 genocide have been *deliberately* "hidden genocides," he adds, not just because of disinterest but because of the determination of influential actors to keep them off the international agenda. It is our hope that the term "hidden genocides" will help to unmask the processes by which this genocide and others are denied or obscured while others are suddenly revealed, thereby providing some measure of historical light for those who suffered and perished at the crux of history's darkest chapters.

Conclusion

Clearly, certain historical events will be held up among others, not necessarily because they are important for the sake of historical truth or abstract notions of justice but because they speak directly to the constitution of power in our current world. Ideological perspectives that derive from political or material interests lead to blind spots in the historical record. Oftentimes, scholars and thinkers are swept up in this wake of history. But history, as Hegel reminds us, is a slaughter-bench where material and political interests underscore the processes by which certain horrors fade into oblivion while others suddenly emerge to the foreground. That is to say, we "remember" and "forget" genocides for reasons that serve greater systems of power than our individual selves. Understood this way, remembering and forgetting are two sides of the same coin. One seeks to reveal, the other to conceal. The relationship is a dichotomy, and there are concrete political, economic, and social interests in both. The blood of the victims whose deaths do not matter to the living is just blood in the sand, Hegel coldly tells us. The blood of those who matter to the living will be remembered.

When genocide studies first emerged as an academic field, for example, it was set to the backdrop of cold war concerns and politics. Even Raphael Lemkin dedicated much of his life in the 1950s toward charging the USSR with genocide in an effort to denounce communism as an economic and political system of social organization.[29] Likewise, Jean-Paul Sartre, the consummate scholar of imperialism who charged European colonial powers and the United States with genocide, diminished genocides that occurred in the wake of decolonization processes he supported.[30]

Today, as Feierstein reminds us in his chapter, ideological blind spots often lead us to conceal past and present genocides committed by strong states while calling attention to the genocides committed by weak states, or so-called pariah states. Indeed, we are also prone to overlooking the genocides upon which our modern states were built—especially the states we view as politically, morally, and socially legitimate. As Helen Fein reminds us, genocidal tendencies are embedded in the myths and ideologies that legitimize the modern state.[31] These include master narratives of benevolence, progress, and state building, which operate under the logic that what *did* happen was what *should have* happened.

From the sixteenth-century Spaniards who conquered the New World to the Khmer Rouge who meticulously photographed their prisoners in S-21, genocidists often provide the most elaborate documentation of their own actions available to the historian or scholar. Obviously, the blood they spill does not embarrass: they celebrate genocide. In a common twist of historical irony, we often find that governments that deny past genocides often violate the desires of the perpetrators of the genocides, who wished for their genocides to be known and remembered. Although hidden in history, the Native American genocide was documented proudly by the United States,[32] the Circassian genocide was chronicled in Russian imperial archives so that it would not be forgotten,[33] and the Armenian genocide was documented as a success by the Turkish state in the years immediately after it ended.[34] This means that the perpetrators believed at the time that it was actually in their interests to prove that the genocides happened. In remembering these genocides, we simultaneously remember how the perpetrator states built their legitimacy upon the bodies of those they killed and drove from their homes. It is entirely possible, therefore, that the perpetrators claimed genocide as a mark of victory—"the closing of the West"—and celebrated their attempt to destroy their victims.

The celebration of genocide places the genocide in full historical view, demanding that what the perpetrators did *not* be forgotten. Perhaps it is remembered not as genocide but as something other than genocide: a war for liberation, the necessary cost of law and order, progress, the cleansing of the social order for the common good, manifest destiny and the closing of national frontiers, or acts of benevolence. In such cases, we confront the paradox that the memory of genocide we seek to preserve might be what the perpetrators wanted to be remembered.

To return to our question about whether or not the slavery and segregation of African Americans was genocide, we would be served well to heed the writing of thinkers such as Paul Robeson. The institutionalized racism of the country, so deeply stitched into the social and political fabric of the nation, led

Paul Robeson to charge the United States with genocide. "We maintain," Robeson wrote in his 1951 petition to the United Nations, "that the oppressed Negro citizens of the United States, segregated, discriminated against and long the target of violence, suffer from genocide as the result of the consistent, conscious, unified policies of every branch of government."[35] Africans entered European modernity as property—not human beings.[36]

The Atlantic slave trade was genocide, trading in the commodity of humans with the intention of transforming the captured into slaves who were bought and sold, tortured, and killed. The Atlantic slave trade resulted in upward of twenty million deaths and the destruction of entire West African societies. As Adam Jones points out in his introductory textbook on genocide, beyond the deaths of those captured, the institution of slavery in the United States meets every criteria of genocide under the Genocide Convention, as well as the broader definition of genocide set forth by Raphael Lemkin.[37] The genocide against Africans captured in the slave trade and their descendants in the Americas had the effect of transforming "white" and "black" into "real" categories in U.S. society—a legacy that still haunts that society.

Long after the institution of slavery came to an end, Robeson contends, the U.S. government on the federal, state, and local levels continued to employ official policies that were intended to destroy, in whole, the population of people of African descent living in the United States. Leading civil society actors in the United States followed this policy directive, embarking on coordinated campaigns of terror and violence toward this genocidal end. As authors and editors of books and conference papers about forgotten or hidden pasts, we would be well served to look within our own pasts in search of hidden genocides and to make bold claims. By using the words "slavery" and "segregation," we in the United States might actually be concealing the genocide that took place against people who were targeted as a group because they drew their ancestry from one particular part of the earth. Such a discourse confines the human suffering caused by slavery to a single moment in history, long ago sealed off as part of a distant past.

Just how hidden is this genocide of slavery? In October of 2009, an Arkansas state representative made national headlines in the United States, stating "the institution of slavery that the black race has long believed to be an abomination upon its people may actually have been a blessing."[38] Echoing the belief that any human suffering was part of a long-distant past, sealed off from the present and vindicated by social progress, the senator reasoned that the descendants of slaves were better off now as Christians and Americans than they would have been if they had been born in Africa. For as much as these comments incited the passions of the public in support and condemnation, public discourse on both sides of the issue accepted the senator's two basic premises: that the legacy of slavery in the United States is part of the past, not the present; and that the descendants of slaves are better off now as Americans (and Christians). Those who criticized the belief that slavery was "a blessing" did so on the grounds of the massive human suffering of the slaves; they did not question slavery as "a blessing" by pointing to the legacy of slavery that lives on to this day, in the form of social and governmental institutions that survive, permutated and incarnate.

Where can we find the legacy of genocide? One location, Michelle Alexander argues, is the mass incarceration system that inherited the legacy of the Jim Crow laws, which were put in place across the United States to subordinate and effectively re-enslave those who were freed after the Civil War.[39] Today, the United States imprisons more of its minorities than any other country in the world, with a percentage of blacks in jail currently exceeding the percentage of blacks in prison in South Africa at the height of apartheid. Nearly 80 percent of young black men who live in the major U.S. cities have a criminal record, setting in motion a process of social and political marginalization that, among other things, strips people of their rights to vote and allows them to be legally discriminated against when seeking employment and housing. While the mass incarceration system in the United States does not exploit labor or subordinate an entire caste of people because of their skin color, as was the case with the institutions it succeeds, America's prisons have proven to be an efficient tool in marginalizing the country's low-skilled and badly educated poor who are labeled as criminals, stigmatized as superfluous, and seen as disposable pieces of a postindustrial economy who deserve to be politically and socially marginalized.

Within the context of the mass incarceration system in the United States, Alexander argues, the accusation of genocide that emerges from the country's poorest communities from time to time is not paranoid. If genocide scholars agree on one thing, it is that marginalizing and stigmatizing groups as disposable—which often entails stripping them of the rights of citizenship—are preconditions of genocide.[40] If the mass incarceration system was the inheritor of the Jim Crow segregation laws, then the history and legacy of genocide in the United States remain hidden in plain sight. By exploring the nexus of knowledge, power, and memory, this volume seeks to unpack the binaries and given assumptions about genocide that have led us to overlook or turn our attention away from hidden genocides.

NOTES

1. Simon Moya-Smith, "Senate Republicans Reject 'Genocide' to Describe Treatment of American Indians," *Indian Country Today*, May 2, 2012, accessed October 19, 2012, http://indiancountrytodaymedianetwork.com/ict_sbc/senate-republicans-reject -american-indian.

2. Ibid.

3. René Lemarchand, ed., *Forgotten Genocides: Oblivion, Denial, and Memory* (Philadelphia: University of Pennsylvania Press, 2011); Donald Bloxham and A. Dirk Moses, eds., *The Oxford Handbook of Genocide Studies* (New York: Oxford University Press, 2010). See also Frank Chalk and Kurt Jonassohn's groundbreaking volume, *The History and Sociology of Genocide: Analyses and Case Studies* (New Haven: Yale University Press, 1990).

4. A. Dirk Moses, "Toward a Theory of Critical Genocide Studies," in *Online Encyclopedia of Mass Violence*, ed. Jacques Semelin (Paris: SciencesPo, 2008), http://www.massviolence .org/Article?id_article=189.

5. Alexander Laban Hinton, "Critical Genocide Studies," *Genocide Studies and Prevention 7*, no. 1 (2012): 4–15.

6. Michel Foucault, *The Archaeology of Knowledge and The Discourse on Language*, trans. A. M. Sheridan Smith (New York: Pantheon Books, 1972), 128.

7. Ibid.

8. "Annual Report of the Commissioner of Indian Affairs, October 24, 1881," in *Documents of United States Indian Policy*, ed. Francis Paul Prucha (Lincoln: University of Nebraska Press, 2000), 154.

9. David Moshman, "Conceptions of Genocide," in *The Historiography of Genocide*, ed. Dan Stone (London: Palgrave, 2010), 86.

10. Ibid.

11. Alexander Laban Hinton, "Genocide and the Politics of Memory in Cambodia," in this volume.

12. Michel Foucault, *Discipline and Punish: The Birth of the Prison*, trans. Alan Sheridan (New York: Vintage, 1979).

13. Hinton, "Critical Genocide Studies."

14. Walter Benjamin, "On the Concept of History," in *Walter Benjamin: Selected Writings*, vol. 4, *1938–1940*, ed. Edmund Jephcot et al., trans. Howard Eiland and Michael W. Jennings (Cambridge, MA: Belknap Press of Harvard University Press, 2003), 392.

15. See the work of R. Brian Ferguson as summarized and cited in his recent article, "Ten Points on War," *Social Analysis* 52, no. 2 (2008): 32–49.

16. Moses, "Toward a Theory of Critical Genocide Studies."

17. Parts of this paragraph and the genocide studies canon chart are adapted from Hinton, "Critical Genocide Studies."

18. Neil Whitehead, "Violence and the Cultural Order," *Daedalus* (Winter 2007): 40–50.

19. Zygmunt Bauman, *Modernity and the Holocaust* (Ithaca, NY: Cornell University Press, 1989); Michael Mann, *The Dark Side of Democracy: Explaining Ethnic Conflict* (Cambridge: Cambridge University Press, 2005).

20. John H. Bodley, *Victims of Progress* (Menlo Park: Cummings, 1975); Ward Churchill, *A Little Matter of Genocide: Holocaust and Denial in the Americas, 1492 to the Present* (San Francisco: City Lights Books, 1997).

21. Jürgen Zimmerer and Joachim Zeller, eds., *Genocide in German South-West Africa: The Colonial War (1904–1908) in Namibia and Its Aftermath*, trans. Edward Neather (Monmouth: Merlin Press, 2008).

22. In a February 15, 2011, lecture at the Center for the Study of Genocide, Conflict Resolution, and Human Rights titled "Studying Genocide, Preventing Genocide," Adam Jones noted the dilemmas inherent in selecting cases and the dangers of canonization. His own efforts at grappling with these problems are illustrated in differences between the first and second editions of his books, with the first-edition chapter "The Armenian Genocide" being recast as "The Ottoman Destruction of Christian Minorities" in

the second edition. Similarly, he expanded the first-edition chapter "Stalin's Terror" to "Stalin and Mao" in the second edition. He noted that he self-consciously attempted to weave in a number of cases, ranging from attacks on witches to Iraq after the U.S. invasion, to cut against the grain of canonization.

23. Chalk and Jonassohn, *History and Sociology of Genocide.*

24. Michel Foucault, *History of Sexuality: An Introduction*, trans. Robert Hurley (New York: Knopf Doubleday, 1990), 137.

25. Douglas Irvin-Erickson, "Genocide, the 'Family of Mind,' and the Romantic Signature of Raphael Lemkin," *Journal of Genocide Research*, forthcoming.

26. Ibid.

27. See David E. Wiklins and Heidi Kiiwetinepinesiik Stark, *American Indian Politics and the American Political System*, 3rd ed. (Lanham, MD: Rowman & Littlefield, 2010).

28. Thomas Grove, "Genocide Claims Complicate Russian Olympics Plans," Reuters, October 13, 2011, accessed October 19, 2012, http://www.reuters.com/article/2011/10/13/us -russia-caucasus-olympics-idUSTRE79C2ST20111013.

29. Anton Weiss-Wendt, "Hostage of Politics: Raphael Lemkin on 'Soviet Genocide,'" *Journal of Genocide Research* 7, no. 4 (2005): 551–559.

30. Jean-Paul Sartre, "On Genocide," *Ramparts* (February 1968): 37–42. Also see Leo Kuper, *Genocide: Its Political Uses in the Twentieth Century* (New Haven, CT: Yale University Press, 1981), 45.

31. Helen Fein, *Accounting for Genocide* (New York: Free Press 1979), 8.

32. Chris Mato Nunpa, "Historical Amnesia: The 'Hidden Genocide' and Destruction of the Indigenous Peoples of the United States," in this volume.

33. Walter Richmond, "Circassia: A Small Nation Lost to the Great Game," in this volume.

34. Taner Akçam, *A Shameful Act: The Armenian Genocide and the Question of Turkish Responsibility* (New York: Metropolitan Books, 2006), 207–208.

35. Paul Robeson, *We Charge Genocide: The Historic Petition to the United Nations for Relief from a Crime of the United States Government against the Negro People* (1951; rpt. New York: International Publishers, 1970), xiv.

36. Cornell West, "The Ignoble Paradox of Modernity," in *The Cornel West Reader* (New York: Basic Books, 1999), 51–53.

37. Adam Jones, *Genocide: A Comprehensive Introduction*, 2nd ed. (New York: Routledge, 2010), 39–41.

38. Chuck Bartels, "Arkansas Rep Calls Slavery 'Blessing in Disguise,'" *Chicago Sun-Times*, October 6, 2012, accessed October 19, 2012, http://www.suntimes.com/news/ elections/15611617–505/arkansas-rep-calls-slavery-blessing-in-disguise.html.

39. Michelle Alexander, *The New Jim Crow: Mass Incarceration in the Age of Colorblindness* (New York: New Press, 2012). The following two paragraphs are drawn from Alexander.

40. Ibid., 218–220.

ONE

Genocide and Ways of Knowing

1

Does the Holocaust Reveal or Conceal Other Genocides?

The Canadian Museum for Human Rights and Grievable Suffering

A. DIRK MOSES

Whether public memory of the Holocaust reveals or conceals other genocides is a common—and controversial—question. Many take it as given that widespread shock about the Holocaust caused the "human rights revolution," crowned by the U.N. Universal Declaration on Human Rights and the Convention on the Prevention and Punishment of Genocide in 1948. By increasing sensitivity about gross violations generally, the Holocaust is said to inspire interest in and research on other genocides. After all, was not the genocide concept itself, coined by the Polish-Jewish lawyer Raphael Lemkin in 1943, modeled on the wartime persecutions, deportations, and mass murder of Jews?[1] The Holocaust's institutionalization in official memorial days by the United Nations, Great Britain, and other countries is held to show that it has become the bedrock of a new, global, cosmopolitan ethic that is newly sensitive to others' suffering. In these ways, it is claimed, the Holocaust reveals other genocides.[2]

Skeptics are not so sure. A close reading of the U.N. debates in the second half of the 1940s shows that its human rights regime cannot be deduced from Holocaust consciousness because no such consciousness then existed. Contemporaries referred broadly to civilian victims of the Nazis rather than only to Jewish ones; Nazi criminality in general rather than the Holocaust in particular was a background context of the U.N. human rights regime.[3] What is more, the Holocaust's later iconic status purveys a false universalism that obscures alternative forms of traumatic violence, let alone other genocides: only that which resembles the Holocaust is a legible transgression—which accounts for the seemingly ubiquitous effort of so many victim groups to affix the term "holocaust" to their suffering.[4] Far from constituting a symbolic idiom that empowers non-Jewish victims to win public recognition, the Holocaust occludes their experiences by establishing an unattainable monumental threshold. In these ways, it is claimed, the Holocaust conceals other genocides.

This debate has come to a head in the controversy about the new Canadian Museum for Human Rights (CMHR) in Winnipeg, Manitoba. The bitter, public wrangle about its projected core Holocaust gallery is a textbook case study of hidden genocides at the intersection of power, knowledge, and memory. Enshrining the Nazi genocide of Jews as the unique lens, template, yardstick, paradigm, or prototype—these are the terms of the discussion—with or through which to understand all genocides and human rights violations satisfies Jewish communal leaders who fear that the Holocaust will be hidden when not specially highlighted, as I explain below. By contrast, leaders of some other migrant groups assert that their powerlessness means the genocides and human rights abuses endured by their compatriots have been hidden from memory and research agendas—and often still are—and are therefore inadequately represented in the museum. Arguing, as many do, that the Holocaust is the "best documented" genocide and therefore best suited for the pedagogical purpose of exemplifying human rights violations misses the point, according to these critics. They think that injustice led to the lack of documentation about other genocides in the past and that the CMHR is compounding it by reproducing historic power imbalances in the exhibition's Holocaust-centric design.

We are left with a standoff in which Jewish communal leaders and their academic supporters maintain that foregrounding the Holocaust "in no way" diminishes other genocides, while the communal leaders who exert proprietary memory rights over those other genocides vehemently dispute this assertion. Indeed, they suggest that dedicating a gallery to the Holocaust while the five genocides recognized by the Canadian state—Armenia, the Holodomor (the Soviet famine genocide against Ukraine in 1932–1933), the Holocaust, Srebrenica (in Bosnia), and Rwanda—are showcased together in the smaller "breaking the silence gallery," evinces prejudice and racism because it prioritizes the one over the many, thereby violating Canada's multicultural consensus about equal treatment of migrant communities.[5] Moreover, how fair is the Holocaust's representation in two galleries, complain communal leaders? As might be expected, they in turn are accused of anti-Semitism.[6]

In a Darwinist zero-sum game, the highlighting of the one group's genocide is experienced as obscuring another's. Moreover, the other's memory also represents a threatening reversion to the dark days of the interwar, war, and immediate postwar years before public recognition of one's genocide. The other's memory even stands as an unbearable reminder of one's former subordinate social status in the country of origin, rekindling traumatic memories of the vulnerability and violence that led to emigration. This constellation inevitably pressures Canada's multicultural tapestry of Indigenous and migrant communities, which ostensibly support the official policy of equity, inclusivity, and social cohesion.

It is noteworthy that these memory wars were unleashed by the imperative for *government* recognition of victim status. After all, communally founded and sponsored museums and memorials to past suffering dot the Canadian urban and rural landscape; there is no shortage of memory about traumas that occurred locally and abroad. The campaigns to have them officially validated seems driven by a fear that if *their* memory is officially recognized, then *ours* is hidden—again. In trying to understand these fraught interactions, Judith Butler's notions of grievability, precariousness, and precarity lay bare the grand psychodrama driving the debate. Ideologically loaded public frames screen out certain forms of human suffering and loss while others "become nationally recognized and amplified": they are grievable, eligible for mourning's affective investment. The Canadian memory competitions concern the "differential allocation of grievability."[7] The competition is driven by an acute sense of precariousness, which connotes not only vulnerability but the fact that one's own existence is ultimately socially dependent, that is, in the hands of others.[8] Far from this realization leading one group to empathize with another group's suffering and to concomitant solidarity, as Butler hopes, the evidence suggests the opposite conclusion, namely that consciousness of precariousness and memories of what she calls precarity—exposure to violence from an arbitrary state or inadequate support networks—lead to frantic efforts to win grievable status, because such status might ensure public safety. Fear of precarity drives the Canadian dispute because contemporary events are interpreted as potential repetitions of past traumas, the "terror of history."[9] Thus Jewish Canadian leaders insist on the centrality of Holocaust memory because they think anti-Semitism is on the rise, yet again, and that Israel is, as always, under siege, while Ukrainian Canadian leaders worry about pernicious Russian influence in sabotaging newly won Ukrainian independence. It is a struggle for permanent security.

Not all migrant community leaders feel this way. Some, like the Chinese Canadian community, do not oppose the CHMR configuration so long as its stories are included. Indeed, its leaders do not feel the need to press for a victim framing of their experiences.[10] The Armenian leadership seems mollified after initial concern, although Armenian Canadian scholars at the Zoryan Institute remain unconvinced.[11] The competitive intersections of specific memories in relation to grievability and precarity need to be carefully identified and explained, for Holocaust memory is plainly experienced in different ways by different community leaders, helping reveal their suffering in some cases while concealing it in others; or so they claim. A related question posed by the participants is whether the Holocaust's intensifying public commemoration is based

on its inherent differences from other genocides or is the result of more successful advocacy, or both. Was the Holocaust *discovered* after decades in obscurity or
made by an upwardly mobile Jewish community?

The power/knowledge/memory nexus and clash of perspectives about the
function of Holocaust memory that I analyze below suggests the impossibility
of appealing to a supposedly authoritative body of facts as a neutral source of
adjudication. The players' partisan rhetorical strategies also render suspect the
universal claims they make. But if an epistemological vantage point for assessing rival frameworks is therefore unavailable, an ethically preferable subject
position may be entertained, namely that of some Indigenous Canadian leaders
and writers. First Nations, Inuit, and Métis, after all, were the initial object of
discourses about humanity in Canada—the notorious trichotomy of savagery,
barbarism, and civilization—in whose name they were conquered, dispossessed,
massacred, and subject to governmentalities, like residential schools and forced
adoptions, designed to culturally destroy them, which had devastating physical
and psychological effects.[12]

As I suggest below, it is with Indigenous Canadians that Butler's ideal of
empathy and solidarity in recognized precariousness is discernible. For in the
manner of a critical theory of genocide studies, their experiences call into question the self-congratulatory human rights project itself, because their suffering
at the hands of European settler colonialism implicates the category of humanity
and the savagery/barbarism/civilization trichotomy that continues to animate
Western political culture.[13] It was with the aim of elevating Aboriginal children
into the full humanity of white civilization that they were taken from their families and placed into residential schools—a policy that persisted into the 1980s.
Holocaust memory does not fundamentally challenge this order because, from
the outset, the Holocaust was coded as the consequence of Nazi barbarism.[14]
Indeed, human rights supplanted the Eurocentric language of civilization after
World War II while performing the same function of distinguishing between the
human and the not-quite or -yet human.[15] And before the residential schools
lies the Europeans' foundational violence to gain possession of this portion of
the continent, violence that was also justified in civilization's name. The human
rights project narrates the past teleologically to culminate in the omniscient
and morally smug humanitarian subject, but it can only extricate itself from
this foundational violence and subsequent policies to "civilize the natives" by a
willful blindness to powerful discursive continuities. The limits of the humanitarian subject's reflexivity are its implications in the genocidal moments it has
perpetrated against Indigenous people.

In view of the intuition that Indigenous experiences ought to be central
in any *Canadian* museum dedicated to human rights, it is remarkable (though
unsurprising) that Indigenous voices were entirely absent in the debates leading

up to the CMHR and that the museum integrates their stories of abuse into a progressive, national, human rights narrative. The grievability of Indigenous victims is a relatively recent development, and the attempt to eliminate their cultures is plainly a question that is difficult for a state-run museum to countenance. To be sure, the Canadian government apologized for the residential school catastrophe in 2008, but not for its own existence.[16] The sovereignty that enabled these polices, far from being questioned, was strengthened by arrogating to itself the ability to selectively condemn the past and incorporate Indigenous people into a redeemed national project. As a proclaimed "human rights leader," it is impossible for the state to admit a genocidal foundation. This is a genocide whose name dare not be spoken in the museum; it is a "conceptual blockage" and will remain concealed, impervious to the progressive narrative of Holocaust consciousness that participates in rather than challenges the enduring savagery/barbarism/civilization categories.[17] Instead of providing a narrative account of the CMHR controversy, this chapter analyzes the background anxieties about "hidden genocides" in the Canadian debate in order to understand its hidden motor.[18]

Entangled Grievability before the CMHR

Long before the dispute's apex in 2010 and 2011, the grievability dispute had been under way in competition between Jews and Ukrainians for public recognition of their suffering in Europe in the 1930s and 1940s. Fatally, their competition is sharpened by the entwinement of these cases, compounding the field's zero-sum logic. For, as we will see, Jewish communal leaders condemn as Holocaust co-perpetrators those Ukrainian nationalists whom many Ukrainians hail as heroic resisters to Polish, German, and Soviet imperial domination, while at least some Ukrainians have accused Jews of collaborating with the Soviet regime in attempting to destroy Ukraine in the 1930s.

The accumulation of grievances stretches back to the First World War, when Canadian authorities interned ethnic Ukrainians—migrants from the Austro-Hungarian Empire—as "enemy aliens" until 1920. Of the approximately 8,500 interned men, 109 died and the others were exploited as virtual slave labor. Some 80,000 others had to register with the police as suspected security risks.[19] The injustice, suffering, and humiliation have been a sore point ever since.[20] Jewish refugees in the 1930s, for their part, were denied entry to Canada—then with the world's most restrictive immigration policies—and could point to prevalent anti-Semitism as one of the reasons. The entwinement of suffering intensified at this moment. For at the same time, Ukrainian Canadian activists for a non-Soviet, independent Ukraine, who were mostly veterans of the war against Poland between 1918 and 1921, complained that recognition of the

Soviet's famine crime of 1932–1933 and Polish repression of its large Ukrainian minority was overshadowed by the Nazi persecution of German Jews. They were incensed by the League of Nations' support of the Polish claim to Western Ukraine and wanted to revise those boundaries. As revisionists, they were open to Nazi anti-Bolshevism and its anti-Polish and anti-Western stance to the extent that it furthered their national liberation project. Some of them shared the Nazis' paranoid views about "Judeo-Bolshevism," a prejudice of a piece with the conviction that Ukrainian Jews were somehow responsible for the loss of the war with Poland. Although the veteran-nationalists represented only a tiny minority of Ukrainian Canadians, the community was largely indifferent to contemporary Jewish suffering in Europe even if it did not share the nationalists' pro-Nazi views.

Herewith began the calculus whose logic dictated that grief for "them" came at "our" expense, particularly when our tolerated or hidden suffering demonstrated that we were profoundly ungrievable. One could not narrate the 1930s in a cogent manner that allowed both groups to be victims. The messiness of history did not lend itself to the morality tale that both needed to make sense of their suffering and to project it publicly. Thus a Ukrainian Canadian newspaper editor declared in 1933 that "the world press writes a great deal about Hitler's 'terror' against the Jews in Germany, although compared to the Soviet terror against Ukrainian people it is like a tiny drop of water in the sea."[21] That was a fair comment in 1933 and even after the Kristallnacht pogrom in 1938 in view of the various forms of violence that Ukrainian civilians had endured from the Polish and Soviet states. The subsequent genocide of European Jews challenged this posited hierarchy of suffering; the task would become to share equal billing.

Nowhere was this challenge more evident than in the shared space of displaced persons (DP) camps in postwar occupied Germany, inhabited by surviving Jews and non-Jewish nationals of the many countries that the Nazis had conquered and from which they had imported slave laborers. In view of their terrible experiences, Jews tended to regard their fellow inmates as co-perpetrators of the Holocaust rather than as fellow victims of the Germans, so much so that many insisted on separate Jewish representation and treatment rather than inclusion as members of the formerly occupied European countries. Here was a key moment in the Zionist ethnogenesis that has animated Jewish communities ever since, whether in Israel or abroad: the thesis of collective world guilt for the Holocaust, the uniqueness of Jewish suffering, and insistence of separate political representation. Solidarity and common projects between Jews and non-Jews proved accordingly difficult, if not impossible, as Anna Holian describes.

> There were also painful efforts at dialogue between Jewish and non-Jewish DPs. In Munich, for example, a group of Lithuanian DPs met with Lithuanian Jewish survivor and DP leader Yosef Leibowitz to discuss the

possibility of working together for the liberation of Lithuania. The meeting ended badly: the Lithuanian delegation was unwilling to provide an unqualified acknowledgment of Lithuanian complicity in the Holocaust, and Leibowitz determined it was impossible to work with them. Such encounters no doubt reinforced support for separation.[22]

Lithuanian nationalists would not be the only Europeans for whom such acknowledgment would be unbearable, because some of their national liberation heroes had used the Nazi occupation to destroy Jewish communities they regarded as loyal to the hated Soviet regime. Moreover, Polish and Ukrainian political prisoners—nationalists who had been persecuted by the Soviets—resented Jewish competition for victim status; such status entailed better treatment in the camp and rehabilitation prospects.[23] The acrimony was a sign of things to come forty years later in Canada.

The question of Nazi war criminals in Canada exercised Jewish leaders who regarded their residence there as a persistence of the anti-Semitism that had callously excluded Jewish refugees in the 1930s. Indeed, "the Jewish community was the first victim of the Canadian post-war system of immunity for war criminals," wrote David Matas, a local lawyer, former chairman of the Canadian Jewish Congress's (CJC) Legal Committee on War Crimes, and representative of the League for Human Rights of B'nai Brith.[24] He and other Jewish leaders bitterly resented that it was apparently easier for such criminals to emigrate to Canada after the war than for Jewish DPs. It was a "moral outrage" that "massive numbers" of them—Germans and their Slavic and Baltic collaborators—had found a "haven" in the country, thereby creating "a political constituency for doing nothing."[25] Tolerating their presence was tantamount to "allowing the victims to be murdered not once, but twice. First their lives would have been obliterated, then their deaths."[26] The government's lack of interest in prosecutions evinced an absence of "any moral sensibility about the Holocaust," complained Irwin Cotler, a legal academic and CJC president between 1977 and 1980. "The Holocaust itself is reduced to a footnote. There is no sense, no appreciation about the horrors of the Holocaust." It also was outrageous that efforts to bring war criminals to justice could be dismissed as "Jewish revenge."[27] Jewish deaths were not grievable in Canada, he and Matas were saying, and it was time to challenge this travesty.

The solicitor general in the Trudeau government in the early 1980s, Robert Kaplan, raised the question at a high level by pushing the investigation of a former Einsatzgruppen member, whom he had extradited from Canada to Germany in 1983. Sol Littman, the Canadian director of the Simon Wiesenthal Center, founding editor of the *Canadian Jewish News*, and first director of League for Human Rights of B'nai Brith, wrote a book about the case and claimed that twenty-eight war criminal suspects who had belonged to the Ukrainian SS units were living in Canada.[28] After questions were raised in Parliament, the Canadian government established the Commission of Inquiry on War Criminals in Canada, known as the Deschênes Commission, in 1985 to investigate such allegations. Cotler became the CJC's chief counsel at the commission in 1986.

The commission's mandate immediately raised the hackles of Ukrainian and Baltic communities, which felt collectively defamed. Two dimensions were particularly vexing; the prospect of the commission's soliciting evidence from the Soviet Union, whose anti-Ukrainian position they naturally distrusted, and the commission's singular focus on crimes committed during the Second World War, which effectively limited them to those against Jews. Stalinist crimes against Ukrainians in the 1930s were omitted. If the Jewish community and government were truly interested in cleansing the country of war criminals, why not included communist crimes and seek out suspects who had migrated to Canada? "Limiting the work of the Deschênes Commission only to Nazi criminals is selective and incomplete justice," complained the Ukrainian Canadian historian Roman Serbyn.[29] Matas's and Cotler's responses to this point could not get around the commission's partial focus.[30] Nor did Cotler deny that ethnic "slurs" had been made against Ukrainian and Lithuanian Canadians as a result of the war crimes campaign. But he wondered why they resisted the commission's work all the same and were so sensitive when other migrants groups like Germans seemed less outraged.[31]

As might be expected, Ukrainian Canadian community activists mobilized against "the unfounded allegations about 'Nazi war criminals' in Canada," establishing the Civil Liberties Commission in 1984; two years later it became the Ukrainian Canadian Civil Liberties Association (UCCLA), one of the main players in the CMHR controversy in addition to the establishment Ukrainian Canadian Congress (UCC).[32] At the same time, the UCCLA launched a campaign for an official accounting of the Ukrainian internment during and immediately after the First World War, including an investigation of the internees' confiscated property. Those victims needed public grieving while Jewish ones were in the headlines. The public memory stakes were escalating.

Ultimately, the Deschênes Commission was a disappointment for Jewish leaders, yielding only a few deportations and no convictions—outcomes they attributed to the bureaucratic inertia and general apathy regarding Jewish suffering about which they had long complained.[33] Another strategy of accumulating grievability lay in having each Canadian province legislate for Holocaust Memorial Day, and this became a major project of the 1990s. Now the Holocaust was not to be remembered only for the victims' sake but was made relevant for all Canadians by drawing human rights lessons from its history. Thus the Manitoban legislation of 2000 for "Yom Hashoah or the Day of the Holocaust" states that it "is an opportune day to reflect on and educate about the enduring lessons of the

Holocaust and to reaffirm a commitment to uphold human rights and to value the diversity and multiculturalism of Manitoban society."[34] The next year saw the introduction of a teacher's guide for Holocaust Memorial Day that included the League for Human Rights of B'nai Brith's "Holocaust and Hope" program.[35]

The League for Human Rights of B'nai Brith is an organization "dedicated to combating antisemitism, racism, and bigotry" and protecting the "human rights of all Canadians."[36] The former Canadian branch of the Anti-Defamation League (ADL) embraced the language of human rights garb as it became prevalent in Canada in the early 1970s.[37] The ADL agenda remained in the league's dual mission of countering both anti-Semitism and "hate group activity" more generally, thereby uniting the particular (protecting Jews) with the universal (protecting everyone).[38] Including the Holocaust in the mandate was straightforward because the league attributed its causes to anti-Semitism: the Holocaust was the ultimate hate crime. Accordingly, the lesson to draw was toleration—along the lines of the Museum of Tolerance of the Simon Wiesenthal Center in Los Angeles.[39] For such institutions, the universal and particular harmonized foremost in the protection of Jews, because they were the universal victim.

The universalizing agenda linking the Holocaust with genocide prevention and human rights was explained in 1992 by Matas in an article revealingly called "Remembering the Holocaust Can Prevent Future Genocides." Extolling the League for Human Rights of B'nai Brith's "Holocaust and Hope" program, "which offers to Canadian educators tours of the death camps of Europe, followed by a visit to Israel," he gave a number of reasons for Holocaust memory's significance. Besides remembering the victims, it was necessary to use the Holocaust as an analogical resource: when we are so moved by the plight of contemporary refugees as to extend them a haven because they remind us of Jewish refugees, the Holocaust was performing its redemptive function. Never subtle, Matas added that the related and primary function of Holocaust memory was atonement: for the world was guilty of having stood by passively while Jews were murdered. "That dismal record means that the world must make atonement." Now it was imperative that this breach of human solidarity never recur, and non-Jews constantly recalling their implication in the genocide of the Jews would provide the necessary impetus.[40] Here a barely concealed sacrificial, indeed pseudo-Christian logic—that the Jews died for the world's moral redemption—combined with the Jewish tradition of *Tikkun olam b'malchut Shaddai*: repairing a (broken) world beneath God's sovereignty.[41]

Nineteen years later, Lubomyr Luciuk of the UCCLA published a book on the Ukrainian internment operations, also declaring a "time for atonement"—with a similar message: "The timely and honourable redress called for will help ensure that no other Canadian ethnic, religious, or racial minority will ever suffer as Canada's Ukrainians once did."[42] For the UCC and UCCLA, Ukrainians were also a universal victim. Two could play the grievability game of atonement. But who would win?

By the late 1990s, the game had moved to a different field: a national Holocaust exhibition or museum. In 1998, the CJC and B'nai Brith managed to have the notion of a dedicated Holocaust gallery placed on the agenda of a revamped Canadian War Museum. A subcommittee of the Canadian Senate considered public submissions on the matter, eliciting by-now-familiar positions. Opposing the proposition were Ukrainian Canadians, whose submission pleaded for a separate genocide museum or a Holocaust exhibition with all victims of Nazism, including Slavs.[43] Further opposition crystallized in the form of Canadians for a Genocide Museum, a new coalition of immigrant communities, established that year. It would become another player in the CMHR debate over the years.[44] The subcommittee rejected the Holocaust gallery in the War Museum but did not rule out "a national Holocaust Gallery" in another context, although neither did it rule out a genocide gallery.[45]

Disappointed but encouraged, Jewish groups pressed on. Eric Vernon, the CJC's director of government relations, was happy with the apparent "commitment on the table to establish a stand-alone Holocaust museum, which we now prefer to refer to as a Holocaust and human rights museum."[46] Unhappy with the drift of the discussion, Sarkis Assadourian, a Syrian-born politician of Armenian descent, tried to force the matter in a private members bill for an exhibition on crimes against humanity in the Canadian Museum of Civilization.[47] While supportive, the UCC continued to advocate a "federally funded Genocide Museum in Ottawa."[48] Caustic comments were irresistible. The *Canadian Jewish News* reported CJC president Moshe Ronen as suggesting that "lobbying for a genocide museum was being orchestrated by individuals who cannot tolerate the notion that the Holocaust was a form of genocide unlike any other, and that it is unique in history in 'terms of the size and scope of its murderous agenda.'" Ever a model of tact, Sol Littman accused John Gregorovich of the UCC of "issue envy" and of trying to portray Ukrainians as "victims." That was not allowed because, for him, they were perpetrators.[49]

Whether the Holocaust reveals or conceals other genocides was the topic of discussion of before the Canadian Parliament's Standing Committee on Canadian Heritage when it invited community and museum representatives to speak in regard to Assadourian's bill in mid-2000.[50] James Kafieh, a former president of the Canadian Arab Federation and later legal counsel for the Canadian Islamic Congress, spoke for Canadians for a Genocide Museum, pleading for the "forgotten victims—the Gypsies, the Ukrainians, the Cambodians."[51] Nate Leipicer, chair of the CJC's Holocaust Remembrance Committee, responded by declaring the Holocaust's uniqueness while trying to avoid giving offense to others: "All genocide, all human tragic events, are of equal importance. There's no question about that. We do not want to get into a contest on whose tragedy was larger or who suffered more." Then came the inevitable qualification: "However, the Holocaust encompasses all genocide and all mass murders, wherever they happen and whenever they occur." On this basis, the CJC proposed "a Holocaust and human rights museum that would focus on the Holocaust as such and would also include the question of human rights."[52] As always now, the human rights pedagogy would revolve around the Holocaust whose exhibition *as such* was the priority because it was an event of universal significance.

For the Jewish representatives like Sheldon Howard, director of government relations at B'nai Brith, it was possible to honor the Holocaust as unique—so it was "not just another example of state-sponsored killing in the 20th century"—"without in any way detracting from the other genocides perpetrated in the 20th century."[53] Here was the central anxiety expressed by Cotler before him. Plainly, Jewish leaders felt that the Holocaust was effectively concealed—a hidden genocide—if regarded as just another genocide. Such a diminution portended grave consequences for Jewish grievability by consigning Jews to the vulnerability they experienced before and during the Holocaust. This is the primal fear that animates the various Jewish memory campaigns. Only the world's recognition of its unique and universal features, with the concomitant atonement effect, would guarantee the safety of a tiny minority in a sea of potentially dangerous strangers. The imperative, therefore, was to have everyone believe that Holocaust memory was a universal good—that is, by deriving human rights from its history. Thus by embodying "universal" lessons, Howard continued, the Holocaust, could be a "central reference point" without "undermining the experience of other ethnic groups."[54] This was a prescient statement, for that is what came to pass at the CMHR. As we will see, Jewish leaders and journalists interpreted criticism of its dedicated Holocaust-centrism as tantamount to effacing the presence of the Holocaust altogether, when the critics were in fact arguing that it should be displayed like other genocides.

Subsequent speakers from other groups gestured to these points before the subcommittee: the Holocaust's universal lessons of antiracism, toleration, and refraining from mass murder could be learned from other genocides, as well. But there was another lesson: the evil of hiddenness. The Serbian representative, Dr. Svetlana Cakarevic, spoke about "the forgotten genocide of Serbs" in World War II and asked why it is "covered up." The Armenian representative, Barry Khojajian, pointed out that Armenians "did not have a Diaspora the way other people had," so the memory of its genocide was constantly threatened with oblivion. Ukrainian, Arab, and Rwandan representatives urged an "equitable" and "inclusive" genocide museum while sometimes pointing out the special, even "unique" dimensions of their own experiences. In the event, the standing committee recommended that academic institutions conduct research on "all genocides and crimes against humanity."[55]

The Absence of Aboriginal Canadians

At no point in these debates did participants consider the question of the first Canadians on whose land they lived. Could they have been victims of genocide as well? It was not as if the question had been ignored in other domains. It had not—but few were listening. At the very same time as the war crimes issue was gathering steam, in 1984, Judge Edwin C. Kimelman was chairing the Manitoban Review Committee on Indian and Métis Adoptions and Placements to investigate the so-called Sixties Scoop, the practice of forced adoption of Aboriginal children into non-Aboriginal families. Reporting that year, he wrote that "having now completed the review of the files . . . the Chairman now states unequivocally that cultural genocide has been taking place in a systematic, routine manner."[56] This finding would be cited by anyone interested in Indigenous affairs in the 1980s and 1990s.[57] Cultural genocide was also regularly alleged at the time by informed commentators, but they were few in number. Indigenous people were not yet fully grievable Canadians, judging by their absence at the parliamentary committee debates.[58]

Events during the 1990s had underlined this outsider status in relation to the unfolding scandal of the residential schools into which Aboriginal children had been forced during most of the twentieth century. After mounting disquiet about the issue in the 1980s, Chief Phil Fontaine publicly disclosed his own abusive experiences in 1990, the same year as the violent land rights dispute by the town of Oka, Quebec, leading to the wide-ranging Royal Commission on Aboriginal Peoples in 1991. The Royal Commission heard testimony about criminal acts of sexual abuse and physical violence by authorities that utterly discredited the residential school system. Even so, the government declined to launch the public inquiry for which the commission called in its 1996 report. Apparently concerned about the legal consequences of an apology, in 1998 it issued a "statement of reconciliation" that was curtly rejected by Indigenous groups.[59] There could be no reconciliation before an apology and compensation. Or education. Some settler Canadians claimed ignorance of the residential schools and few registered the depth of Aboriginal feeling about the issue; after all, the residential schools had been designed for Indigenous uplift, they thought. Adoptions and residential schools, however coercive, did not resemble genocide in the public mind. The Holocaust did. The residential schools policy was a genocide that an activist clergyman claimed was "hidden from history."[60] Writing in 1996, the historian J. R. Miller aptly observed that the Europeans' "sin of interference has been replaced by the sin of indifference."[61]

In response, Indigenous Canadians sought redress in the courts. Even the mixed results—nearly 15,000 survivors had tried to sue the government in individual and class actions, winning some $110 million—brought pressure to bear on the government and churches, which had administered the residential schools. Along with the Aboriginal Healing Foundation, which raised awareness of the residential schools' effects on Indigenous people, the suits led to negotiations that culminated in the Indian Residential Schools Settlement Agreement of 2006.[62] The agreement provided for a compensation process, support measures, commemorative activities, and establishment of a Truth and Reconciliation Commission (TRC) that sits to this day.[63] The government apologized two years later. The first decade of the twenty-first century saw the eventual intersection of these Indigenous issues and the broader genocide debate.

The Unstable CMHR Synthesis

In the meantime, the Winnipeg-based media magnate Israel Asper was formulating an ingenious synthesis of these developments. The bitterness of the Deschênes Commission issue and the state's reluctance to sponsor a Holocaust gallery or museum indicated the futility of memory wars with Ukrainian communal leaders who purported to represent over one million Canadians of Ukrainian descent, more than three times the number of Jewish Canadians. Moreover, Indigenous questions were now firmly on the table. Since 1997, Asper's philanthropic foundation had run a Human Rights and Holocaust Studies Program in the venerable tradition of the League of Human Rights of B'nai Brith and the Simon Wiesenthal Museum of Tolerance.[64] Might not the state support a human rights museum that included all citizens, especially Ukrainian and Indigenous Canadians? In 2003, Asper's proposal of just such a project won the approval of the UCC with the promise that the "Ukrainian Famine/Genocide" would feature "very clearly, distinctly, and permanently," as would the internment of Ukrainians during World War I.[65] "The museum will be the first place in the world where the famine will be given attention," gushed the UCC's executive director, Ostap Skrypnyk, gratified by the Jewish recognition of their grievability.[66] A separate Indigenous gallery also featured in the proposal.

Asper understood the line to take with the general public. His was to be a "museum for human rights, not the Holocaust," and it was to "be totally apolitical and antiseptic in terms of trying to preach a message of one kind of inhumanity over another." His staff spoke about "an all-inclusive Canadian genocide museum," using the rhetoric of Canadians for a Genocide Museum and the UCCLA.[67] Nonetheless, the latter organizations opposed the Asper plan as a Holocaust museum in human rights disguise, because a central Holocaust gallery remained in the mix. True to their principles, they wanted equal treatment for all genocides, which meant no special treatment for the Holodomor or Indigenous people, either.[68] The envisaged outcome was the same as the UCC position, however: whether the Holodomor received a gallery like the Holocaust or they were both integrated into thematic exhibitions, each would be placed on pedestals of equal height. That was the point.

Jewish groups and supporters did not interpret the new venture as primarily a human rights museum, either. It was never meant to be like the International Red Cross and Crescent Museum in Geneva. To them, the CMHR's attraction was the Holocaust focus. The Asper Foundation press announcement about the project also made the Holocaust's centrality perfectly clear: a Holocaust gallery would be one of the permanent ones. "You may ask why there is a focus on the Holocaust in the Consequences Gallery. The Holocaust represents a singular, unprecedented event in human history."[69] Other Nazi victims were tacked on as if they were afterthoughts. In 2008, Gail Asper—who led the foundation after Israel's death in 2003—praised the fact that the CMHR "will contain the first national gallery in Canada dealing with the Holocaust." Here she reflected the official summary of the legislation that converted the Asper-led project into a national museum of the Canadian state. It reads: "The first national museum to be located outside of the National Capital Region, the CMHR is to be built in Winnipeg. It will house the largest museum gallery in Canada devoted to the subject of the Holocaust." Then follows the universal pitch a few lines later: "One of the goals of Canada's museum policy is to facilitate the access of all Canadians to their cultural heritage."[70] The government legislative summary thereby mirrored the Holocaust–human rights relationship advanced by Jewish organizations since the 1970s. If the reconciliation of the particular and universal was perfectly obvious to Asper and his supporters, the reaction of other Canadians suggests that it was not readily apparent to them. The CHMR controversy shows that fulfilling both of these intentions is a Sisyphean task.

Academics from both sides weighed in on the matter. Barney Sneiderman, a law professor at the University of Manitoba in Winnipeg, had objected to "Holocaust bashing" and "the profaning of history," arguing that the "Holocaust is unique" after Lubomyr Luciuk had contested the Asper Foundation statement that "the Holocaust stands out as a unique event in history."[71] Luciuk, the son of Ukrainian nationalist refugees, a political geography academic at the Royal Military College of Canada and a leading figure in the UCCLA, responded by declaring that "all genocide victims must be hallowed." It is worth considering his case in detail because it contains all the elements of the Ukrainian campaign for the Holodomor's equal, grievable status in the CMHR.

If the continental reach of the Holocaust was remarkable, he wrote, so were features of the Holodomor: "more Ukrainians perished in the terror famine than all the Jews murdered in the six years of the second world war," citing a much-disputed statistic. Moreover while the Holocaust was ended by conquering armies, the "man-made Famine started and ended when Stalin said so." Although Holocaust survivors could speak out, Holodomor survivors were fearful because they had to cover up their Ukrainian nationality to emigrate to Canada. It was therefore difficult to challenge the genocide deniers—even in

Ukraine, where former Soviet "apparatchiks remain influential." So while "the Holocaust's engineers were punished, Ukraine's reapers haven't faced justice." What is more, Luciuk continued, Moscow could restrict the archives with impunity. "The Russians even lobbied at the United Nations to ensure the Holodomor was not declared genocide. Would German diplomats dare to sidebar the Shoah? Inconceivable." He concluded by declaring "unique" the Holodomor's obscurity and advocating for continuing efforts to "ensure we never learn more."[72] The museum would only be successful if it meant that "many millions of Ukraine's victims are not marginalized, somehow made less worthy of memory than the Holocaust's victims. The Holodomor was arguably the greatest act of genocide in 20th century Europe. Recognizing that would not only ensure that the proposed Canadian Museum for Human Rights is a unique institution, it would make it a truly world class one as well."[73] Luciuk was saying that part of the trauma of the Holodomor was its hiddenness.

At the same time, Luciuk was campaigning to revoke the Pulitzer Prize for Walter Duranty because he had concealed the Holodomor as a *New York Times* journalist in the 1930s. By calling his book *Not Worthy: Walter Duranty's Pulitzer Prize and the New York Times*, Luciuk was underlining the message of the Ukrainians' ungrievability. It was time to teach the world otherwise: "This project was launched with very modest resources by a small group of activists who were able to remind the world of what arguably was the single greatest act of mass murder to take place in Europe during the 20th century."[74] The Ukrainian communal organizations competed with Jewish ones in accessing the levers of power. In 2005, a private member's bill to recognize the "internment of persons of Ukrainian origin" was passed, providing for compensation, the mounting of commemorative plaques by the UCCLA, and other memorializing activities at former internment sites. However gratifying, these minor victories did not translate into the ability to determine the contents of the CMHR. The Ukrainians were losing this game.

After building construction commenced in April 2009, the museum leadership established a Content Advisory Committee (CAC) "comprising 17 human rights scholars and acknowledged experts from across Canada." As its 2010 report states, "Many of its members had been part of a previous Human Rights Advisory Committee established in 2005 by the Friends of the Canadian Museum for Human Rights to provide guidance during the planning process of the Museum, or part of its successor, the Friends Content Advisory Committee." The report notes further that "the initial advisors to the Friends and the exhibition designers Ralph Appelbaum and Associates for the Exhibit Master Plan (2005) were Yude Henteleff, Constance Backhouse, David Matas, Ruth Selwyn and Ken Norman."[75] Henteleff, like Matas, a lawyer and Asper confidante, was also a B'nai Brith leader, serving on its Advisory Board on National Holocaust Task Force Leadership.[76]

These figures, with the exception of Selwyn, "led the story-gathering tour across Canada" on which the report was based; the idea was to have the museum incorporate Canadians' human rights stories in its exhibition.

In the event, the report bears a remarkable resemblance to Matas's views. Those who ventriloquized the Asper Foundation and B'nai Brith line are given disproportionate space in the report, especially in comparison with Ukrainian-Canadian voices. Summaries of the interviews conveniently supported the B'nai Brith vision and the Asper vision:

> Those [interviewees] who advocated that the Museum should recognize the centrality of the Holocaust emphasized that it is the Holocaust that provides our paradigm for understanding the causes and processes of all mass, state-sponsored violence, as well as provides the inspiration for human rights protection on a world-wide scale. As such, it merits a permanent home and a major focus within the Museum. With such an essential foundation secured, the Museum can and should explore relationships between other genocides and the Nazi atrocities: for example, how the Nazis learned from the earlier genocide in Armenia.[77]

No effort was made to conceal Matas's involvement in the story-gathering process. One Holocaust survivor referred to a film about Raoul Wallenberg that "also emphasized the involvement of Canada and Canadians such as David Matas, a member of the CAC, in the efforts to discover the fate of Mr. Wallenberg."[78] No reader would be surprised to come to the report's fifteenth recommendation that simply repeated the gist of these statements and cited two papers by Matas as authority in the accompanying endnote.

> 15. The Museum should position the Holocaust as a separate zone at the centre of the Museum, showing the centrality of the Holocaust to the overall human rights story and in prompting the creation of the Universal Declaration of Human Rights, with its grounding in the idea of common humanity. The story of human rights told in other parts of the Museum should bring home to visitors the core messages of the Holocaust, including the message that learning and acting on the lessons of the Holocaust—that respecting human rights—give hope that nothing like the Holocaust will ever happen again.[79]

In retrospect, it is astonishing that the museum leadership thought no one would notice the transparent attempt to lend the air of consultative legitimacy to the imposition of a partisan vision on a national museum. Other Canadians did notice. And they complained bitterly.[80]

Needless to say, the UCC felt that the deal sealed in 2003 had been broken.[81] The feared trauma of renewed hiddenness was now a real prospect. The presence of so many communal Holocaust museums and memorials in Canada meant that it was "in no danger of being forgotten," wrote Luciuk, while the "catastrophe that befell many millions of non-Jews enslaved or murdered by the Nazis—including the Roma, Catholics, the disabled, Poles, Ukrainians, Soviet POWs, homosexuals and others—will be obfuscated in the proposed museum."[82] Being "lumped" in the mass atrocity gallery was considered particularly objectionable. As before, the UCC wanted a Holodomor gallery like the Holocaust one, while the UCCLA advocated a nonhierarchical vision of twelve galleries that are "thematic, comparative and inclusive." Otherwise, in the words of the Ukraine-born consultant and former UCC office bearer Oksana Bashuk Hepburn, "It's as if the museum's, indeed, Canada's message is to exonerate the Soviet crimes."[83]

Ukrainian Canadians were not the only ones to complain. Roger W. Smith, chair of the Armenian-affiliated International Institute for Genocide Studies, wrote in support of the genocide concept at the museum, arguing that

> [t]here must be a scientific and scholarly basis for the CMHR's decision-making process, including the designation of its galleries. It is our belief that the comparative approach to various cases of genocide, based on the principle of inclusiveness, provides such a scholarly standard, whereas allocating a whole gallery to only one case, while lumping all others into a single gallery called "Mass Atrocity," relativizes and thereby trivializes those other cases.[84]

George Shirinian, executive director of the Armenian Zoryan Institute, was happy for the Holocaust to be a "prime model of how to teach genocide"—but not the only one: "it is critical to realize that other cases are necessary, as each provides its own particular lessons to be learned." This was an argument echoed by University of Ottawa political scientist David Petrasek, who had worked for Amnesty International and the U.N. High Commission for Human Rights. In his experience, he observed, "each genocide unfolds in its own unique and uniquely horrible ways. The truth is that a deep understanding of the Holocaust provides few parallels that would aid in understanding the events leading up to, for example, the genocidal Anfal against the Kurds of Iraq in 1988 (other than the banal lesson that dictators can't be trusted)."[85] In other words, contrary to arguments of Jewish communal leaders, the Holocaust did not encompass all other genocides and could not function as the "ultimate prototype."[86] Political benefits also accrued to a comparative approach, Shirinian averred.

> Taking a comprehensive and comparative approach to genocide as the ultimate violation of human rights would complement perfectly the objectives of Canada's official policy of multiculturalism. It would avoid differentiating and dividing communities. It especially would make those

communities who feel their histories have been neglected or denied feel more welcome. One can not overestimate the psychological trauma of those who are part of a nation that has experienced genocide.[87]

The Ukrainian-led campaign began to bite by early 2011 as politicians lined up to plea for the Holodomor's equal status in the museum.[88] In the face of scholarly criticism—Sam Moyn, author of an influential book on human rights in history, was flown in from New York—the museum also revised its claim that the Holocaust had animated the human rights revolution. It now stressed that, since Nazi Germany was the best-documented and best-known assault on human rights, it would have the greatest pedagogical impact and should therefore receive its own gallery.[89] Although non-Jewish victims of the Nazis and Lemkin's generic genocide concept would be included in that gallery, it would still be named after the Holocaust—as Asper and so many donors had expected and as the museum's legislative summary indicated.

Even so, the impression that academic consultants were diluting the Content Advisory Committee Report vision set off alarm bells in the Jewish community. Yude Henteleff told a University of Manitoba audience, "If this [position of the Holocaust separate zone] is in any way diminished it will significantly impair the museum in carrying out its stated objectives as noted in its enabling legislation."[90] The anxiety that the Holocaust would be hidden if its specific gallery was abandoned was acutely expressed by the editor of the *Winnipeg Jewish Review*, Rhona Spivak. "Should we as a Jewish community keep in mind that in the not too distant future there will be no more survivors alive, to educate first hand about the Holocaust—which will make exhibits in museums all the more important educational tools?"[91] Journalist supporters like Martin Knelman hoped that "sanity will prevail" with the failed "effort to reduce the destruction of European Jewry to just another genocide."[92] Plainly, having the Holocaust depicted as just another genocide was an unbearable proposition that would undermine the project of Jewish grievability.

At length, David Matas, now the senior honorary counsel to B'nai Brith Canada, spoke out to defend his vision of the museum. This time he argued that the Holocaust lens illuminated Aboriginal Canadian suffering while persisting with the now discredited myth about the causal relationship between the Holocaust and the so-called human rights revolution. "Revulsion to the Holocaust generated a paradigm shift from the stratification of humanity to the equality of humanity," he declared. Consequently, "the notion of aboriginals as equals became prevalent. The shift to human rights meant discriminatory and abusive practices inflicted on aboriginals either ended or lessened." What is more, he continued, the United Nations' human rights regime "resonated with the global aboriginal community," conveniently omitting the fact that cultural genocide was cut from the Genocide Convention and needed to be compensated in other instruments decades later as a result of persistent Indigenous activism rather than Holocaust memory. In a remarkable display of special pleading, he went so far as to argue that "without the commitment to human rights generated by the Holocaust experience, non-aboriginals might be continuing those abusive practices [of residential schools and forced adoptions] to this day."[93] That it was in the name of the human right to education and other emoluments of civilization that Indigenous children were taken does not appear to have been considered.

An alternative vision was expressed by Canadians for Genocide Education—the rebadged Canadians for a Genocide Museum—in their submission to a CMHR roundtable discussion. Rather than arguing that the Holocaust should be privileged in order to draw attention to Indigenous suffering, the group—or, rather, the Palestinian Canadian lawyer James Kafieh who signed the submission[94]—argued that Indigenous suffering warranted the privileged position because of its intrinsic relationship to Canada.

> It is our position that the genocide of Canada's First Nations and Inuit is the only case of genocide that deserves special status in the CMHR as this genocide happened in Canada and is a defining aspect of all that Canada is today. Our prosperity is premised on the resources taken from and then denied to our First Nations and Inuit. In addition, this human rights museum is to be built on their stolen land.[95]

Here was an anticolonial manifesto that would challenge Asper's vision of the CMHR—and the State of Israel, as Kafieh perhaps intended. It is no surprise that its recommendation to weight the displays "towards lesser-known cases of human rights abuses and genocide that have been historically marginalized or neglected" was ignored.[96]

Indigenous Analogizings

First Nations, Inuit, and Métis people did not need settler Canadians to represent them in this debate. Their leaders spoke out clearly enough about genocide and destruction—although not in relation to the CMHR, perhaps because some of them were consulted about the Indigenous gallery and museum site. In 2011, Daniel N. Paul, a Mi'kmaq elder, made the headlines when his article "The Hidden History of the Americas: The Destruction and Depopulation of the Indigenous Civilisations of the Americas by European Invaders," published in the Australian-based journal *Settler Colonial Studies*, was picked up by Canadian newspapers. Exasperated by European cultural arrogance, he reversed the barbarism/civilization binary by accusing the Europeans of barbarism for their blindness to "American Indian civility" and their attempt to destroy Indians and exploit the environment. Indeed, he averred, these actions were unique though unacknowledged. It was "a long denied fact: the dispossessing of the Indigenous Peoples of the Americas by Europeans, and the near extermination of them in the process, is the greatest inhuman barbarity that this World has ever known." What prevented this recognition was Indians' "ongoing invisibility."[97] Indigenous grievability was hindered by its hiddenness.

In this case, the genocide concept's popular association with the Holocaust concealed rather than revealed the Indigenous experience, contrary to Matas's claim. For the historian John Reid denied Paul could use "essentially a 20th century term . . . to understand 18th century realities," although he conceded that "what happened in the 18th century is a process of imperial expansion that was ruthless at times, that cost lives."[98] Indignant at Paul's argument, Kyle Matthews, the senior deputy director at the Montreal Institute for Genocide and Human Rights Studies, complained that genocide was "a divisive term," pointing to the CMHR controversy: "You can see different cultural communities in Canada wanting their collective human suffering recognized with the same weight as others." He too was prepared to concede that European colonial rhetoric about Indians evinced "some genocidal intent" but declined to use the genocide term because of its problematic "overuse."[99] A proponent of the Responsibility to Protect doctrine, Matthews presumably would have denied that genocide was taking place against Indians during colonial conquest and would not have supported the West's humanitarian intervention to protect them; after all, Europeans were committing the genocide.[100] The next year, in 2012, the chairman of Truth and Reconciliation Commission (TRC), Justice Murray Sinclair, used the term in relation to the residential schools policy: "the reality is that to take children away and to place them with another group in society for the purpose of racial indoctrination was—and is—an act of genocide and it occurs all around the world."[101] Predictably, he too met resistance, and the term did not make it into the TRC's interim report. Government officials fell about themselves to avoid the topic.[102]

Understandably, some Indigenous leaders are angered and frustrated by the treatment their peoples have endured and continue to experience. Sometimes these traumatic associations were expressed in attention-grabbing slogans and blunt equations. For example, in October 2012, two former chiefs, Terry Nelson and Dennis Pashe, appeared on Iranian television to denounce Canada's reserve system as "concentration camps" and the six hundred First Nations women who have disappeared over the past decade as "part of the ongoing effort by the Canadian government to exterminate us."[103] Needless to say, these statements—and the location whence they were uttered—generated momentary controversy, but more significant was the rebuke of other Indigenous leaders. "I'm scared to even compare that tragedy [the Holocaust] with our history," said Birdtail Sioux First Nation Chief Kenneth Chalmers. "That's not acceptable. It's totally different. We're not lining up for gas chambers."[104]

On another occasion, Chief Phil Fontaine criticized Nelson for making anti-Jewish remarks on behalf of the Assembly of First Nations, because First Nations people should know better than to trade in stereotypes. Indeed, he continued, "no group in Canadian society is more familiar with racism, racial hatred and violence than the First Nations. Not only do our people put up with individual acts of discrimination on a daily basis, we continuously struggle with the effects of systemic discrimination designed to wipe out our languages and culture." Striking about Fontaine's statement was his invocation of this particular experience to connect with other Canadians by using a spatial metaphor of nonhierarchical partnership rather than a temporal one of precedent or a visual one of a lens or prism through which others' experiences must be telescoped, focused, or refracted.

> There is certainly a need for greater public education about issues such as the Holocaust. As well, we need public education about the history of First Peoples in Canada and the cultural genocide perpetrated by the Indian Residential Schools. Our goal in learning about one another, however, is to build bridges, not to burn them or to block them. There is no place for over-the-top rhetoric or unacceptable statements.
>
> First Nations, Jews, gays and lesbians, Muslims, people of colour and others are targeted by hate mongers because of our differences. We must support each other and in so doing we will send a strong message to those who would discriminate against us.[105]

Here was the solidarity that Judith Butler anticipated when a person apprehends his or her precariousness.[106] Because Indigenous people are subject to the greatest degree of precarity, it is perhaps no surprise that their leaders are able to reach out like this. Not from a claim of primacy, or from one of a hidden genocide, still less because one regards the other as threatening, but out of recognized suffering and mutual empathy—this is the basis of the ethically preferable subject position.

So does the Holocaust reveal or conceal genocides? The answer depends on how one analogizes. The David Matas approach is indentured to the atonement effect and sets up a monumental threshold that provokes the very people whom he thinks he is helping. An alternative is presented by the Métis literature scholar Warren Cariou in his remarkable reflection, "Going to Canada."[107] Visiting Auschwitz, he was shocked to see a building called Canada marked on a map of the Auschwitz camps. It must have been named by Canadians, he surmised, because it was "a byword for freedom, for human rights and for justice." Or because the building was source of hope or a hiding place. In fact, it was where the Nazis stored loot stolen from inmates. This was his second shock.

Going to see the site, he saw that the Nazis had burned down the building; now all that remained were stumps, piles of ashes, and a few twisted spoons.

This unsettling experience led to an unsettling analogy, "not because Canada has any real connection to the horrific events that occurred in Birkenau, but because the juxtaposition of the two Canadas in my mind brings up a disturbing metaphor, a different lens for picturing my home." The new vision was of Canada as at once a storehouse of vast, stolen wealth and a place of burned ashes, "as if to obliterate the traces of what has happened there." Cariou stresses that he is "not interested in arguing for equivalences among the various atrocities the world has known." In this he differs from Nelson and Pashe. He does not "want to make any claims that anything has happened in Canada is equal to what happened in the holocaust, or that arithmetic of any other quantifiable method can be used to calculate the degree of any crime against humanity." Echoing Fontaine's noncompetitive ethic, he continues that "each group of victims deserves the dignity of not having their suffering measured against anyone else's." What interests him are parallels and contiguities so he can answer "the most difficult questions that the twentieth century left with us: Why do these terrible things happen again and again?" Like Daniel Paul, he challenges the civilized conceit of the West: "How can they occur in supposedly civil societies, in communities that think of themselves as generous and enlightened?"[108]

In the end he does not try to answer this question. Instead, he is interested in Indigenous authors' responses to their experiences. He observes that these authors "expose a legacy of theft and dehumanization that indigenous people in this country have had to live with for many generations." They challenge the redemptive view of Canadians "as people of justice and civility and freedom and generosity" that Cariou dismisses as "simply a product of those cover-up stories that almost always come after violence." Such stories have replaced the older heroic colonial narrative but perform the same function.[109] Referring to the CMHR, he notes that it promotes itself as "a powerful symbol of Canada's unwavering commitment to recognizing, promoting and celebrating human rights," commenting that "this characterization of Canada bespeaks either a breathtaking naiveté or a willful ignorance. Anyone familiar with our colonial history knows that Canada has 'wavered' a great deal on the questions of human rights over the generations."[110] Will the CMHR be able to disavow the founding violence that made the state and its museum a possibility?

Cariou's analogizing also went in the other direction. His witnessing of the Canadian oil sands region where the life and lands of the local peoples were devastated by mining and development reminded him "of that obliterated warehouse in Birkenau. It is a place of almost unbelievable wealth, but at the same time a place of ashes, a place in which the land itself is literally being stolen from the people who have depended upon it for generations." The oil goes to power the Canadian economy at expense of native peoples and the environment.[111] In this link, he discovered Canada's "suppressed histories, silenced people, uncomfortable juxtapositions." This use of the Holocaust reveals another Canada, but not that about which Matas and the Asper family, proud patriots, were thinking.

Conclusion

The passionate if ill-tempered CMHR debate is more significant than the much-derided competition for victimhood. Rival conceptions of evil are being advanced for public consideration and official endorsement. Where supporters of the CMHR constantly point to the fact that the Holocaust is the "best documented"—that is, most recognized—genocide as grounds for its central gallery, Ukrainians and most other migrant and Indigenous groups contend that the salient lesson—and evil—is the fact that their story of suffering has been so overlooked and hidden compared to the Jewish one. The evil lies in nonrecognition. Indeed, far from making the case for the Holocaust gallery, the abundant documentation and high profile of the Holocaust could be grounds *against* granting central status in the museum. The next attendant question inevitably concerns why some genocides are hidden—or not even considered genocides—and others are not. Is it a question of power making knowledge, as Roman Serbyn, the Ukrainian Canadian historian and onetime chair of the UCC's Subcommittee on a Genocide Museum, suggests about the Jewish success in establishing the Holocaust in public consciousness? Or do specific features of the Holocaust mark it as uniquely unique, as the CMHR advocates suggest, invoking supposedly neutral academic writers like Steven Katz?[112]

That particular interests are advanced under the guise of universal claims is difficult to ignore. For one thing, the insistence on the universal Jewish victim is indentured to the conviction that Jewish welfare is an index of welfare for everyone—a conviction that James Kafieh would justifiably dispute. At the same time, is it true, as Lubomyr Luciuk avers, that "being inclusive and equitable takes nothing away from hallowing the Shoah"?[113] Certainly, the Canadian Jewish leaders, journalists, and academics cited here would disagree. But it is not as if the Ukrainians and Canadians for Genocide Education are blind to the Holocaust's obviously distinctive features; that much is clear after a decade of debate. Perhaps that is why they want lesser-known cases of genocide and human rights violations displayed. If so, are genocide and crimes against humanity adequate memory concepts when they are being deployed specifically *against* the Holocaust?[114] If Jews claim universal significance for their particular experience, can it be said that particular interests are being advanced by the universal concept of genocide? Such use of Lemkin's concept would not accord with his intentions. The new Institute for Research of Genocide in Canada is plainly a Bosnian operation, just as Canadians for Genocide Education includes virtually every

Canadian migrant and ethnic group except Jewish ones, who have declined invitations to join.[115]

What about the power/knowledge/memory nexus with which we began? The success of the UCC's own memory activism suggests that it is difficult to pry them apart. Its National Holodomor Education Committee can boast advances in having Holodomor Memorial Day commemorated in some school districts, and in introducing teachers to its Holodomor pedagogical resources.[116] This strategy sounds familiar. Not to be outdone by the Jewish effort to erect a Holocaust memorial (rather than a museum) in Ottawa—the national Holocaust monument was approved in March 2011—Ukrainians and other groups founded Tribute to Liberty in 2009 to lobby and raise money for a memorial to victims of "totalitarian communism" in the national capital as well. "Victims of the atrocities committed by Communist regimes have not received recognition for their suffering," it declared. "This is beginning to change: archives have been opened and the truth can no longer be hidden." The theme of hidden suffering featured in the organization's newsletters, which carried a story on "history unhidden" in each issue.[117] The memorial also "will raise Canada's and the world's awareness of 'the most colossal case of political carnage in history' (*The Black Book of Communism*)."[118] Here was a uniqueness claim of a different type. So far, the campaign has succeeded in having the government set aside a plot of land, and it is only a matter of time before the funds are raised to erect it there. Then Ottawa will have Holocaust and Holodomor monuments.

Finally, does the CMHR debate do justice to the Indigenous experience—the most Canadian of them all—when it mostly concerns wrangling over events that occurred in Europe more than a half-century ago? The UCCLA position entails removing the Indigenous gallery as well, after all. The virtually exclusive attention on the European theater casts most settler Canadians as victims, conveniently hiding the settler-Indigene binary and settler racism toward Aboriginal peoples. Memory debates in settler colonial states like Canada and Australia necessarily must contend with the particular legacies of those states' foundations, yet there seems little interest in an unflinching examination of this legacy at the CMHR beyond the platitudes of the human rights agenda. This agenda, it could be said, is implicated in the attempted erasure of Indigenous cultures by the forcible imposition of "civilization" upon them. The (cultural) genocide concept is apposite for such collective experiences, but it is conspicuously absent from the museum in this case. Significantly, the Harper government's 2008 apology to Canada's First Nations people is never mentioned during these CMHR debates. The Holocaust gets a national remembrance day in Canada, but not Canada's treatment of Indigenous people.

The power/knowledge/memory nexus lies at the heart of these disputes; Indigenous peoples simply do not dispose over the resources—recall the migrant-group organizations' government liaison staff and various national committees with their grandiose titles—to lobby extensively for their memory claims. Any advances they have achieved have been won through persistent activism, like the individual and class action lawsuits that brought the government to the negotiating table about the residential schools. They have been the authors of their own success rather than passive beneficiaries of Holocaust memory, contrary to David Matas's fable. While some settler Canadians may regard them as privileged because of the dedicated Indigenous gallery, will the question of Indigenous genocide be raised in the museum? The Canadian Museum for Human Rights has raised the public profile of genocides, if only by the controversy it has unleashed, but in doing so has it hidden others?

ACKNOWLEDGMENTS

Thanks to Avril Alba, Neil Levi, Sam Moyn, and Natasha Wheatley for invaluable comments on earlier drafts.

NOTES

1. This is a widely believed misconception. See A. Dirk Moses, "The Holocaust and Genocide," in *The Historiography of the Holocaust*, ed. Dan Stone (Houndmills, UK: Palgrave Macmillan, 2004), 533–555.

2. On the Holocaust and cosmopolitan ethics, see Daniel Levy and Natan Sznaider, *The Holocaust and Memory in the Global Age* (Philadelphia: Temple University Press, 2006); Daniel Levy and Natan Sznaider, *Human Rights and History* (Philadelphia: Temple University Press, 2010), 80–82; and Jeffrey Alexander, Bernhard Giesen, Martin Jay, Michael Rothberg, Robert Manne, Nathan Glazer, Elihu Katz, and Ruth Katz, *Remembering the Holocaust: A Debate* (New York: Oxford University Press, 2009). On the Holocaust and human rights, see Thomas Buergenthal, "International Law and the Holocaust," in *Holocaust Restitution: Perspectives on the Litigation and Its Legacy*, ed. Michael J. Bazyler and Roger P. Alford (New York: New York University Press, 2006), 17–29; Johannes Morsink, *The Universal Declaration of Human Rights: Origins, Drafting, and Intent* (Philadelphia: University of Pennsylvania Press, 1999), 37.

3. Sam Moyn, *The Last Utopia: The Holocaust in* History (Cambridge, MA: Harvard University Press, 2010); Marco Duranti, "The Human Rights Revolution and the Holocaust: Revisiting the Foundation Myth," *Journal of Genocide Research* 14, no. 2 (2012): 159–186.

4. Vinay Lal, "The Concentration Camp and Development: The Pasts and Future of Genocide," *Patterns of Prejudice*, 39, no. 2 (2005): 220–243; Donald Bloxham, *The Final Solution: A Genocide* (Oxford: Oxford University Press, 2009), ch. 8.

5. James Kafieh and Canadians for Genocide Education, Submission to the CMHR, Roundtable Discussion, Ottawa, 11 June 2009, 1, http://instituteforgenocide.org/en/wp-content/uploads/2012/03/CMHR-Submission-Nov-20-2009-2.pdf; Ross Romaiuk, "No Genocide Should Be Above All Others: Luciuk," *Whig Standard*, 11 April 2012.

6. Adam Muller, "Proposed Plans for the Holocaust Gallery in CMHR Are Perfectly Justifiable," *Winnipeg Jewish Review*, 13 April 2011.

7. Judith Butler, *Precarious Life: The Powers of Mourning and Violence* (London: Verso, 2004), xiv.

8. Judith Butler, *Frames of War: When Is Life Grievable?* (London: Verso, 2009), 14.

9. A. Dirk Moses, "Genocide and the Terror of History," *Parallax* 17, no. 4 (2011): 90–108.

10. Geoff Kirbyson, "Content Focus of Human Rights Museum: Chinese Group Wants Story Told," *Winnipeg Free Press*, November 27, 2011.

11. Armenian National Committee of Canada Statement on Human Rights Museum, 20 May 2012, http://asbarez.com/101787/anc-of-canada-issues-statement-on-human-rights-museum; Zoryan Institute/George Shirinian, "How Will the Canadian Museum for Human Rights Represent Genocide?" 17 February 2012, http://genocidestudies.org/Announcements/How%20Will%20the%20Canadian%20Museum%20for%20Human%20Rights%20Represent%20Genocide.pdf.

12. On this general problem, see Alex L. Hinton, ed., *Annihilating Difference: The Anthropology of Genocide* (Berkeley: University of California Press, 2002).

13. A. Dirk Moses, "Toward a Theory of Critical Genocide Studies," in *Online Encyclopedia of Mass Violence*, ed. Jacques Semelin (Paris: SciencesPo, 2008): http://www.massviolence.org/Article?id_article=189; Alexander Laban Hinton, "Critical Genocide Studies," *Genocide Studies and Prevention* 7, no. 1 (2012): 4–15.

14. George Steiner, *Language and Silence* (New York: Atheneum, 1977), viii; A. Dirk Moses, "*Das römische Gespräch* in a New Key: Hannah Arendt, Genocide, and the Defense of Republican Civilization," *Journal of Modern History* 85, no. 4 (2013).

15. Jack Donnelly, "Human Rights: A New Standard of Civilization?" *International Affairs* 74, no. 1 (1998): 1–23.

16. Indigenous activists found the 2008 government apology wanting for its failure to mention genocide: Mike Krebas, "'Sorry for Genocide'? Residential School Apology in Context," *Dominion*, 18 July 2008, http://www.dominionpaper.ca/articles/1928.

17. A. Dirk Moses, "Conceptual Blockages and Definitional Dilemmas in the Racial Century: Genocide of Indigenous Peoples and the Holocaust," *Patterns of Prejudice* 36, no. 4 (2002): 7–36.

18. I have undertaken this task in A. Dirk Moses, "The Canadian Museum for Human Rights: The 'Uniqueness of the Holocaust' and the Question of Genocide," *Journal of Genocide Research* 14, no. 2 (2012): 215–238.

19. Canadian War Museum, "The Internment of Ukrainian Canadians," http://www.warmuseum.ca/cwm/exhibitions/guerre/internment-e.aspx.

20. Lubomyr Luciuk, *Searching for Place: Ukrainian Displaced Persons, Canada, and the Migration of Memory* (Toronto: University of Toronto Press, 2000); Lubomyr Luciuk, *Without Just Cause* (Kingston, ON: Kashtan Press, 2006).

21. Orest T. Martynowych, "Sympathy for the Devil: The Attitude of Ukrainian War Veterans in Canada to Nazi Germany and the Jews, 1933–1939," in *Re-Imagining Ukrainian Canadians: History, Politics, and Identity*, ed. Rhonda Hinter and Jim Mochoruk (Toronto: University of Toronto Press, 2011), 185–189, 203.

22. Anna Holian, *Between National Socialism and Soviet Communism: Displaced Persons in Postwar Germany* (Ann Arbor: University of Michigan Press, 2011), 172.

23. Ibid., 246–249.

24. David Matas, "The Struggle for Justice: Nazi War Criminals in Canada, from Immigration to Integration," in *The Canadian Jewish Experience: A Millennium Edition*, ed. Ruth Klein and Frank Dimant (Institute for International Affairs B'nai Brith Canada, 2001), http://www.bnaibrith.ca/institute/millennium/millennium06.html.

25. David Matas, "War Crimes Prosecution in Canada: 2010," 44, http://www.bnaibrith.ca/files/03032011.pdf.

26. Matas, "The Struggle for Justice."

27. George Fletcher, Henry Friedlander, and Fritz Weinschenck, "Canadian Responses to World War Two War Criminals and Human Rights Violators: National and Comparative Perspectives," *Boston College Third World Law Journal* 8, no. 1 (1998): 45.

28. Sol Littman, *War Criminal on Trial: The Rauca Case* (Toronto: Lester and Orpen Dennys, 1983).

29. Roman Serbyn, "Alleged War Criminals, the Canadian Media, and the Ukrainian Community," in *Ukraine during World War II: History and Its Aftermath—A Symposium*, ed. Yuri Boshyk (Edmonton: Canadian Institute of Ukrainian Studies, 1986), 121–130; Roman Serbyn, "Echoes of the Holocaust in Jewish-Ukrainian Relations: The Canadian Experience," *Ukrainian Quarterly* 60, no. 12 (2004): 215–226; Lubomyr Luciuk, "Accusations of War Crimes against Ukrainian Canadians: 'Go After the Real Culprits,'" *Kingston Whig-Standard*, 19 January 2003.

30. David Matas, "Bringing Nazi War Criminals in Canada to Justice," in Boshyk, *Ukraine during World War II*, 113–120; David Matas, *Bringing Nazi War Criminals in Canada to Justice* (Downsview, ON: League for Human Rights of B'nai Brith Canada, 1985); David Matas with Susan Charendoff, *Justice Delayed: Nazi War Criminals in Canada* (Toronto: Summerhill Press, 1987); David Matas, *Nazi War Criminals in Canada: Five Years After* (n.p.: Institute for International Affairs of B'nai Brith Canada, 1992).

31. Fletcher, Friedlander, and Weinschenck, "Canadian Responses to World War Two War Criminals and Human Rights Violators," 43; Irwin Cotler, ed., *Nuremberg Forty Years Later: The Struggle against Injustice in Our Time* (Montreal: McGill-Queens University Press, 1995).

32. UCCLA Mission Statement, http://www.uccla.ca/mission_statement.htm; Ukrainian Canadian Congress, http://www.ucc.ca.

33. Matas, "War Crimes Prosecution in Canada: 2010"; Howard Margolian, *Unauthorized Entry: The Truth about Nazi War Criminals in Canada, 1946–1956* (Toronto: University of Toronto Press, 2000).

34. The Holocaust Memorial Day Act, http://web2.gov.mb.ca/laws/statutes/ccsm/h068e.php.

35. Yom ha-Shoah Holocaust Memorial Day Teacher's Guide, http://www.bnaibrith.ca/league/hh-teachers/guide00.html.

36. League for Human Rights of B'nai Brith, http://www.bnaibrith.ca/league/league.htm.

37. On the 1970s turn to human rights rhetoric in Canada, see Dominique Clément, "Human Rights in Canadian Domestic and Foreign Politics: From 'Niggardly Acceptance' to Enthusiastic Embrace," *Human Rights Quarterly* 34, no. 3 (2012): 751–778.

38. The ADL founding Charter of October 1913 puts it thus: "The immediate object of the League is to stop, by appeals to reason and conscience and, if necessary, by appeals to law, the defamation of the Jewish people. Its ultimate purpose is to secure justice and fair treatment to all citizens alike and to put an end forever to unjust and unfair discrimination against and ridicule of any sect or body of citizens." About the Anti-Defamation League, http://www.adl.org/about.asp.

39. Simon Wiesenthal Center Museum of Tolerance, http://www.museumoftolerance.com.

40. David Matas, "Remembering the Holocaust Can Prevent Future Genocides," in *Genocide*, ed. William Dudley (San Diego: Greenhaven Press, 2001), 119–123. Excerpted from

"Remembering the Holocaust," in *Genocide Watch*, ed. Helen Fein (New Haven, CT: Yale University Press, 1992).

41. For elaboration of this notion, see A. Dirk Moses, "Stigma and Sacrifice in Postwar Germany," *History and Memory* 19, no. 2 (2007): 139–180.

42. Lubomyr Luciuk, *In Fear of the Barbed Wire Fence: Canada's First National Internment Operations and the Ukrainian Canadians, 1914–1920* (Kingston, ON: Kashtan Press, 2001), 51.

43. Stefan Petelycky, *Into Auschwitz, for Ukraine* (Kingston, ON: Kashtan Press, 1999/2008), 50. The following paragraphs draw on my "Canadian Museum for Human Rights."

44. Raja George Khouri, "There Is No Hierarchy in Genocide," *National Post*, August 11, 1999. Khouri was vice president of the Canadian Arab Federation.

45. Quoted in *Guarding History: A Study into the Future, Funding, and Independence of the Canadian War Museum*, Report of the Subcommittee on Veterans Affairs of the Standing Senate Committee on Social Affairs, Science and Technology (May 1998).

46. Quoted in Standing Committee on Canadian Heritage, Minutes-Evidence (7 June 2000), 1645.

47. Jeff Sallot, "PM Urged to Set Up Genocide Museum," *Globe and Mail*, 27 January 1999.

48. Andrij Kudla Wynnyckyj, "Canadian MP Submits Bill Supporting Genocide Exhibit in Ottawa," *Ukrainian Weekly*, 7 March 1999.

49. David Lazarus and Paul Lungen, "Holocaust Museum May Be Derailed: Ukrainian-Led Effort Could Disrupt Plans," *Canadian Jewish News*, 9 April 1999; Sol Littman, *Pure Soldiers or Bloodthirsty Murderers? The Ukrainian 14th Waffen-SS Division* (Toronto: Black Rose Books, 2003).

50. Standing Committee on Canadian Heritage, Minutes-Evidence (7 June 2000), 1545.

51. Ibid., 1555–1600.

52. Ibid., 1615–1620.

53. Ibid., 1625–1630.

54. Ibid.

55. Third Report of the Standing Committee on Canadian Heritage, Subject-matter of Bill C-224, *An Act to establish by the beginning of the twenty-first century an exhibit in the Canadian Museum of Civilization to recognize the crimes against humanity as defined by the United Nations that have been perpetrated during the 20th century*, Clifford Lincoln, Chair (June 2000).

56. Edwin Kimelman, *File Review Report: Report of the Review Committee on Indian and Métis Adoptions and Placements* (Winnipeg: Manitoba Community Services, 1984), 51.

57. Michael Downey, "Canada's Genocide," *MacLeans Magazine* 112, no. 16 (1999), rpt. as "Canada's Genocide: Canada's Struggle to Repair the Past," in *The Genocide Reader: The Politics of Ethnicity and Extermination*, ed. *Marnie J. McCuen* (Hudson, WI: GEM Publications, 2000), 87–92, and as "Canada's Cultural Genocide: Forced Removal of Native Children," in *Genocide*, ed. William Dudley (San Diego: Greenhaven Press, 2001), 155–158; Clem Chartier, *In the Best Interest of the Métis Child* (Saskatoon: University of Saskatchewan Native Law Centre, 1988), 55; Geoffrey York, *The Dispossessed: Life and Death in Native Canada* (Toronto: Lester and Orpen Dennys, 1989), 214; Margaret Philps, "Land of the Lost Children," *Globe and Mail*, 21 December 2002.

58. Deborah Jones, "Cultural Genocide: Canada Puts Race before Children's Welfare," excerpted from "Canada's Real Adoption Crisis," *Chatelaine*, May 1998, rpt. in McCuen, *Genocide Reader*, 93–98.

59. Kim Stanton, "Canada's Truth and Reconciliation Commission: Settling the Past?" *International Indigenous Policy Journal* 2, no. 3 (2011), http://ir.lib.uwo.ca/iipj/vol2/iss3/2; Statement of Reconciliation, http://www.edu.gov.mb.ca/k12/cur/socstud/foundation_gr9/blms/9–1-4e.pdf.

60. Rev. Kevin Annett, *Hidden from History: The Canadian Holocaust—The Untold Story of the Genocide of Aboriginal Peoples by Church and State in Canada* (2001): http://canadian genocide.nativeweb.org/genocide.pdf. See also http://hiddenfromhistory.org.

61. J. R. Miller, *Shingwauk's Vision: A History of Native Residential Schools* (Toronto: University of Toronto Press, 1996), 435. He, too, speaks of cultural genocide: 10. See also John S. Milloy, *A National Crime: The Canadian Government and the Residential School System—1879 to 1986* (Winnipeg: University of Manitoba Press, 1999).

62. The government established the Aboriginal Healing Foundation in 1999 after its Statement of Reconciliation. Aboriginal Healing Foundation, http://www.ahf.ca.

63. Stanton, "Canada's Truth and Reconciliation Commission"; Indian Residential Schools Settlement—Official Court Website, http://www.residentialschoolsettlement.ca/english .html; Truth and Reconciliation Commission, http://www.trc.ca.

64. Asper Foundation Human Rights and Holocaust Studies Program, http://humanrights .asperfoundation.com.

65. See the UCCLA submission to the CMHR, "The Canadian Museum for Human Rights: A Canadian Ukrainian Perspective," 11 June 2009, http://www.uccla.ca/CMHR_11June09 .pdf.

66. David O'Brien, "Museum to Respect Ukrainian Rights," *Winnipeg Free Press*, 1 December 2003.

67. Bill Gladstone, "Canadian Philanthropist Wants New Museum with Holocaust Gallery," Canadian Jewish Congress/Jewish Telegraphic Agency, 19 May 2003: http://www.cjc .ca/2003/05/29/canadian-philanthropist-wants-new-museum-with-holocaust-gallery; UCCLA, "The Canadian Museum for Human Rights."

68. Paul Samyn, "Asper-Led Museum Sets Off Alarm Bells: View of Genocide Said Too Exclusive," *Winnipeg Free Press*, 27 February 2003.

69. Asper Foundation, "Israel Asper Announces Plans to Create Canadian Museum for Human Rights," 17 April 2003, http://www.friendsofcmhr.com/news_room/news _releases/index.cfm?id=23.

70. Rhonda Spivak, "Tanenbaum Donates $1 Million to Rights Museum," *Canadian Jewish News*, March 13, 2008; Legislative Summary, LS-57E, Bill C-42, An Act to Amend the Museums Act and to Make Consequential Amendments to Other Acts, 22 February 2008 (Library of Parliament: Parliamentary Record and Information Service), 4–5.

71. Barney Sneiderman, "Holocaust Bashing: The Profaning of History," *Manitoba Law Journal* 26, no. 3 (1999): 319–334; Barney Sneiderman, "Holocaust Is Unique in Way," *Winnipeg Free Press*, 13 December 2003.

72. Lubomyr Luciuk, "All Genocide Victims Must Be Hallowed," *Ukrainian Weekly*, March 7, 2004.

73. Lubomyr Luciuk, "The Holodomor Was Unique," UCCLA, 5 February 2004, http://www .ukemonde.com/holodomor/unique.html.

74. Lubomyr Lucuik, "Introduction: Not Worthy?" in *Not Worthy: Walter Duranty's Pulitzer Prize and the New York Times*, foreword by Roger Daniels (Kingston, ON: Kashtan Press, 2004), vi.

75. Canadian Museum for Human Rights (CMHR), *Content Committee Advisory Report* (25 May 2010), 3, 74, http://humanrightsmuseum.ca/programs-and-events/programs/ content-advisory-committee-final-report.

76. http://www.bnaibrith.ca/files/211009.pdf.

77. CMHR, *Content Committee Advisory Report*, 74, 43.

78. Ibid., 43.

79. Ibid., 43, 75n62. The papers are quoted as "David Matas The Holocaust and the Canadian Museum for Human Rights 8 March 2010 and The Holocaust Lens May 1, 2010 on deposit at the Museum."

80. Ira Basen, "Memory Becomes a Minefield at Canada's Museum for Human Rights," *Globe and Mail*, 20 August 2011.

81. "UCCLA: Broken Promise Made to Ukrainian Canadians Provoked Controversy," 17 December 2010, http://www.ucc.ca/2010/12/17/uccla-broken-promises-made-to -ukrainian-canadians-provoked-controversy.

82. Lubomyr Luciuk, "Canadian Museum for Human Rights Is Quite Un-Canadian," *Whig Standard*, 17 December 2010.

83. Oksana Bashuk Hepburn, "Canadian Museum for Human Rights: Right the Wrong," *Hill Times*, 16 April 2012; Bill Redekop, "Let Museum Tell of Holodomor: Prof; A Prime Chance to Recognize Ukraine's Great Tragedy, He Says," *Winnipeg Free Press*, 3 June 2012.

84. Roger W. Smith, "How Genocide Should Be Represented in the Canadian Museum for Human Rights," 24 February 2011, http://www.zoryaninstitute.org/Announcements/How %20Genocide%20Should%20be%20Represented%20in%20the%20CMHR%20v20.pdf.

85. David Petrasek, "Forward—to the Past? Re-thinking a Human Rights Museum," Centre for International Policy Studies Brief, No. 17 (March 2012).

86. The term was used by the Jewish Federation of Winnipeg in an online petition to support a permanent Holocaust gallery. See http://www.jewishwinnipeg.org/page .aspx?id=211471.

87. George Shirinian, "Genocide Is Not Genocide in the Canadian Museum for Human Rights," 22 August 2011, http://www.genocidestudies.org/Announcements/Genocide %20Multiculturalism%20and%20the%20CMHR.pdf.

88. Details of this campaign are in Moses, "The Canadian Museum for Human Rights," 228–231.

89. Cf. Muller, "Proposed Plans for the Holocaust Gallery."

90. Yude Henteleff, "Critical Conversations with Canadians: The Work of the Content Advisory Committee," University of Manitoba, 5 January 2012, http://law.robsonhall .ca/the-distinguished-visitors-lecture-series/now-playing/753-yude-henteleff-critical -conversations-with-canadians-the-work-of-the-content-advisory-committee.

91. Rhonda Spivak, "Open letter to Lubomyr Luciuk, Director of Research, Ukrainian Civil Liberties Association, Re: CMHR," *Winnipeg Jewish Review*, 31 March 2011.

92. Martin Knelman, "Gail Asper Never Gave Up on Rights Museum Dream," *Star* (Toronto), 6 November 2011; Martin Knelman, "Bumps in the Road for Human Rights Museum," *Star* (Toronto), 6 January 2012.

93. David Matas, "Human Rights Born of Holocaust's Horror," *Winnipeg Free Press*, 4 July 2012. On the cultural genocide question, see A. Dirk Moses, "Raphael Lemkin, Culture, and the Concept of Genocide," in *The Oxford Handbook on Genocide Studies*, ed. Donald Bloxham and A. Dirk Moses (Oxford: Oxford University Press, 2010), 19–41.

94. Kafieh participates in Palestinian politics. James Kafieh, "Working towards a Palestinian National Voice," Electronic Intifada, 3 October 2007, http://electronicintifada.net/ content/working-towards-palestinian-national-voice/7165.

95. Kafieh and Canadians for Genocide Education, Submission to the CMHR, 3–4.

96. Ibid., 2.

97. Daniel N. Paul, "The Hidden History of the Americas: The Destruction and Depopulation of the Indigenous Civilisations of the Americas by European Invaders," *Settler Colonial Studies* 2, no. 1 (2011): 168, 178.

98. Kathryn Blaze Carlson, "European Settlers Sought 'Genocide' on Mi'kmaq: Historian," *National Post*, 16 September 2011.

99. Ibid.

100. Kyle Matthews, senior deputy director, http://migs.concordia.ca/W2Ibios.html.

101. Chinta Puxley, "Residential School Called a Form of Genocide," *Globe and Mail*, 17 February 2012; Christopher Powell, "Sinclair Is Correct—It Was Genocide," *Winnipeg Free Press*, 24 February 2012. Important background is provided in Andrew Woolford, "Ontological Destruction: Genocide and Canadian Aboriginal Peoples," *Genocide Studies and Prevention* 4, no. 1 (April 2009): 81–97.

102. Jorge Barrera, "Federal Official Wanted Emails Deleted Outlining Plan to Stonewall on Residential School Genocide Questions," *National News*, 13 January 2012.

103. Kevin Engstrom, "Canada Trying to 'Exterminate' Aboriginals: Terry Nelson," *Winnipeg Sun*, 15 October 2012.

104. Joyanne Pursaga, "Tehran Terry Nelson's Tall Tales 'Not Acceptable': Chiefs," *Winnipeg Sun*, 16 October 2012.

105. Phil Fontaine, "Like Jews, Natives Know that Racism Hurts," *National Post*, 14 April 2005.

106. David W. McIvor, "Bringing Ourselves to Grief: Judith Butler and the Politics of Mourning," *Political Theory* 40, no. 4 (2012): 409–436.

107. Warren Cariou, "Going to Canada," in *Manitowapow: Aboriginal Writings from the Land of Water*, ed. Niigaanwewidam James Sinclair and Warren Cariou, foreword by Beatrice Mosionier (Winnipeg, MB: Highwater Press, 2011), 320–328.

108. Ibid., 324.

109. Ibid., 325.

110. Ibid., 326.

111. Here Cariou links up with Indigenous activists and commentators who decry the exploitation and destruction of the environment in terms of genocide. See Mike Mercredi, "Slow Industrial Genocide," *Dominion*, 23 November 2008, http://www.dominionpaper.ca/audio/mike_mercredi; Chuck Wright, "What They Call Development, We Call Destruction," *Dominion*, 23 March 2012, http://www.dominionpaper.ca/articles/4391; Dawn Paley, "Oil, Gas, and Banks Head South," *Dominion*, 24 April 2012, http://www.dominionpaper.ca/articles/4439; Jennifer Huseman and Damien Short, "'A Slow Industrial Genocide': Tar Sands and the Indigenous Peoples of North Alberta," *International Journal of Human Rights* 16, no. 1 (2012): 216–237.

112. Serbyn, "Echoes of the Holocaust," 215; Sneiderman, "Holocaust Is Unique."

113. Luciuk, "Canadian Museum for Human Rights Is Quite Un-Canadian."

114. Charles Lewis, "Controversial Poll Shows Opposition to Rights Museum: Pollster Says Results Were Misinterpreted," *National Post*, 31 March 2011.

115. Institute for Research of Genocide Canada, http://instituteforgenocide.org/en.

116. Ukrainian Canadian Congress, http://www.ucc.ca/2011/04/13/national-holodomor-education-committee-report.

117. Tribute to Liberty, "About Us," http://www.tributetoliberty.ca/aboutus.html. For the newsletter *Tribute to Liberty News*, see http://www.tributetoliberty.ca/newsletter.html.

118. Tribute to Liberty, "Impact on the Community," http://www.tributetoliberty.ca/impact.html.

2

Hidden in Plain Sight

Atrocity Concealment in German Political Culture before the First World War

ELISA VON JOEDEN-FORGEY

In our thinking about genocide, it is often assumed that genocides are hidden primarily through intentional acts of denial, that is, through propaganda and deception orchestrated by the perpetrating state or armed force. This chapter will examine a less intentional, much more long-term process of "atrocity concealment" involving the creation of official legal categories that encourage widespread delusions about state policy, thereby gradually eroding those public values that shore up polities against genocidal tendencies and hiding future genocidal policies from public recognition. The specific case I will examine is imperial Germany, where potentially genocidal categories were created from the experience of the first fifteen years of overseas colonization; these categories eventually helped further a genocide (against the Herero and Nama peoples in German Southwest Africa), and in the long term they contributed significantly to the erosion of public commitment to those humanist values that can serve as strong bulwarks against genocide, rendering Germany much more vulnerable to the perpetration of human rights abuses and genocide during and after World War I.

During Germany's era of direct overseas colonization (1884–1918), the German state, along with a host of public pressure groups, constructed a category of belonging called *Eingeborene* (a translation of the English "native") that was to account for the millions of new colonial subjects who had quite suddenly come under German sovereign authority. The term was initially descriptive—it signified all the people in the colonies who could not easily be counted as "citizens" or "foreigners" in existing citizenship and naturalization law. Eventually, however, the category served to erase completely the common law traditions of the nineteenth century that had organized German diplomatic relations with the non-Western world, opening up dangerous new territory in German traditions of belonging. In this sense, *Eingeborene* was a *lieu de l'oubli*, a space of forgetting (to play on Pierre Nora's famous phrase).[1] It evoked, when used, a whole world whose existence rested on the forgetting of the past, and it ended up serving the purpose of forgetting atrocities as they were happening. This category, because it was an entirely new phenomenon within German constitutional and citizenship law, erased legal traditions of incorporation that had existed up to that point and that Germans were using as models for understanding their expansion overseas. The way it redefined the people who fell into its grasp created in effect a radically new—and wholly illusory—group of people who were scientifically destined to be the repository of the pure will of the state. The category of *Eingeborene* ultimately created a discursive world in which atrocity could be committed without "registering" in political culture, eventually setting the stage for both the committing and the forgetting of the genocide against the Herero and Nama peoples in German Southwest Africa between 1904 and 1907. The world of the *Eingeborene* ultimately became what we might now call a "black site": a legal space in which atrocity could be committed without risk of public recognition or remembering, where it could happen in the shadows, even if everyone knew about it.

The Colonial Background: Unsovereign Land/Unsovereign People

Imperial Germany declared sovereignty for the first time over overseas territory in the spring and summer of 1884, when it claimed both Togo and Cameroon for the empire. At its height Germany's share of the globe consisted of Togo; Cameroon; South West Africa (Namibia); German East Africa (Tanzania); northeastern New Guinea; part of Samoa; the Bismarck, Marshall, Carolina, and Mariana Islands in the Pacific; and Qingdao in Shandong, China. In comparison with Britain and France, Germany's colonial empire was quite small. It was comparably short-lived—Germany lost all of its colonies as a result of the First World War. It was also financially unprofitable from the viewpoint of the national economy, due to the state subsidies required. For all these reasons, Germany's experiment with overseas governance has long been viewed as an insignificant sideshow to the great drama of German history.

This is not entirely the case. The German colonial empire had lasting effects on German political discourse, a fact that is gaining increasing recognition among historians.[2] While one can debate how intense its impact was and what it contributed to some of the larger events in twentieth-century German history, the German colonial project initially constituted a major and, I would say, radical challenge to German legal norms and its evolving democratic and humanist values.[3] Unlike the other major European imperial powers at the time, especially Britain and France, Germany did not have more than a century of overseas colonial activity to draw from by the time the era of high imperialism came around. It began its engagement suddenly and with several political weaknesses: a central state that had only recently come into being (German unification occurred in 1871), liberal political institutions that were weak and lacked historical depth, and the absence of an overarching rationale and justification for colonial engagement. One consequence of this was that colonial enthusiasts, who were looking to encourage popular support for colonial enterprise, attempted to use colonialism to build stronger national institutions, making colonialism a key component in public discussions about German unity and strength. A second consequence is that German liberalism, which was developing within a colonial context, became split over critical differences in colonial policy. Finally a large proportion of the German population, while embracing expansion as such, believed that new colonial subjects would be integrated into the body politic as fellow imperial subjects, perhaps even citizens, as had been done in previous waves of German, especially Prussian, expansion on the continent. All of this came together to create a very potent and contradictory political brew that led to pitched public battles over colonial atrocities and high-stakes debates about the nature and future of German governance. These battles in turn required that the state and supporters of its colonial ventures redouble their efforts to hold on to the colonial project. In an effort to put to rest the chaotic public discourse on colonialism, reformers and government officials eventually constructed a legal category of radical alterity, a state of nonbeing into which colonial subjects were thrown.

As is well known, German Chancellor Otto von Bismarck embraced imperialism, seemingly out of the blue, in order to increase Germany's international political leverage. Colonies were useful foreign policy chits.[4] The problem for Germany was that these chits were full of people, and nobody had put much thought into what it was going to do with them, what their standing would be in legal terms, and what would happen to the preexisting states and polities in the regions it had just claimed. Unified Germany had little constitutional experience in this department, with the slight exception of the annexation of Alsace-Lorraine after the Franco-Prussian war. Alsace-Lorraine was incorporated into the German Reich according to a special law that made it an imperial province (*Reichsprovinz*) that would eventually gain legal parity with the federated German states (*Bundesstaaten*). The law granted the denizens of Alsace-Lorraine a special form of citizenship called *Reichsangehörigkeit* that was only formally different from the local *Staatsangehörigkeit* held by most Germans.[5] So, arguably, Alsace-Lorraine could have offered a model for the incorporation of new colonial territories.

Most observers in the German parliament seemed to agree that Africa and Asia were significantly different from Alsace-Lorraine. The arguments made to this effect drew on the nineteenth-century standard of civilization, according to which African and Asian peoples were too distant from European civilization to warrant full incorporation into the German constitution as sovereign legal entities. So, unlike Alsace-Lorraine, colonized peoples, Africans in particular, were believed to lack any institutions that could be built upon and Prussified. This imperial assumption stood in stark contrast to the complex negotiations that were going on in the colonies over the terms of their disposal by Germany. On the Cameroon coast, to cite one example, the merchant kings of the Duala polity had been requesting European annexation for years as part of a strategy to counter the unfair practices of European merchants there. There existed a Court of Equity that had been established in the 1850s to regulate commerce, on which the four Duala kings sat alongside British and German representatives. Duala leaders hoped that "annexation" (their word) would lead to greater justice as well as public investment in schools and other infrastructure. They realized that somebody was going to annex them, since both British and German gunboats were in their coastal waters, and were trying to negotiate the best possible outcome for their interests.[6]

Representatives of the German government on the Cameroon coast were negotiating with people they perceived to be representatives of foreign political entities; they appear to have imagined a colonial arrangement that would develop out of existing trade relationships and the assumptions about sovereignty that were intrinsic to them. The German consul of Gabon, Emil Schultze, who ultimately ratified the treaty of annexation with the Duala kings, first signed a memorandum written by Duala notables in English in which they expressed that they expected to retain local control over trade and markets, among other things, and stated that their desire for annexation grew from their need to protect these things from rapacious British and German merchants.[7] When Duala leaders finally signed a treaty of annexation with Germany, Gustav Nachtigal, the first imperial commissioner to West Africa, did not believe this should cut the Duala leaders out of all institutions of governance.[8] He even imagined a future Cameroon that would be governed by a "Cameroon Council" that would include African members.

At the Foreign Office in Berlin there was similar uncertainty about the future of African political leaders. There was not even any agreement about whether colonial territories were to be considered foreign or domestic territory for legal purposes—a question that would not be settled until Germany lost its colonies in World War I. The state was happy to leave vague the position of new colonial subjects, so that it could pursue whatever policies best suited Bismarck's hopes for a loose protectorate arrangement overseen by German merchants. In the absence of an official decision, German officials were suggesting all sorts of options that were drawn from traditional German models of incorporation. One Foreign Office official referred to colonial subjects in Germany as "consular subjects" who had, according to him, the same rights and privileges as German nationals.[9]

The Category

For many people in the German state, however, it was clear from the outset that any kind of incorporation of new colonial subjects based on older models would cause too many headaches, especially as the objectives of German merchants usually clashed with the economic interests of African and Asian polities and would, therefore, require force to impose. It was clear that a new model of incorporation would have to be devised, one that excluded subjects from the constitutional protections given to both citizens and foreigners.

In early parliamentary debates about Germany's annexation of new territories in Africa, parliamentarians referred to the new subjects as *Eingeborenen* (plural of *Eingeborene*, a direct translation of the English "native"). The term at this point was descriptive and signified those persons in the colonies who were not European. The term was only gradually incorporated into colonial laws, and even then only to define the category in the negative, in terms of what *Eingeborenen* were not. The term really began to take on legal and political content through official usage—through debates, reports, correspondence and policies related to this new type of German.

The term *Eingeborene* did not catch on very quickly within the German public; many Germans—within both official and public circles—continued to speak of new colonial subjects in traditional and cosmopolitan terms. Documents from the first twenty years of colonization demonstrate the widespread usage of pre-existing legal and descriptive terms of belonging to refer to colonial subjects, including *Schutzgenosse* (consular subjects), *Reichsangehörige* (citizens of the Reich), and *Landesleute* (countrymen). By the turn of the century, these claims had become political weapons used by German Social Democrats and left liberals to oppose the autocratic German state. In 1901, for example, the liberal Frankfurt newspaper *Für Wahrheit und Recht* (For truth and justice) printed the following:

> In the interest of trade with the colonies, we believe it is absolutely necessary that, firstly, the *Eingeborenen* of these lands be put on equal legal footing as us Germans in the mother country, for they pay taxes just as we do, have mostly taken up Christianity, and are mostly very useful merchants. The judiciary must be just as fair to these people as to us and then the question of jurisdiction must at once be brought to discussion in the Reichstag.[10]

The Social Democrats simply made colonial subjects into de facto citizens by referring to them as *Reichsangehöriger* both in parliamentary debates and in newspaper articles. This was particularly embarrassing for the central government in Berlin, which was then accused of committing atrocities on a regular basis *against its own citizens.*

The extent to which similar cosmopolitan commitments were taken seriously by ordinary Germans is evidenced by the correspondence in the 1890s between a widow in the small eastern German town of Görlitz and the Foreign Office, which, at the time, was tasked with overseeing German colonization. Frederika Dörfling had been caring for two young boys from the port city of Duala, Cameroon, for four years by the time she was in contact with the Foreign Office in 1893 regarding their schooling. The two boys had been brought back to Germany by her brother, a sea captain, for further education. This arrangement was quite common at the time, and the powerful Duala merchant families in particular showed a keen interest in sending young men to the new empire for training. Dörfling wrote to the Foreign Office that "their future is very important to me and to my brother, since they have been close to me as children in my house for four years already and have always given me reasons for satisfaction with their aspirations and mistakes."[11] She looked after the boys as her own, referred to them as "foster sons," and oversaw their apprenticeship with local craftsmen, taking great pride in their successes. In 1897 the Foreign Office sent the young men back to the colonies for what Dörfling believed would be respectable positions in the service of the German Empire; instead they were poorly housed, poorly fed, flogged, and generally mistreated. Upon receiving distraught letters from both of them, she fired off an angry letter to the Foreign Office that read in part: "It has already been underscored repeatedly that my foster sons are free people and not slaves. Similarly they did not enjoy their training here to be common workers in Cameroon and to be treated in such a dishonorable way, even though they have black skin. They were often presented here to the whites as role models!"[12]

Frau Dörfling was not alone in her surprise about the treatment her young charges received at the hands of the German government in Cameroon. The colonial contradiction between the rather positive reception of Africans in Germany and the dehumanization they faced in the colonies was the source of much anticolonial opinion. And even among civil servants there was a general confusion about the status of these subjects and the rights they had. This meant that once the German state began to integrate the term *Eingeborene* formally into colonial law, it had to use it not only to legalize and legitimize what it was doing on the ground in the colonies but also to emphasize to Germans that colonial subjects were so different that they required the creation of a radically new legal status. This was not easy. It required that Germans be made to forget the cosmopolitan instincts that grew out of nineteenth-century humanism, political liberalism, and a form of political belonging that emphasized loyalty to the monarch above nationality, ethnicity, or color. The conversion of Africans (and Asians) into *Eingeborene* required that German social practices be altered—that German elites, for example, inside and outside the state, cease treating visiting Africans as foreign dignitaries based upon older patterns of cultural contact (it was a constant thorn in the side of colonial administrators that some German aristocrats socialized with African princes). And it required that colonial subjects themselves somehow be brought to forget their former sovereignty.

Political Realities

Once defined legally, even if only on very vague terms, the term *Eingeborene* was given the status of a state-sanctioned category of belonging, a category complementary to "foreigner" (*Ausländer*) and "citizen" (*Staatsangehöriger/ Reichsangehöriger*). It thus became a political identification, a way of defining the legal basis of the relationship of state power to a specific class of people. Unlike foreigners and citizens, the persons labeled *Eingeborenen* had no recognized protections against raw state power. Given that such protections had evolved out of notions of popular sovereignty and political legitimacy that invested each individual human being with intrinsic value, the creation of the *Eingeborenen* was simultaneously the creation of a political space in which human beings had no intrinsic worth. *Eingeborene* was, therefore, a radical concept of nonbeing right from the beginning.

It certainly set in motion a process of political radicalization, both in the colonies and in Germany. The term *Eingeborene* required the erasure of the previous human status of African and Asian people who came under its jurisdiction. The German state claimed not only total sovereign powers over colonial matters with respect to domestic institutions; it also claimed total sovereign power over its new subjects—obsessively so, one could argue.[13] The total sovereign authority that German officials in Berlin both imagined and demanded denied any options that would allow for multiple sovereignties or layers of authority. This move flattened out any recognition of social hierarchy and differentiation in colonized polities, essentially creating a democracy of terror, where the colonized were completely devoid of any customary or legal protection from the state. In the absence of a territorial extension of citizenship and normative German civil and criminal law over all colonial subjects, the state's attempts to enforce total sovereignty took on a new form. It was pure state violence emptied of any customary limiting factors.

The term *Eingeborene* legalized this world of pure state violence and opened it up to be filled by the caprices of local colonial bureaucrats. The obsessive need to prove Germany's total domination over colonial subjects created a situation in which every subject—and especially former political, cultural, and economic leaders—fell under suspicion of "arrogance," either for using noble titles or for otherwise continuing to conduct themselves in ways that harkened to the pre-annexation past. Societies that had enjoyed established sovereign relationships with European merchants prior to annexation suffered particular humiliations. This prompted the most powerful king on the coast of Cameroon to plead with the Foreign Office, "Please let me know if there is no respect of [the] person in Germany. I am the man who gave my country to you the government of Germany, but I am very much surprised how I am daily brutally treated by your governor. . . . Instead of treating me as a King, or respectable man, he is treating me as a dog."[14]

The conversion of sovereign peoples into unsovereign subjects required the widespread use of daily humiliations against colonial subjects as well as the rampant commission of atrocities by civilian and military authorities in the colonies. Foremost among these atrocities was the routine use of flogging for minor infractions of largely unwritten rules. Flogging was so widespread that the colony of Cameroon popularly became known as "the twenty-five country," referring to the number of lashes regularly given.[15] A sentence of twenty-five lashes was enough to kill the victim, especially if the whip being used cut deeply into the flesh and damaged the internal organs. Every punishment with flogging was, therefore, a potential death sentence.[16]

The routine use of flogging by German administrators and private persons alike led to rather vocal outrage in Germany, where flogging became a metonym for colonial abuse in general. Several colonial scandals in the 1890s also fanned the flames of colonial opposition, which was institutionalized within the center-left and left parties. One high-profile scandal originated out of Germany's push into the southwestern interior of Cameroon, where a judge named Wehlan ordered that several villages be burned to the ground; the men, women, and children killed; and prisoners beaten to death. According to one witness, his soldiers cut off the heads of their victims and took them home as mementos. Wehlan's superior, the interim governor Karl Theodor Heinrich Leist, who was also a jurist, became famous for flogging and raping the wives of officers on Cameroon's only police force, thereby sparking a revolt.[17]

Supporters of the colonial project responded to these atrocities in two different ways. Many imperial officials, the Prussian bureaucrats and officers sent to govern the colonies, simply defended their right to dispose of *Eingeborenen* as they saw fit. This approach rather quickly lost ground as these Prussian bureaucrats found themselves facing parliamentary investigations into their conduct in the colonies and involuntary early retirement. The second approach was promoted by the National Liberal Party and other pro-colonial forces, who sought to put German colonization on a more modern footing. They launched a very effective colonial reform movement that eventually institutionalized the term

Eingeborene within German political discourse. The term ended up supplanting the use of cosmopolitan terms like "citizen" and "countryman" and helped bring about the widespread racialization of the entire colonial project within the German public.

An important early work in the colonial reform movement was a book published in 1898 by the reformer Franz Giesebrecht entitled *Die Behandlung der Eingeborenen in den deutschen Kolonien* (The treatment of the natives in the German colonies), which sought to create a science of colonial governance. In it Giesebrecht collected the opinions of civil servants, jurists, officers, scholars, missionaries, explorers, and others on what was coming to be known as the *Eingeborenenfrage* (native question). The book framed colonial atrocities as a problem of individual civil servants rather than as a constitutional problem raised by the invention of the term *Eingeborene*. The essays in general pointed to better training of colonial authorities as well as ethnological studies of colonized populations as the solutions to what were seen to be colonial "excesses." In advocating these things, the book—along with the larger colonial reform effort—cemented the idea of a separate world of the *Eingeborene* in the discourse on colonialism. This was a world governed not by laws but by the scientific implementation of governance strategies geared toward the particular needs and requirements of this strange legal term that was now supposed to exist—the new race of the *Eingeborene*.

The essays in the book use the term *Eingeborene* synonymously with *Neger*, a term which, by this time, was beginning to connote a specific racial group at the bottom of the Great Chain of Being. Contributors wrote in terms of *Negerbehandlung* (treatment of the Neger), the *Negerfrage* (Neger question), and the usefulness of *Rassenpsychologie* (racial psychology) alongside the use of composite nouns created from *Eingeborene*. Although most contributors agreed with the editor Giesebrecht that colonial reformers must advocate humanitarian policies with respect to the *Eingeborene/Neger*, an effort was made to distinguish humanitarianism from what they called *Humanitätsduselei* (sentimental humanitarianism). *Humanitätsduselei* was the belief that colonial subjects were equal to Europeans. Reformers cast this belief as an extremist one, which they juxtaposed to genocide on the other extreme:

> If one looks over the history of all colonies, one will recognize that up to the present day there are two directions among the colonizers: the first leads a war of extermination against the black race with brutal, raw violence to eradicate them from this earth; the other, inspired by a certain *Humanitätsduselei*, tries to educate the members of this race for culture and civilization and to bring them onto the same footing as the Europeans.[18]

In other words, the cosmopolitan options being bandied about by ordinary Germans were nothing more than weak sentimentalism, out of step with the brutal colonial realities. In between raw force and foolishness, the reformers advocated a "middle way," in which there was even room for flogging (when fairly administered). A colonial administrator from East Africa distinguished flogging from brutality in the following way:

> The main principle in contact with the *Neger* should be: *Streng, aber gerecht* [Strict, but just]! Strictness must naturally not develop into brutality; on the other hand, however, the level of punishment must not be so measured, especially with flogging, that one [negatively] affects the feelings of honor with the handing out of only a small number of lashes. . . . Physical pain is a better method of education than the harm of the sense of honor, which is only little developed in the average *Neger*. That the *Neger* will feel that five to ten lashes is a punishment will only be the case when he himself is from a high position. . . . otherwise the minimum number of lashes must be fifteen in my opinion.[19]

In line with the general view of *Eingeborene* nature in this collection, this administrator believes that a higher number of lashes is a sign of justice (and humanitarianism) that is shared between the colonizer and the colonized. Along these lines, one contributor even suggested that the flogged person would come to thank his punisher afterward, so long as he had been informed of the reasons for his flogging beforehand.

Giesebrecht's book gives us a sense of the imaginary worlds that were being constructed around the *Eingeborene* in the minds of colonial enthusiasts. Reformers constructed scenarios of power that required the ritual reiteration of humiliation and brutality. Not only were these rituals believed to be just and humane, but also they were described as scientifically grounded in the radical alterity of the *Eingeborene*. Even genocide was not off limits. Giesebrecht, though a staunch critic of colonial "excesses," as he called them, still believed that genocide theoretically constituted a legitimate policy—so long as it was pursued by the state and not individual administrators:

> Admittedly, life is more brutal than the man, and when in the struggle of the races [*Rassenkampf*] the extermination of the population of an entire continent is postulated, that is certainly a standpoint of monstrous cruelty, a standpoint that we hold to be false and therefore that must be fought with all our energy, but that we must recognize as an historically and philosophically legitimate [one]. In contrast, we refuse all brutality that is committed by one colonizer against individual *Eingeborene*.[20]

The problem for reformers was that the atrocities being reported in the German press were indeed being committed by individual colonizers against individual *Eingeborenen*. Reformers thus began to advocate for the routinization of colonial brutalities, a policy initiative they justified with reference to the separate, distant world of the *Eingeborene*.

Colonial reformers, who often made their arguments—in Germany as in other colonial empires—on humanitarian grounds, faced the task of supporting the colonial project and its economic goals while also finding ways of explaining and refining daily colonial brutalities as a part of civilized legal and political practice. A racialized interpretation of *Eingeborene* status, as well as the invention of *Eingeborenenrecht* (native custom), became the explanatory mechanism that allowed brutality and humanitarianism to exist in the same legal realm. The claims of humanitarianism made by German colonial reformers were thus not really hypocritical, as colonial reform has often been characterized. Humanitarianism had become so uprooted from its universalist foundation in nineteenth-century humanism that reformers could advocate it while also supporting practices of governance that Europeans would have considered appalling (and that had been abolished) in the home country. So long as brutalities could be reinvented as "native custom," there was no reason for Germans to concern themselves with the glaring contradiction between the liberal laws they enjoyed at home and the space of autocratic terror that existed overseas.

Colonial reform eventually grew into a strong force in German politics and society. It came to the rescue of Germany's colonial effort during the so-called Hottentot elections of 1906, when the chancellor dissolved the parliament after it refused to pass a colonial budget in protest against colonial atrocities, including the genocidal war against the Herero people in South West Africa. The colonial reform agenda helped elect a pro-colonial parliamentary majority in the new elections in 1907. The ideas promoted by reformers were institutionalized in the Colonial Institute, founded in 1908 to train German administrators, and within various new fields of study, such as colonial law, colonial politics, and native custom. The creation of a freestanding Colonial Office in 1907 was also in part the consequence of reformist efforts. All of these things were built on the assumption that there existed something called an *Eingeborene* and that this category of person lived in a world so distant from European norms that routine flogging was a legitimate tool of governance. We should not be surprised, then, that the evidence shows that conditions for colonial subjects actually worsened after the institutionalization of colonial reform. Incidents of flogging seem to have risen, for example, in part because colonial reformers lent to that punishment the aura of legitimacy. In Cameroon, the official number of floggings per year jumped from 315 in 1901–1902 to 4,800 in 1912–1913.[21]

The entire movement for colonial reform rested, of course, on a collective delusion—that there existed a space occupied by human beings so radically alterior to Germans that they should be governed not simply by autocratic institutions but by the scientific application of force, including flogging and even genocide. This was a powerful argument, for it eroded the cosmopolitan language used by a wide variety of Germans in first decade of colonization. It also erased the cosmopolitan institutions that existed to govern trade prior to annexation. And it dealt what could be characterized as a mortal blow to the humanist principles of much nineteenth-century thinking about the world outside of Germany, which were a core element in Germany's early movement for political liberalization. Terms like *Eingeborene* (and its partner, *Neger*), *Eingeborenenrecht*, *Eingeborenenpolitik* (native politics), and the *Eingeborenenfrage* created entirely new possibilities for modern governance. *Eingeborenenrecht* in particular provided a powerful space for forgetting atrocity and eventually genocide. The more people talked about these things, the more real they became, and the less possible it was for colonial opponents to gain any traction. How could one argue for the extension of the protection of citizenship to people who were so different that the same ethical considerations did not apply to them? How could one argue even for the basic application of German legal and penal norms to colonial subjects if they did not occupy—by virtue of biology—the same "universe of moral obligation" (to borrow a term from Helen Fein)?[22] One could not—and after the Hottentot elections, when the colonial reform effort was made into official German policy to save the empire from itself, one finds fewer and fewer echoes of the more cosmopolitan past.

Conclusion

The long-term impact of the collective delusion regarding a race of nonbeings called the *Eingeborenen* still remains to be assessed. It is fair to say that the institutionalization of colonial reform and its vision of humanitarianism created a language of respectable racism that made German political culture more vulnerable to the threat of fascism after World War I. In the short term, the effect of the invention of the *Eingeborene* is evident: it introduced a particularly toxic framework into thinking about colonial exploitation that sucked atrocity down a black hole called colonial humanitarianism and colonial reform. Its new form of humanitarianism vis-à-vis the *Eingeborene* in particular fed right into the thinking of General Lothar von Trotha, the architect of the 1904 genocide in which nearly 80 percent of the Herero population perished. His famous statement—"My intimate knowledge of many central African tribes, Bantu and others, has everywhere convinced me of the necessity that the *Neger* will never submit to a treaty but only to naked force"[23]—could have been a chapter contributed to Giesebrecht's reformist *Behandlung der Eingeborenen.* Like other reformists, Trotha was operating according to the scientific rules of racially based governance. Speaking of the genocide after the fact, he noted, "As yet I have only been accused [in international circles] of excessive inhumane treatment of the natives, which gives me the right to oppose such views. Peaceful natives must be treated humanely in all events. But to adopt the same approach toward rebellious natives *is to be inhumane toward our own fellow countrymen.*"[24]

Trotha's logic neatly summarizes the important shift in perspective that occurred over three decades of colonial domination. Colonial subjects in Africa and Asia went from being members of lesser cultures who could nonetheless be embraced as fellow subjects with rights to life and property to being alterior racialized bodies requiring institutionalized brutality, even mass murder, to be properly governed. His nightmarish vision of a race war had become so normative in some circles by 1904 that General von Schlieffen, chief of the General Staff, could remark: "One can agree with [Trotha's] plan of annihilating the whole people or driving them from the land. The possibility of whites living peacefully together with blacks after what has happened is very slight unless at first the blacks are reduced to forced labor, that is, a sort of slavery."[25] Such a view was frequently expressed during the protracted war against the Herero and Nama from 1904 to 1907, and it was not particularly extreme. As we have seen, a moral argument for a rational plan of genocide was already being crafted in the mid-1890s by colonial reformers.

The German imperial state did not set out to create a radically new concept of belonging that would facilitate genocide. It was acting pragmatically when it decided to create a category that gave the state ultimate powers over the disposal of the bodies and the lives of new colonial subjects. This category, however, in requiring the enforcement of a total form of sovereignty, also required rather widespread popular forgetting, both among colonial subject populations and among Germans themselves. People who refused to forget, and hence demanded that colonial subjects be treated as the human beings that they were, found themselves in increasingly intense opposition to the imperial state and its officials. In the colonies, such opposition often resulted in bloodshed and, at the very least, the stepping-up of routine humiliations. In Germany, it resulted in a concerted and successful campaign of colonial reform that sought to create a scientific category out of the fictitious term *Eingeborene.* Once the world of the *Eingeborene* was brought into existence, once it was spoken about as if it signified a real space occupied by real people, it became a *lieu de l'oubli* that could be filled with all sorts of fantasies about the humanitarian nature of flogging and massacre. The ultimate result of this was that anything that happened in the space of the *Eingeborene* stayed in the space of the *Eingeborene.* Colonial brutalities could be forgotten—they did not even need to register in the first place—because they were all part of the proper scientific management of an alien species.

As we know, genocide denial starts with the genocide, where it is meant to camouflage facts that "everyone knows" in order to perpetuate the killing. Post-genocide denial strategies draw their main frameworks and terminology from what Raul Hilberg aptly called the "verbal camouflage" of the genocidal regime, but they do so to with the goal of permanently erasing any remaining evidence of killing.[26] And yet, the words themselves are still about killing, and, at some level, everyone knows it. Speaking the language of denial is, therefore, a violent act, part and parcel of the genocidal process.[27] This may help explain why deniers of one genocide tend to deny others, and why official genocide denial is an important red flag for the perpetration of human rights abuses and genocide in the future.

When we consider the history of genocide denial, it is important that we look not only for the intentional verbal denial strategies of the perpetrator—before, during, and after the commission of the crime—but also for other, less instrumental spaces of atrocity concealment that can feed into the development of genocidal ideologies and capacities: legal categories, discursive strategies, simple words that are introduced into public debate that serve the purpose of hiding atrocity in plain view. There are many different historical pathways that can contribute to the development of genocidal processes down the road, some of which develop around the commission of other atrocities and human rights abuses decades and sometimes generations before the genocide. By looking at links that exist outside of the established histories of perpetrator parties and ideologies, we get a better sense of how a policy of genocide is historically connected to other forms of political violence. In fact, casting our net widely in considering precursors to genocide can help us understand how the crime can develop out of long-term social processes linked to the infliction of institutionalized and often normalized human rights abuses and to a society's efforts either to recognize and confront them for what they truly are or to ignore and forget them by accepting and promoting the terrifying, delusional world of the *lieux de l'oubli.*

NOTES

1. Pierre Nora, "Between Memory and History: Les Lieux de Mémoire," trans. Marc Roudebush, *Representations* 26, Special Issue: Memory and Counter-Memory (Spring 1989): 7–24.
2. Woodruff Smith, *The German Colonial Empire* (Chapel Hill: University of North Carolina Press, 1978); Jürgen Zimmerer and Joachim Zeller, eds., *Völkermord in Deutsch-Südwestafrika: Der Kolonialkrieg (1904–1908) in Namibia und seine Folgen* (Berlin: Christoph Links Verlag, 2003); Shelley Baranowski, *Nazi Empire: Colonialism and*

Imperialism from Bismarck to Hitler (Cambridge: Cambridge University Press); Volker Langbehn and Mohammad Salama, eds., *German Colonialism: Race, the Holocaust, and Postwar Germany* (New York: Columbia University Press, 2011).

3. See, for example, Elisa von Joeden-Forgey, "Race Power, Freedom, and the Democracy of Terror in German Racialist Thought," in *Hannah Arendt and the Uses of History*, ed. Richard King and Dan Stone (London: Berghahn Books, 2007), 21–37; Andrew Zimmermann, *Anthropology and Antihumanism in Imperial Germany* (Chicago: University of Chicago Press, 2001); Pascal Grosse, *Kolonialismus, Eugenik und bürgerliche Gesellschaft in Deutschland 1850–1918* (Frankfurt: Campus Verlag, 2000).

4. For an overview of the history of German colonization, see Smith, *The German Colonial Empire.*

5. *Reichsangehörigkeit* signified a form of citizenship that was granted directly by the central imperial state; *Staatsangehörigkeit*, in contrast, was a form of citizenship gained within one of the federated states that made up the empire. Although formally different in legal terms, both forms of citizenship accorded people the same obligations and privileges.

6. The classic history of the Duala is Ralph Austen and Jonathan Derrick's *Middlemen of the Cameroons Rivers: The Duala and Their Hinterland, c.1600–c.1960* (Cambridge: Cambridge University Press, 1999).

7. Shirley Ardener, *Eyewitness to the Annexation of Cameroon, 1883–1887* (Buea: West Cameroon Antiquities Commission, 1968), 70.

8. Stenographiasche Berichte über die Verhandlungen des Reichstages, 11. Legislaturperiode-II. Session, erster Sessionsabschnitt 1905/1906, vierter Anlageband, Aktenstück Nr. 294.

9. Königlich Preußische Gesandschaft in Mecklenberg and the Hanseatic Cities, 9 February 1886, Bundesarchiv-Berlin R1001 5581.

10. *Für Wahrheit und Recht* 5, no. 11 (1901), 3–4.

11. Frau Dörfling to the Colonial Department of the Foreign Office, 20 November 1893, Bundesarchiv-Berlin R1001 5572.

12. Frau Dörfling to the Colonial Department of the Foreign Office, 29 October 1897, Bundesarchiv-Berlin R1001 5574.

13. Early on in the colonial project, the state launched a campaign to deprive colonial subjects of the right to use precolonial noble titles, arguing that their use challenged the final sovereignty of the German emperor. See, for example, Bismarck to Soden, 5 July 1888, Bundesarchiv-Berlin R1001 4297.

14. Bundesarchiv-Berlin R1001 4297, 36.

15. Helmuth Stoecker, "The German Empire before 1914: General Questions," in *German Imperialism in Africa*, ed. Helmuth Stoecker (London: C. Hurst, 1986), 206.

16. F. F. Müller, *Kolonien unter der Peitsche* (Berlin: Rütten und Loening, 1962), 99.

17. Helmuth Stoecker, *Drang nach Afrika* (Berlin: Akademie Verlag, 1991), 59–60; L. H. Gann and Peter Duignan, *The Rulers of German Africa, 1884–1914* (Stanford, CA: Stanford University Press, 1977), 145–146. According to Gann and Duignan, Leist moved to the United States and became a successful lawyer in Chicago.

18. Wilhelm Vallentin, *Die Behandlung der Eingeborenen in den deutschen Kolonien* (Berlin: S. Fischer Verlag, 1898), 143.

19. Franz Giesebrecht in *Die Vehandlung dee Eingeborenen in den Deutschland Kolonien*, ed. Franz Giesebrecht (Berlin: S. Fischer Verlag, 1898), 182.

20. Ibid., 183.

21. Helmuth Stoecker, "The German Empire before 1914: General Questions," in *German Imperialism in Africa* (London: C. Hurst, 1986), 207. The unofficial figures for each year were probably much larger, as plantation owners and private persons frequently resorted to flogging.

22. Helen Fein, *Accounting for Genocide* (New York: Free Press, 1979), 4.

23. Geneal Lothar von Trotha, explaining his call to exterminate the entire Herero people in 1904. This letter has been widely reproduced and discussed in works on the Herero genocide. See Gesine Krüger, *Kriegsbewältigung und Geschichtsbewußtsein* (Göttingen: Vandenhoeck & Ruprecht, 1999); Jan-Bart Gewald, *Herero Heroes: A Socio-Political History of the Herero of Namibia, 1890–1923* (Oxford: James Currey, 1999), 173; John Bridgman and Leslie J. Worley, "Genocide of the Hereros," in *Century of Genocide: Eyewitness Accounts and Critical Views*, ed. Samuel Totten, William S. Parsons, and Israel W. Charny (New York: Garland, 1997), 15; Helmut Bley, *Namibia under German Rule* (Hamburg: Lit Verlag, 1996), 163–165.

24. Bley, *Namibia under German Rule*, 93 (my emphasis).

25. Letter reproduced in Bridgman and Worley, "Genocide of the Hereros," 15.

26. Raul Hilberg, *The Destruction of the European Jews* (New York: Holmes & Meier, 1985), 621.

27. Israel W. Charny, "The Psychology of Denial of Known Genocides," in *Genocide: A Critical Bibliographic Review*, vol. 2, ed. Israel W. Charny (London: Mansell; New York: Facts on File, 1991), 3–37.

3

Beyond the Binary Model

National Security Doctrine in Argentina as a Way of Rethinking Genocide as a Social Practice

DANIEL FEIERSTEIN

Genocide studies emerged from a fertile intersection of law, history, and social science. However, a shift in emphasis from understanding to prevention has gradually led to the current "binary model" that reduces genocidal social practices to an eternal struggle between good and evil in which the only problem is whether the "good guys" have enough "political will" to neutralize and defeat the "bad guys." The result has been a growing trivialization of the term *genocide* since it was coined nearly seventy years ago. A simplistic model has emerged that requires each case of genocide to have one and only one victim and one and only one perpetrator. Victims, perpetrators, and accomplices that do not fit the model are ignored or rendered invisible.

This chapter will show how attempts to prosecute the perpetrators of state terror in Argentina under the Genocide Convention led to a much deeper understanding of genocidal processes in general: the idea that genocide is essentially a partial destruction of the perpetrators' own national group—a destruction that is intended to transform the survivors through the annihilation of the victims. The case of Argentina will be discussed less for its intrinsic interest than as a means of understanding and making sense of the powerful and all-embracing effects of genocidal social practices in those societies in which they are implemented. Moreover, this interpretation is already present in Raphael Lemkin's thinking about genocide and is closely linked to other highly promising approaches to fighting the consequences of genocidal processes, such as that of the Lithuanian-Jewish philosopher Emmanuel Levinas.

In order to understand how this radical change in perspective affects memory processes, let us examine a few well-known examples from history. The Holocaust is often reduced to the idea of the persecution of Jews by Germans under the Nazi regime. Little attention is given to other victims of Nazism—three million non-Jewish Poles, 3.3 to 3.5 million Russian prisoners of war, and hundreds of thousands Sinti and Roma. Even less attention is given to the hundreds of thousands *German* victims, including not only Jews, Sinti, and Roma but also political dissidents, Jehovah's Witnesses, homosexuals, the unemployed, and the handicapped. Similarly, the Austrians, Croatians, French, Hungarians, Italians, Latvians, Lithuanians, Poles, and Romanians who killed and tortured are also forgotten. In the same way, genocide scholars tend to focus on the massacre of Armenians between 1915 and 1923, ignoring the large numbers of Greek and Syrian Christians who were also murdered by the Young Turk Ittihadist party.

More recently, "Hutu moderates" who were killed in the Rwandan genocide in which Hutu militias mainly targeted Tutsis have been relegated to oblivion. The complex system of interrelated conflicts in the former Yugoslavia has proved it is impossible to overcome employing a banal dualism of "goodies" and "baddies," even if the Serbs could play the role of the bad guys. Attempts to label the current conflicts in the Sudan in terms of Arab Muslims against black Christians have similarly turned out to be oversimplified. Most of the groups involved are Muslims *and* blacks and define themselves as Arabs.

It is not then a question as to whether or not certain historical processes are found to be hidden from the gaze but rather that what is actually hidden is the type of process that the genocide implies. The binary gaze that attempts to embrace the notion that one group (the Germans, the Turks, the Hutus) has annihilated another group (the Jews, the Armenians, the Tutsis) manages to obscure not only other perpetrators and other victims but, more importantly, it prevents us from making sense of these very genocides.

Restoring the complexity of the historical process of each individual genocide is a necessary requisite so that one can manage the consequences of the genocide and even prevent future genocides. This approach clearly goes beyond simple pronouncements of "innocence" or "guilt" assigned wholesale to entire groups of people. The Argentine case proves to be particularly fruitful for this discussion, since it does not easily lend itself to the construction of this binary gaze. The perpetrators as well as the victims were Argentine. Although one could say the same about other cases (first the Germans and then Europeans were perpetrators and victims of Nazism; perpetrators and victims alike who were both part of the Ottoman Empire fell under the drive of the Ittihadist State; and indeed Rwandans were perpetrators as well as victims of the massacres of 1994). The binary "ease" with which these three classic cases have come to be understood cannot be easily reproduced in the Argentine case even if one wishes to emulate dyads such as the "military perpetrators" and the "leftist victims." Therefore this chapter aims to dismantle the binary approach to the understanding of genocidal processes by analyzing the mass killings in Argentina as way of "awakening" the hidden genocides that lie dormant within visible genocides.

The Question of Definitions: Law and Social Sciences

Genocide studies first emerged largely as a result of legal and sociological debates about the adequacy of the Genocide Convention adopted by the U.N. General Assembly in 1948. Most earlier works highlighted the serious shortcomings of the legal definition of genocide (especially the exclusion of political, economic, social, gender or sexual groups, among others) and thus proposed new definitions. Examples of this approach can be found in Vahakn Dadrian, Irving Louis Horowitz, Frank Chalk and Kurt Jonassohn, Helen Fein, Israel Charny, Barbara Harff and Ben Kiernan, and Greg Stanton, among others.

Disagreements over definitions led scholars to develop a wide and rich variety of concepts based on alternative definitions of genocide. However, there was no consensus about which of these definitions could replace the one contained in the Genocide Convention. Thus, it was not always clear whether different authors were talking about the same social practice.

During the negotiations leading up to the Rome Statute for an International Criminal Court (ICC) in 1998, all attempts to introduce a broader definition of genocide failed, and the formal definition of the Genocide Convention was adopted. At the same time, the Rome Statute introduced a new, extended definition of "crimes against humanity." This persuaded many scholars to change their approach and accept the inadequate definition of the Convention as the only possible way of establishing common ground within the academic community.

Some scholars suggested that the debate over definitions be closed. In William Schabas's words, it would be more useful to "[relegate] the concept of genocide in favor of the more general and more easily applicable concept of crimes against humanity."[1] While this position has been accepted by many pioneers of Genocide studies, this mainly Anglo-Saxon consensus has been and should be strongly interrogated for two reasons:

1) The concept of crimes against humanity often refers to the indiscriminate killing of civilians and so lacks the explanatory power of the concept of genocide—which refers to the attempted destruction of a group.
2) The wording of Article 2 of the 1948 Genocide Convention (reproduced in the Rome Statute for the ICC) violates the principle of equality before the law by placing some target groups under its protection and not others. To violate this principle is to violate the concept of law itself.

Partial Destruction of One's Own National Group: New Possibilities

Because political groups were not explicitly protected by the 1948 Genocide Convention or the 1998 Rome Statute, it is easy to confuse attempts to destroy political groups with the murder of individual politicians or activists. By reducing genocide to crimes against humanity, there is a real danger that we may lose sight of the ways in which the social practices of genocide systematically destroy identity. The destruction of identity has been a key element in the conceptualization of genocide since Raphael Lemkin's pioneering work.[2]

The Convention and the Rome Statute fortunately do not completely close the door on new interpretations of genocide, and thus the experience of the trials in Argentina offers the possibility of exploring new interpretations and ways with which to dismantle the binary model of genocide thinking, without any change to the Convention.

In Spain, Baltasar Garzón's interpretation in 1998 of the extermination of political groups in Argentina as the destruction of a part of a national group (in this case, the Argentine national group) has proved to be particularly illuminating. In Argentina, the Federal Oral Criminal Tribunal No. 1 for La Plata convicted the former police commissioner Miguel Etchecolatz in 2006 and the former police chaplain Christian Von Wernich in 2007 for crimes against humanity "committed in the context of genocide." In this landmark ruling, the court considered the systematic nature of the crimes and their effect on society as a whole, urging other courts to use the concept of "destruction of part of the national group" to resolve a number of conceptual and legal issues surrounding Argentina's State Terrorism. Some other Argentine courts have continued such rulings, and as of mid-2012, six different courts have accepted this interpretation in nine separate trials. Argentina's Human Rights Secretariat has adopted this as its official view, as was declared by the secretary for human rights, Eduardo Luis Duhalde, at the opening of the Ninth International Conference of the International Association of Genocide Scholars (IAGS) in Buenos Aires on July 19, 2011.[3]

This concurrence makes it possible to deal with the backbone of genocidal logic: the use of terror and annihilation as a strategy to eradicate identity. According to Lemkin, the main purpose of genocidal practices is to destroy the oppressed group's identity. The fact that all national genocide laws explicitly forbid the partial destruction of national groups should allow an increasing number of cases to be successfully prosecuted in national courts.

The distinctive feature of genocide, according to Lemkin, is that it aims to destroy a group rather than the individuals that make up the group. The ultimate purpose of genocide is to destroy the group's identity and impose the identity of the oppressor on the survivors. This idea gives us a useful insight into the workings of power systems in the modern era. In particular, the nation-state has tended to destroy the identities of ethnic and religious minorities within its boundaries and impose a new identity on them: the national identity of the oppressor.

What tends to be hidden in these processes is that, in many cases, the perpetrators and victims shared a previous identity (German, Polish, Ottoman,

Rwandan, Yugoslavian), and it is precisely *this* plural identity that is destroyed by transforming it into a homogeneous identity (German Aryan, Ottoman Turk–Muslim, Rwandan Hutu), altering it radically (as occurred in Argentina, Chile, Cambodia, or Indonesia), or completely eliminating it (as is in the Yugoslavian case, where the identity seems to be only legible as Serbian, Croatian, or Bosnian, thus preventing us from remembering or from reconstructing the previous Yugoslavian identity). In this way, what remains hidden is precisely the identity that they sought to annihilate, and it is replaced by the binary model of clashing preexisting identities as such Germans versus Jews, Turks versus Armenians, or Hutus versus Tutsis.

Although the notion of genocide as a destruction of any group is to some degree present in the two earlier drafts (the Secretariat Draft and the Ad Hoc Committee Draft) of the Genocide Convention written in May 1947 and April 1948, it was carefully edited out of the final text, which was approved only after two years of intense disagreements. By excluding political groups, delegates were able to pretend that genocide was an irrational and therefore "nonpolitical" form of racism or religious bigotry far removed from the rational logic of state oppression.

The illegitimacy of excluding political groups in this way has been discussed by authors in different works.[4] However, the Genocide Convention still offers a way of linking the crime of genocide with the systematic destruction of national identity through the concept of partial destruction of a national group.

The concept of "partial destruction of a national group" is contained in the 1948 Convention and all subsequent legal definitions of genocide, and it summarizes the essence of genocidal practices as Lemkin understood them. The oppressed group might live under colonial rule, as was common in Lemkin's time, or form part of a nation-state, as tended to be the case in the second half of the twentieth century, when the national security doctrine of the cold war period brought a resurgence of military regimes around the globe and turned national armies into armies of occupation within their own borders, replacing the colonial armies of the past. In the second half of the twentieth century, national armies have repeatedly behaved like armies of occupation in their own countries.[5]

Many legal analysts and scholars have argued that the national group must necessarily be different from the perpetrator group. However, this idea is not supported by the Convention itself, which states only that genocide occurs when there is "intent to destroy, in whole or in part, a national, ethnical, racial or religious group, as such,"[6] without saying anything about the identity of the perpetrators.

Assumptions about the relationship between victims and perpetrators lie at the heart of different conceptions of genocide. Those who argue that "partial destruction of the national group" does not apply when victims and perpetrators belong to the same group tend to see genocide as resulting from a confrontation between two or more groups, fueled by "ancestral hatred" or "irrational discrimination." Supporters of this view tend to focus on genocides currently occurring in Africa, where rival groups are assumed to have reverted to tribal savagery and ancestral hatred in its most ethnocentric form. This explains the emphasis of the media and many academics on conflicts in Nigeria, Rwanda, or Sudan. However, more careful analysis shows that these conflicts are far from being mere "tribal confrontations." Moreover, they are not the only phenomena of mass destruction in recent decades.

Interestingly, the conflict in the former Yugoslavia also tends to be seen as a tribal clash. Thus, a modern conflict was explained in some cases in terms of fourteenth-century struggles between Christians and Muslims, which of course is exactly how today's extreme nationalists in the Balkans—whether they be Serbs, Croats, or Bosnians—wish to portray the conflict.

In contrast, those who argue that the "partial destruction of the national group" constitutes genocide even if the perpetrators are members of the same group tend to see genocide mainly as a power strategy. In this view, the ultimate purpose of genocide is not the destruction of a group as such but the transformation of society as a whole. This was the aim of the Nazis in Germany and Axis-occupied Europe as well as of the perpetrators in Yugoslavia, Rwanda, Indonesia, Cambodia, and Latin America, to point out just a few cases in which terror has been used as an instrument of social transformation.

In other words, even though the Genocide Convention makes no claims about the underlying causes of genocide, the way in which the "national group" is interpreted has profound consequences for our understanding of genocidal processes.

Effects on Social Memory Processes

As a paradigmatic case of genocide, the Holocaust provides a good example of how different interpretations can promote ownership of experience or, conversely, alienation. If we analyze the Holocaust only in terms of the Jewish and Roma communities annihilated in Germany, Poland, or Lithuania, "ordinary" Germans, Poles, and Lithuanians seem to have remained largely unaffected except for possible feelings of solidarity with the victims. Once stripped of their German, Polish, or Lithuanian identities, Jews and Gypsies could only be seen through the eyes of the perpetrators, as being "outside" of the German, Polish, or Lithuanian national group, indeed even as being outside of the European identity, since Nazism was in fact a continental project, especially at the beginning of the World War II.

On the other hand, if we can envision the Nazi genocide as a partial destruction of the German, Polish, or Lithuanian national groups, we can reinstate the victims as full citizens and confront the goals of Nazism, which proposed the need for a Reich that was "free of Jews." The aim of Nazism was not only to exterminate certain groups (ethnic, national, and political, among others) but to completely transform German and European society through the absence of such groups, a transformation that proved to be quite successful. In particular, one of the most enduring effects of the Nazi genocide of Jews and Gypsies was the disappearance of internationalism and cosmopolitanism as constituent parts of the German and European identity.

The key feature, then, of this more recent interpretation of "partial destruction of the national group" is that it focuses our attention on the wider purpose of genocide and the way it targets the whole population of a particular territory. It invites societies to reflect on how destruction has shaped their *own* social practices, avoiding the alienation inherent in treating genocide as the suffering of *others*. In such a way, even the Nazi genocide is somehow a "hidden genocide," as its main consequence on European society was forgotten.

Understanding genocide as the partial destruction of one's own group also widens the sphere of complicity in the planning and execution of murder. We are forced to ask who has benefited from the disappearance of certain groups and—more importantly—from the social transformation generated by the processes of annihilation and terror. The business and political sectors behind many genocides have often remained invisible and unpunished, since responsibility is usually attached only to the direct perpetrators, whether military or police, but not to their paymasters.

The Processes of Constructing Identity and Otherness

We need to remember that genocide, like other social practices, is a process that unfolds over time. It is not possible to develop a set of social practices involving genocide without first building models of identity and otherness, symbolic representations that suggest ways of perceiving ourselves and those whom we cast in the role of "other." Moreover, although the two occur more or less simultaneously, the "other" may not be demonized until much later in the process.

The formulation of separate ethnic and national identities is a distinguishing feature of modernity even if some of its features predate the modern era. Negative typecasting has taken various forms, from a simple dichotomy between civilization and barbarism to sophisticated racial theories or the racialization of class relations.[7] Whatever the case, stereotyping is a necessary step on the path toward genocide, and detecting and deconstructing negative labels while they are still being formed may help prevent genocide or at least prevent it being repeated.

Although identity is dynamic and multiple, the construction of a "negative other" forces us to limit our own identity to a narrow set of criteria. In the modern period these criteria have mostly been nationalistic, sometimes tinged with religion (as in the case of "Western Christian" values), secularism (as in the case of French citizenship), or even agnosticism and racism (as in the case of the "new man" of the Third Reich).[8]

Without this way of getting rid of the otherness within ourselves—an otherness that is part of both personal identity and the identity of every modern nation-state—the dehumanization of other human beings required to commit genocide would simply not be possible. It is not at all easy to kill people we think of as belonging to our own community. It is much easier to kill or help to kill those we consider to be strangers or aliens. Zygmunt Bauman has coined the term *adiaphorization* to describe the deactivating or suppressing of one's sense of right and wrong and insensitivity to the suffering of strangers—an attitude that tends to be combined with negative stereotyping among the direct perpetrators.[9]

As I have pointed out elsewhere,[10] this way of constructing identity involves several interlocking processes:

- Reduction of the multiple dimensions of identity to just one (national, religious, ethnic, or another)
- Creation of a "normal" identity, including acceptable and unacceptable forms of deviance for different categories of social actors
- Alienation and dehumanization of collective identities that fall outside the accepted limits of deviance and indifference toward the possible fate of deviants

Therefore, any attempt to tackle or prevent genocidal social practices must begin with this construction of identity and otherness. Indeed, it is precisely these constructions that the perpetrators set out to impose, not only through terror but later through the memory of genocide in post-genocide societies. Thus, genocidal social practices will be difficult to prevent unless we question the paradigm of identity by exclusion, with its accompanying processes of normalization, alienation, dehumanization, and adiaphorization.

Similarly, perpetuating binary visions of "us" and "them" after genocide has occurred simply serves to legitimize future acts of counter-genocide by the "victimized group." Israel's violations of human rights in the occupied Palestinian Territory (supposedly legitimized by the suffering of European Jews under Nazism), the terrorist attacks by Palestinians living under Israeli occupation, the killings of Hutus in the Democratic Republic of Congo as revenge for the genocide against the Tutsis in Rwanda, the killings of Serbs in Kosovo in revenge for the murder of Kosovar Albanians, and the killing and expulsion of the German

population by the Soviet Union from those areas of eastern Europe in which
the Nazis had committed atrocities are just a few examples where debates rage
about who is "good" and who is "bad." Part of this binary way of thinking is that
each group must be, intrinsically, either perpetrators or victims within a binary
paradigm that can only conceive of whole groups of the population as perpetrators or as victims—a logic that eternally relegates them to bearing the burden
of the above-mentioned characteristics—and thus prevents us from recognizing
the complexity of the historical processes as well as the dynamism and artificial-
ity of the processes of constructing identity.

Politics and Ethics: Some Suggestions by Emmanuel Levinas

If reversing the consequences of a "reorganizing genocide"[11] is a decidedly political act, so too is confronting the conditions that make genocide possible in the
first place. It is also an ethical issue because we are responsible for the ways in
which we conceptualize our own identity and the identities of others, as well
as for any limits we may place on this responsibility. In this sense, the Jewish
philosopher Emmanuel Levinas has suggested a way of looking at this ethical
dimension that is eminently political.[12]

Levinas understands otherness as a fundamental fact of human life. But
unlike more philosophical interpretations of otherness or politically correct discourses about "respect" and "tolerance" for others, Levinas is not interested in
just *any* "other," and certainly not in abstractions. On the contrary, Levinas sees
the other as the foundation of ethical life. The other is the face of the widow, the
orphan, the beggar, and the stranger—figures that emerge straight from the Bible.
These figures are repeated each time Levinas refers to otherness. They do not
speak to us simply from the fact of their existence but from their pain, their dispossession, their need, and a responsibility that makes us—the holders of wealth,
power, knowledge, health, happiness, or whatever—guilty of the other's suffering.

Levinas poses a *nonsymmetrical* and *nonallergic* relationship with otherness.
This is not just any otherness but a "deprived" otherness in which our responsibility for them is not balanced on their part by any responsibility toward us.
There is no moral quid pro quo, and our actions expect no response in return.
Unlike the contractual model of ethics, which in the final analysis is based on
the market metaphor, Levinasian responsibility is not guided by any expectation about the other's past or future actions. Responsibility for others derives
entirely from their dispossession or need.

This radical ethical-philosophical view of the dispossessed other as one
whose life and well-being demand our *total responsibility*, a duty of service, provides a starting point—although others are possible—for designing a policy to
confront the genocidal potential that resides in every modern human being,

while offering a profound way of reshaping the way we understand our moral responsibility and, therefore, our own identity.

In any situation where another human being is disparaged, harassed, reviled, isolated, stigmatized, kidnapped, tortured, or killed, we have absolute and total responsibility in ethical terms for that person's fate. Responsibility is thus shared by everyone; family members, friends, and acquaintances but also witnesses of kidnappings, neighbors of victims, and acquaintances of their torturers.

Genocidal social practices could not progress if we moved toward a moral reformulation of this type, and the concept of genocide as the partial destruction of our own national group is a crucial step in that direction, making visible what the most common understandings of genocide used to hide. Genocides need the *active consensus* of the population through shared prejudices, or at least a *passive consensus* in the form of a numbing of moral values and indifference toward the fate of persecuted people (what Bauman calls adiaphorization). Rethinking our moral approach in a Levinasian sense could jeopardize our welfare (perhaps "comfort" would be a better word) and even endanger our own lives in order to save another. However, it is one of the most promising ethical and moral strategies for challenging the growing hegemony of genocidal practices as ways of reorganizing social relations across national groups by means of terror.

Without a major transformation of our processes of identity construction, without a restatement of the limits of our responsibility for others, and without understanding that each of us is an inseparable part of any social practice prevailing in our society, and therefore morally responsible for its effects, there will be no chance of banishing genocide as a tool of social engineering. This new approach is both ethical and political, and its success or failure will determine the type of society that we and our children will inhabit and engage with.

Conclusions

We have seen that the Genocide Convention allows for an interpretation of genocide based on Lemkin's notion of "partial destruction by the perpetrators of their own national group." This explanation makes the Convention applicable to a potentially large number of politically motivated annihilations, including nearly all modern genocides. This is true even when a group appears *at first sight* to have been targeted for religious or ethnic reasons. At the same time, Lemkin's interpretation is much more enriching for social memory processes, restoring ownership of the past to the victims rather than letting it be appropriated by the perpetrators.

There is a growing tendency to include non-state actions within the category of "crimes against humanity," thus confusing acts of terrorism and even political dissent with state-sponsored atrocities. This blurring of conceptual boundaries is making the notion of "crimes against humanity" so open-ended that it could eventually be used to persecute any civilian group that opposes the status quo.

It is therefore important to emphasize the distinctiveness of the concept of genocide, which requires "intent to destroy a group in whole or in part." We should not devalue international criminal law with a host of new concepts ("atrocity crimes," etc.) that lump together crimes that are qualitatively different (for example, state-sponsored crimes as compared to non-state crimes). Clear legislation is needed to protect individuals from arbitrary state persecution and to guarantee fundamental rights, which have taken centuries to evolve.

Contrary to the hegemonic trend in international law, which seeks to replace the term "genocide" in almost all cases with "crimes against humanity," I feel it would be much more useful if the ICC called cases of genocide by their proper name. It should stop putting the actions of insurgent movements in the Congo, Uganda, or Colombia on the same level as mass murder committed by the state.

In the case of Argentina, it is particularly useful to understand the entire process of genocide and its consequences for the whole of society. Some specifics of the Argentinean case (the nonexistence of ethnic groups before and after the genocide as "separate identities" inside the Argentine national group, the trials in the national courts, the interpretation of the facts by some tribunals as "partial destruction of the Argentine national group") help us to break away from the binary model of "goodies" and "baddies," one group annihilating another group, and to better understand the effects of genocide on our own national group and in our own lives. But the Argentine case provides a perspective that is also useful in addressing other cases, a perspective that was precisely Lemkin's when he created the concept of genocide: that genocide is always a destruction of the patterns of identity of the national group (in his case, the "Polish national group").

So, the principal danger of viewing genocide as irrational is binary thinking. The sanctification of the Holocaust as "incomprehensible," a conflict in which German "willing executioners" killed innocent Jews—diminishes other processes of disappearance and annihilation viewed as "understandable" by blaming the victims. It is almost as if an unconscious and therefore innocent "being in itself" is accusing a conscious and clearly political "being for itself." If we accept this logic, then the scholar's job becomes primarily one of deciding in which direction to tip the scales: innocent or guilty. And if only the "innocent" deserve protection, then the law can be ignored. "Victimized groups" will always be supported and legitimized, whatever they do. "Perpetrator groups" will always be persecuted, even though their role has changed and they are now suffering human rights violations. This binary logic leads to a world vision that is void of critical thinking, one in which good and evil are inherited, and even the grandchildren of those who suffered genocide can believe they are morally justified in violating the rights of others because of the suffering of their grandparents.

What the genocidal cases have in common is that the perpetrators sought to annihilate their enemies both materially and symbolically. Not just their bodies but also the memory of their existence was intended to disappear, forcing the survivors to deny their own identity, as a synthesis of *being* and *doing* defined like any other identity by a particular way of life. In this sense, the disappearances outlast the destruction of war: the effects of genocide do not end but only begin with the deaths of the victims. In short, the main objective of genocidal destruction is the transformation of the victims into "nothing" and the survivors into "nobodies."

And it is this situation in which we should attempt to understand, to resist, and to reverse—not in any individual or partisan fashion, but for all peoples and, in a utopian sense, for the good of humankind.

NOTES

1. William Schabas, *Genocide in International Law*, 2nd ed. (Cambridge: Cambridge University Press, 2009).

2. Raphael Lemkin, *Axis Rule in Occupied Europe* (Washington DC: Carnegie Endowment for International Peace, 1944).

3. Eduardo Luis Duhalde, Opening Act, Ninth Biennial International Conference on Genocide, IAGS-UNTREF, Buenos Aires, 19 July 2011.

4. Authors with very different approaches who have challenged the exclusion of political groups include: Frank Chalk and Kurt Jonassohn, *The History and Sociology of Genocide: Analysis and Case Studies* (New Haven, CT: Yale University Press, 1990); Ward Churchill, *A Little Matter of Genocide: Holocaust and Denial in the Americas, 1492 to the Present* (San Francisco: City Lights Books, 1997); Helen Fein, *Accounting for Genocide* (New York: Free Press, 1979); Leo Kuper, *Genocide: Its Political Use in the Twentieth Century* (New Haven, CT: Yale University Press, 1981); Vahakn Dadrian, "A Typology of Genocide," *International Review of Modern Sociology* 15 (1975): 204; Barbara Harff and Ted Gurr, "Toward Empirical Theory of Genocides and Politicides," *International Studies Quarterly* 37, no. 3 (1988): 359–371; Matthias Bjornlund, Eric Markusen, and Martin Mennecke, "¿Qué es el genocidio? En la búsqueda de un denominador común entre definiciones jurídicas y no jurídicas" [What is genocide? In search of a common denominator between legal and nonlegal definitions] in *Genocidio: La administración de la muerte en la modernidad* [Genocide: The management of death in modernity], ed. Daniel Feierstein (Bueno Aires: EDUNTREF, 2005).

5. This is clearly the case in Latin America, Indonesia and several other countries during the 1960s, 1970s, and 1980s, and even in Rwanda during the 1990s.

6. Convention on the Prevention and Punishment of the Crime of Genocide, Article 2.

7. See Mario Margulis and Marcelo Urresti, *La segregación negada: Cultura y discriminación social* [Segregation denied: Culture and social discrimination] (Buenos Aires: Biblos, 1998).

8. An interesting reflection on the functioning of these processes with reference to the notion of "Arabs" and the way they are perceived in Argentina can be found in Hammurabi Noufouri, *Del Islam y los árabes: Acerca de la percepción argentina de lo propio y de lo ajeno* [Islam and the Arabs: About Argentine perceptions of self and others] (Buenos Aires: Cálamo, 2001).

9. See Zygmunt Bauman, *Postmodern Ethics* (Oxford: Blackwell, 1993).

10. See, for instance, Daniel Feierstein, *El genocidio como práctica social: Entre el nazismo y la experiencia argentina* (Buenos Aires: FCE, 2007) (to be published as *Genocide as Social Practice* by Rutgers University Press).

11. For the idea of "reorganizing genocide" see Feierstein, *El genocidio como práctica social.*

12. For a more complete version of Emmanuel Levinas's ideas on this subject, see his books: *Totalidad e infinito* [Totality and infinity] (Salamanca: Sígueme, 1999) and *De otro modo que ser o más allá de la esencia* [Otherwise than being: Or beyond essence] (Salamanca, Sígueme, 1987).

TWO

Power, Resistance, and Edges of the State

4

"Simply Bred Out"

Genocide and the Ethical in the Stolen Generations

DONNA-LEE FRIEZE

After a series of legislative enquiries and reports, statements and apologies, the Australian Labour leader Paul Keating initiated the Report of the National Inquiry into the Separation of Aboriginal and Torres Strait Islander Children from Their Families, titled *Bringing Them Home (BTH)*, in 1995.[1] The *BTH* report sought testimony from Aborigines who had been forcibly removed from their families between the early years of the twentieth century to the 1970s, formally known as the Stolen Generations.[2] As Rosanne Kennedy states: "The report was historically significant because it was the first time this history of separation was officially acknowledged by the Australian federal government, and for the first time it received a prominent place in Australian culture."[3] The report concluded that this act of separation was an act of genocide. The Genocide Convention states in Article 2(e) that "Forcibly transferring children of the group to another group" may constitute genocide, if the group mentioned in this point is a member of a "national, ethnical, racial, or religious group,"[4] with the intention of destroying this group in whole or in part. By the time the report was presented to the Australian parliament, Keating had gone and was replaced by the conservative Howard government. This history, largely written by descendants of perpetrators, was now being challenged by Aboriginal voices through oral and written testimonies.

The *BTH* report sparked a very public debate in which issues of benevolence (or motivations) and genocide (or intentions) abounded. The arguments supposed that because genocide is the "crime of crimes," acts of benevolence are evidently the antithesis to these heinous acts. The arguments exposed the lack of knowledge of what genocide is and illuminated the normative notion that genocide is only associated with mass murder and hence the Holocaust. Another reason why some could not equate the case of the Stolen Generations with the

Holocaust is that, "unlike the ideology of racial purity that emerged in Germany from eugenics, according to which 'impure races' had to be prevented from 'contaminating' the pure Aryan race . . . [the perpetrators] argued the advantages of 'miscegenation' between Aboriginal and white people."[5] The Stolen Generations are a clear example of genocide, where the "out" group is destroyed through absorption into the "in" group. As these issues impinge on notions of responsibility and duty, this chapter will consider Emmanuel Levinas's philosophical approaches to these ideas in relation to the biological absorption policy of the Western Australian government in the 1930s. These notions of responsibility, duty, and biological absorption are concealed aspects of a genocide that does not exhibit normative understandings of genocide-as-mass-murder.

It must be clear that even though each state enacted its own legislation, from 1937 it was clear that the "destiny of the natives of aboriginal origin . . . lies in the their ultimate absorption by the people of the Commonwealth."[6] The period of forced removal was from 1909 and conducted with different policies in different states in Australia,[7] but I will be focusing on the interwar period in Western Australia because the 2002 film *Rabbit-Proof Fence*, which depicted these events, became part of the collective consciousness of Australians five years after the publication of the *BTH* report.[8] The ideology and philosophy behind Western Australia's abduction policy was also well documented by its chief protector of Aborigines from 1915 to 1940,[9] A. O. Neville, dubbed "Australia's most enthusiastic exponent of absorption,"[10] who is also depicted in the film. Neville's philosophy draws on "anthropologists in Australia [in the 1930s who] were convinced of the validity of biological race as a real factor."[11] His logic was brilliantly simple and shockingly racist: his focus was skin color and he believed that if Aborigines became lighter in skin color over time, their cultural behavior would simulate white people's cultural characteristics.[12] In a demonstration regarding this process, Neville states: "The continuing infiltration of white blood finally stamps out the black color. The Aboriginal has simply been bred out."[13] As "Aboriginal" is an adjective, Neville implies that the entire physical, cultural, and biological characteristics of the Aborigine are forced to disappear, and, in turn, ensure that the Stolen Generations are hidden from an understanding of this case study as a genocide.

Removal of "Half-Castes": Benevolence or Genocide?

In her formidable article "Unspeakable Pasts as Limit Events," Simone Gigliotti questions (the no less impressive historian) Inga Clendinnen's defiant refusal to identify the actions against the Stolen Generations as "genocide." Clendinnen argues: "When I see the word 'genocide' I still see Gypsies and Jews being herded into trains, into pits, into ravines, and behind them the shadowy figures of Armenian women and children being marched into the desert by armed men. I see deliberate mass murder."[14] Gigliotti rightly asserts that Clendinnen reads genocide as an "extreme practice as intentional physical wounding and homicide."[15] Clendinnen's narrow definition of genocide represses the voices of many victims of genocide, including the thousands of children forcibly removed from their families.

Before examining *Rabbit-Proof Fence* in the context of Emmanuel Levinas's ethical theses of responsibility and duty, this section places the genocide in its historical context by considering the *BTH* report, which stimulated debate and feelings of shame and denial throughout academia, the popular press, and the general populace.[16] The immediacy of the *BTH* report meant that *Rabbit-Proof Fence* was perceived to be of direct relevance.

As pointed out in *BTH*, Australia was under no legal obligation to sign the nonbinding U.N. declarations of 1945 and 1948, nor was it pressured to ratify the binding Genocide Convention of 1948 and the Convention of 1965.[17] However, the policy of child removal "continued to be practised as official policy long after being clearly prohibited by treaties to which Australia had voluntarily subscribed,"[18] and decades after Australia's ratification of the Genocide Convention.[19] That the official policy contradicted many articles and points in the conventions and declaration suggests that the policy makers were inattentive to, or ignorant of, the contents of these documents after Australia's ratification. Arguably, during the interwar period that *Rabbit-Proof Fence* depicts, the policies were believed to emanate from benevolence and therefore were excluded from accusations of unethical behavior.[20] If the policy of biological absorption was so benevolent, it must be asked, why only half-castes and not full-bloods (terms used to segregate Aborigines from mainstream society)? Because Neville believed the government could not alleviate the situation of full-blood Aborigines (who, according to Neville, were "dying out"), but he argued that half-caste Aborigines could be biologically absorbed into the white community.[21] Ironically, then, in Western Australia there was no intention "to destroy in whole or in part" full-bloods, as "Neville waited for interracial relationships and high rates of poverty and disease"[22] to destroy the full-bloods, according to Katherine Ellinghaus. As Alan Charlton notes, this notion of full bloods "dying out "had a long auspicious heritage and Neville was only one of many to subscribe to it."[23]

In the section on reparation, *BTH* debates whether the policies directed at the Stolen Generations constituted genocide. Intention is a key concept in the crime of genocide, and Neville's intentions, as stated here, are clear: "The decision made by the Commonwealth Government to adopt as definite policy the encouragement of marriages of white men and half-caste women with a view to raising the standard of mixed blood to that of whites, is nothing new in this State [Western Australia]. I have foreseen it for years, and sponsored it as the only outcome of the position. The blacks will have to go white."[24] As Ellinghaus points out, the policy was not directed at removal alone, but half-castes were viewed as "prime candidates for sexual relationships or marriages with whites."[25] In addition, Neville's last sentence indicates the intention was to destroy part of the group through biological absorption rather than cultural assimilation.[26]

Neville contends: "The native must be helped in spite of himself! Even if a measure of discipline is necessary it must be applied, but it can be applied in such a way as to *appear to be* gentle persuasion" (emphasis added).[27] Supercili ousness and conviction tinge Neville's words rather than vitriol. The "gentle persuasion" implies the Indigenous population will in time understand what is "good" for them. Of course, forcible seizure of children does not equate with "gentle persuasion," but Neville's intentions (biological absorption) are motivated by the *appearance* of "gentle persuasion." The appearance of motivations does not necessarily reveal intentions (of genocide, or any other crime), but it does suggest Neville and the perpetrators are hiding more sinister motives.

BTH suggests that the chief protector's acts were motivated by goodwill. For instance, at the Royal Commission inquiry into the conditions of Aborigines in the 1930s, Neville argued that "if we are going to fit and train such children for the future they cannot be left as they are. . . . I want to give these children a chance. . . . Unless those children are removed, social conditions in those places will go from bad to worse. . . . I want to teach them right from wrong. How are the children to fight against these conditions?"[28] However, the report puts forward a key argument: "To constitute an act of genocide the planned extermination [or intended destruction] of a group *need not be solely motivated by animosity or hatred*" (emphasis added).[29] Indeed, it is possible to argue that other forms of genocide, such as killing members of the group, are well intended on the part of the perpetrators in order to "purify" a national, racial, ethnic, or religious group. Regardless of the motivation behind the intent, the effects of a policy decision cannot be ignored.

Forcibly removing children caused serious mental harm to indigenous Australians through the loss and traumas of having the children removed (Article 2[b]), and the removal of the children prevented births within the group (Article 2[d]). The state used racial persecution to change the ethnicity through the forced cultural assimilation and biological absorption of young Australian children to transform race. Thus, Colin Tatz contends that by applying the definition of the Genocide Convention, "Australia is guilty of at least three, possibly four, acts of genocide [Article 2(a), (b), (d), and (e)]."[30] Bain Attwood, however, suggests that intentions without empirical actions may not be genocidal.[31] Nevertheless, Tatz argues persuasively that the "twentieth-century official state policy and practice of forcibly transferring children [intent *and* action] from one group to another [was] with the express intention that *they cease being Aboriginal*."[32] This clearly distinguishes motivation from intent, a distinction also made by Helen Fein.[33]

Gigliotti points out that Sir Ronald Wilson, one of the authors of *BTH,* expressed unease at the use of the word "genocide" in the report.[34] He felt that the word was too controversial and, in hindsight, should not have been used. The problem with the term "is that you are arguing about intent,"[35] writes Sir Ronald. While "intent" and "motive" are often muddled, it is more likely that some find it difficult to conceive of genocide as anything but mass murder. According to Patrick Carlyon, "the report's justification for the use of the word relied on an interpretation of a 1948 United Nation definition, and that was a long way from the everyday *perception* of genocide" (emphasis added),[36] which is mass murder. Tatz suggests the evasion of the term *genocide* may be due to the cultural image Australians want to project: "Almost all historians of the Aboriginal experience—black and white—avoid it. They write about pacifying, killing, cleansing, excluding, exterminating, starving, poisoning, shooting . . . but avoid genocide. Are they ignorant of genocide theory and practice? Or simply reluctant to taint 'the land of the fair go,' the 'lucky country,' with so heinous and disgracing a label?"[37]

This pervasive insistence on not referring to the removal of half-caste Aborigines as genocide reflects a limited understanding of the term under international law. Forcible removal (and biological absorption), it seems, is one crime, and genocide—in the minds of many—is another. As Robert Manne argues, "The administrators advocating absorption did not advocate violence as a solution to the Aboriginal problem."[38] Although corporeal violence was not the method used to implement biological absorption, the intentions were nonetheless genocidal, even though the forcible transference of children for biological absorption was often viewed as responsible and dutiful not only at the time but continuing to this day, ensuring that the Stolen Generations remain behind a veneer of decency and thus hidden as a genocide.

Responsibility and Duty

The issue of responsibility highlights the philosophical contribution of Emmanuel Levinas's concept of the Other. A philosophy of the ethical, the Other is every being I encounter and who I hold in the highest respect: "the relationship to the [O]ther is asymmetric: the [O]ther is always greater than me"[39] and hence its capitalization.[40] For Levinas, responsibility for the Other is the utmost ethical stance. However, in the following quotation he appears to argue for a lack of liability in our responsibility: "The unlimited responsibility in which I find myself comes from the hither side of my freedom, from a 'prior to every memory,' an 'ulterior to every accomplishment,' from the non-present par excellence, the non-original, the anarchical, prior to or beyond essence."[41]

Colin Davis argues, "Such responsibility [of the dutiful and benevolent kind] would be an attribute or property of the subject; Levinassian [*sic*] responsibility is less generous, more imperious and ineluctable."[42] Responsibility for the Other is then inevitable (whether I choose to exercise it or not) but "natural benevolence" is indeterminate. Seen in this way, Neville refutes his a priori responsibility to the Other and determines that what he is doing for the Aborigine is benevolent. Such acts may seem innocuous, but they are, on the one hand, effective tools in implementing the genocide and, on the other, secure means of keeping this genocide hidden.

On a collective scale, Neville misplaces responsibility to the Aborigines. He states that Western Australian Aborigines "have been indulging in practices calculated in time to wipe them out of existence without any help from us."[43] Not only does this obliterate the history of colonization of Australia by the English-born chief protector, it places his attempt at biological absorption as an act of "natural benevolence," helping the "natural" process along. Neville does not conform to the conventional images of perpetrators of genocide (more often than not, the state and the military) but rather the image of a citizen executing his three watchwords: "Duty, service, responsibility."[44]

The disengagement with the Other is elucidated in *Rabbit-Proof Fence* in a sequence at the Moore River Settlement, where the children, who have been stolen from their families to be absorbed into Anglo culture, reveal the color of their skin to Neville. The whiter ones will be sent elsewhere to be "educated," as the biological advantage of having white skin putatively equates with intelligence. Molly cautiously approaches Neville and the matron. This is shot from Molly's point of view to enhance the frightening experience and accompanied "by the overdubbing of Molly's breathing," which is, as Tony Hughes D'aeth contends, to enhance the child's perspective of fear.[45] Neville is shot from sharp side angles—as if Molly can never engage with such strangeness—utilizing his "gentle persuasion" to coerce her with his three "watchwords." After assessing her, he utters a hardened, uncompromising "no," indicating that she is not white enough to be educated. The alien world into which Molly and her family are forcefully plunged is depicted as claustrophobic, without alterity. The harsh climate of the Australian outback through which the girls travel over 1,500 miles for nine weeks appears, by comparison, to embrace them.

The resistance to alterity—or the Other's Otherness—is linked with speech. Levinas argues that the saying (that is, the preverbal, the ethical, the "listening to a voice")[46] is inextricably correlated with responsibility for the Other, and like responsibility for the Other, the saying cannot be captured as it changes over time: "saying, in the form of responsibility for another, is bound to an irrecuperable, unrepresentable, past, temporalizing according to a time with separate epochs, in a diachrony."[47] In *Rabbit-Proof Fence*, the customary language of the Aboriginal children at the settlement is explicitly and unequivocally suppressed. On their first night in the dormitory, the matron orders "no talking" and again the following morning at breakfast. When the girls attempt to speak their native language, the matron accuses the children of speaking "jibber." Levinas writes, "To communicate is indeed to open oneself, but the openness is not complete if it is on the watch for recognition."[48] The absence of a common language renders the "opening up of one's self" impossible for the girls and the matron.

Davis remarks that "prior to choice, commitment, activity, or passivity, the subject is exposed to the Other, capable of speaking and responding to the discourse of [O]thers."[49] The chief protector's agents are exposed to the Others[50] but opt instead to treat Aborigines as alien others. Removing the language of the children at the settlement is not just an act of folly and cruelty; it precisely modifies the children to suit a mirror image of Neville and his agents, so they can "recognize" themselves in the other. As Genevieve Lloyd astutely observes in relation to the treatment of the Stolen Generations: "the connecting thread in the policies was not discrimination against something seen to be different, but, on the contrary, a failure to recognise difference."[51] This is not ethical language "for the Other" but rather ontologically "by the other";[52] the Other is reduced to a reflection of the self, who is there *for* me. As Bauman writes, "It is this . . . non-reversibility of my responsibility . . . which puts me in the . . . [ethical] relationship."[53] In Levinasian discourse, Neville's expectation of the response to his captives—to oblige by accepting their pact in the relationship of responsibility—is unethical.

As a filmic text, *Rabbit-Proof Fence* engages with the ethical notion of responsibility through the visual image of the face. It is not a film dominated by dialogue, and thus, the director often focuses on the faces of the three girls as they journey home. But how is this linked with responsibility? Levinas writes, "the approach of the face is the most basic mode of responsibility";[54] thus, responsibility begins with the epiphany of the face of the Other. However, it is important to understand Levinas's ambiguity regarding the face. While the face is the empirical object we see, it is more often the "meaning of poverty [the Levinasian term for vulnerability], of helplessness, of being exposed,"[55] in other words, the Other's very Otherness or essence. The *expression* of poverty, enhanced subliminally through the cinematography and poignant music, is reflected in the faces of the three girls.

Encounters with Others sporadically intersect the girls' experience through the 1,500-mile trek home. As one would expect, the trek is extraordinary. The film focuses on the experience the girls have of encounters with the Other on the way home. The girls meet white and black Australians, some helpful, others untrustworthy. Unlike their captors, the girls look beyond skin color in their ethical encounters with Others, reversing the dehumanizing actions of the chief protector and the staff at the settlement. In short, the film seems to exemplify the Levinasian dictum that a "face is pure experience, conceptless experience."[56]

The face for the genocidal perpetrator, however, does not reveal itself in ethical experience but is masked by knowledge, a supposed knowledge that governs this hidden genocide. In order to dehumanize with the intent to destroy, the perpetrator professes to "know" the members of victim groups through defined facial or cultural characteristics.

Responsibility is depicted in the film as an ideology of "rationality" that confers universality on the actions in the chief protector's circles. In other words, the perpetrators believe that their actions are reasonable because other white Australians share their values. As Bauman writes: "Responsibility does not have a 'purpose' or 'reason' . . . it is not an effect of 'will' or 'decision.'"[57] However, a general category or definition of responsibility produces, for Levinas, a more sinister quality and effect. According to Bauman: "stripping him or her of *their* responsibility, which constitutes *their* alterity, their *uniqueness* . . . is most certainly not the outcome my responsibility may pursue or contemplate without denying itself, without ceasing to be . . . [an ethical] stance."[58] Thus, a so-called benevolent obligation, which equates reason with morality, disengages the victims from ethical responsibility. It is in short, a violation of alterity.

Having realized that the three girls are following the rabbit-proof fence to their home in Jigalong, Neville caustically tells the police inspector: "Just because people use Neolithic tools, Inspector, doesn't mean they have Neolithic minds. This makes our task much easier."[59] As in all forms of racism, on which the dehumanizing aspect of genocide is premised, Neville's prejudice locates the girls in a space that occupies all others as Same, and yet inferior. This way, Neville, like other perpetrators, believes he can engage in the freedom of the self through the demonization of the Other, a point that Levinas reiterates throughout his writing in relation to Heidegger.

The Heideggerian ontological concept of "other" revolves around a power struggle. Peter Sedgwick argues in relation to Heidegger's philosophy that in our concern "with . . . [others] we define ourselves in relation to them. We want to make sure that . . . [others] do not outstrip us in some ways . . . or, if we have some kind of priority over them in some manner, we are keen to maintain this priority."[60] The other is there to threaten my freedom and therefore the relationship between the other and me is based on authority. In this sense, the chief protector and his agents engage with a Heideggerian concept of power and are devoid of the ethical. The Levinasian ethical philosophy sees the Other as "my 'judge' and 'master,' higher than I am, calling me to responsibility for my thoughts and actions . . . I am required, in the course of this meeting, to justify my existence."[61] Clearly, in the process of genocide, whether intentional mass murder or biological absorption, the power relationship is ethically contorted.

Conclusion

The claim that the removal of indigenous Australian children from their parents was the product of innocuous government policy and was not genocidal is inextricably linked to the debates surrounding responsibility and duty. *Rabbit-Proof Fence* portrays the intentions of the policy makers who insisted that half-caste children be biologically absorbed into white Australian culture, without any contact with their biological parents or access to their cultural practices. Despite the motivations of the policy makers, intentional destruction of a racial group occurred through the absorption methods. Genocide is concerned with intentional destruction, and as the case of the Stolen Generations evidently demonstrates, there are many ways to destroy a group.

It is clear, in the wake of the Keating government's enquiry that initiated the *BTH* report, the Howard government's refusal to express any regret over the Stolen Generations, and finally the apology made by the Labour Rudd government, that Australians are now aware, from a collective perspective, of the existence of the Stolen Generations, even though these events are hidden from public consciousness as a genocide. Rudd's speech was deeply moving; he also made many specific and explicit references to the Stolen Generations. As such, very early on in his apology he stated: "We reflect in particular on the mistreatment of those who were Stolen Generations—this blemished chapter in our nation's history."[62] But a "blemished" nation-state does not (could not) commit genocide: Rudd refused to mention the act of genocide in relation to the Stolen Generations.

Less than ten years after the *BTH* report, the Supreme Court of South Australia made a landmark decision on August 1, 2007, when it compensated Bruce Trevorrow for having been stolen from his family.[63] Slowly, through court decisions like this, the voices of the victims can rightfully eclipse the white utterances on this genocide. However, since the Rudd government's apology, the issue of genocide and the Stolen Generations has, in Tony Barta's words, "been buried in public discourse . . . [and have] again been driven underground."[64] The public discourse includes issues of duty and responsibility, benevolence and noncorporeal violence, issues that, if allowed to continue to dominate the popular discourse, will ensure that the genocide remains hidden, cloaked behind "goodwill." Rudd had the opportunity to acknowledge the genocide and ratify the Genocide Convention in Australian domestic law. However, it is probable, as A. Dirk Moses ascertains, that the term "genocide" has a moral overtone to it, and to call Australia's history "genocide" could appear to "criminalize it." Rudd asserted he understood the term, and thus he "knew" to avoid it.[65] The law was used to biologically absorb the Stolen Generations; however the law is ignored when it comes to admonishing the acts.

Indeed, those laws of child removal presume that there is no relationship between the child and the family, whereas Emmanuel Levinas attempts to achieve, in Davis's words, "a philosophy of self and Other in which both are preserved as independent and self-sufficient, but in some sense in relation with one another."[66] Because the relationship with the Other is asymmetrical, it challenges the essence of universalism and codes imposed on us by the law.[67] Prior to the law, I have a responsibility to the Other to be regarded as Other. As Levinas writes, "Does not justice consist in putting the obligation with regard to the [O]ther before obligations to oneself, in putting the [O]ther before the [S]ame?"[68] In this regard, responsibility, as espoused by the duty enacted in the law in Western Australia prior to the Second World War, and resonating in *Rabbit-Proof Fence*, is unethical but also genocidal.

ACKNOWLEDGMENTS

The author would like to express gratitude to Daniel Feierstein and Joyce Apsel for their close reading and insightful comments on this essay.

NOTES

1. Human Rights and Equal Opportunity Commission, *Bringing Them Home,* Report of the National Inquiry into the Separation of Aboriginal and Torres Strait Islander Children from Their Families (hereafter *BTH*), Part 2: "Tracing the History," 1997, accessed 22 June 2011, http://www.hreoc.gov.au/social_justice/bth_report/report/index.html.

2. A term first coined by Peter Read in 1981. See Peter Read, *The Stolen Generations: The Removal of Aboriginal Children in New South Wales, 1883 to 1969* (Sydney: NSW Department of Aboriginal Affairs, 1998).

3. Rosanne Kennedy, "The Affective Work of Stolen Generations Testimony: From the Archives to the Classroom," *Biography* 27, no. 1 (2004): 52.

4. United Nations, *Convention on the Prevention and Punishment of the Crime of Genocide*, Office of the High Commissioner for Human Rights, 1948, Article 2, accessed 22 June 2011, http://www2.ohchr.org/english/law/genocide.htm.

5. *BTH*, Part 2. This did not stop Neville from quoting Hitler to strengthen an argument regarding procreation and legislation. He writes: "It has often been said that you cannot make people moral by Act of Parliament or, as Hitler once put it, you cannot abolish sexual intercourse by decree nor eliminate the instinct to possess. True enough, but laws and punishment are good in their way, serve to check illicit intercourse and regulate responsibility for the care and maintenance of children." As Alan Charlton writes, "It is difficult to say which is more stunning . . . that anyone could use Hitler to bolster an argument in such as off-hand manner in a book published in 1947, or that Neville seems to think Hitler too soft on this particular subject." See A. O. Neville and Alan Charlton in Alan Charlton, "Conceptualising Aboriginality: Reading AO Neville's Australia's Coloured Minority," *Aboriginal Studies* 2 (2002): 57.

6. Commonwealth of Australia, *Aboriginal Welfare: Initial Conference of Commonwealth and State Aboriginal Authorities, Held at Canberra, 21st to 23rd April, 1937* (Canberra: L. F. Johnston, 1937), 3.

7. The official policy began in 1909: "Towards the end of the 19th century authorities started to take children away without a legal framework. A framework was established in 1909 with the Aborigines Protection Act." See Creative Spirit, "Australia's Stolen Generations," accessed 19 August 2011, http://www.creativespirits.info/aboriginalculture/politics/stolen-generations.html#stolen-generations-guide.

8. ReconciliACTION Network, "Stolen Generations Factsheet," accessed 27 June 2011 http://reconciliaction.org.au/nsw/education-kit/stolen-generations/#forced.

9. *BTH*, Part 8: "The History—Western Australia."

10. Russell McGregor, "Governance, Not Genocide: Aboriginal Assimilation in the Postwar Era," in *Genocide and Settler Society: Frontier Violence and Stolen Indigenous Children in Australian History*, ed. A. Dirk Moses (New York: Berghahn Books, 2004), 293.

11. Charlton, "Conceptualising Aboriginality," 47.

12. Terms such as "white," "half-caste," "full-blood," and "black" for example, are inappropriate and racist terms, but this was the language used by the protectors for their genocidal theory and, as such, will be used throughout this essay. *BTH*, Part 2.

13. A. O. Neville quoted in *Rabbit-Proof Fence*, directed by Phillip Noyce (South Australia: Australian Film Finance Corporation, 2002), DVD, ch. 4.

14. Inga Clendinnen quoted in Simone Gigliotti, "Unspeakable Pasts as Limit Events: The Holocaust, Genocide, and the Stolen Generations," *Australian Journal of Politics and History* 49, no. 2 (June 2003): 165.

15. Gigliotti, "Unspeakable Pasts as Limit Events," 165.

16. See, for instance, Robert Manne, "In Denial: The Stolen Generations and the Right," *Australian Quarterly Essay*, no. 1 (2001); and Frank Devine, "Unscrupulous Genocide Claims Don't Help Aborigines," *The Australian*, 5 April 2001, 11. See also Russell McGregor, who argues that postwar biological absorption was not the intent of the governments, but, rather, assimilation, and, therefore, not genocide: McGregor, "Governance, Not Genocide," 290–311.

17. Charter of the United Nations of 1945, the Universal Declaration of Human Rights of 1948 and the International Convention on the Elimination of All Forms of Racial Discrimination of 1965.

18. *BTH*, Part 4: "Reparation."

19. See Australia's ratification status of the CPPCG on 8 July 1949 at United Nations, *United Nations Treaty Collection: Convention on the Prevention and Punishment of the Crime of Genocide—Participants*, accessed 29 June 2011, http://treaties.un.org/Pages/showDetails.aspx?objid=0800000280027fac.

20. In relation to his biological absorption plan, Neville said, "The sore spot requires the application of the surgeon's knife for the good of the patient, and probably against the patient's will." A. O. Neville quoted in Robert Manne, "Aboriginal Child Removal and the Question of Genocide, 1900–1940," in Moses, *Genocide and Settler Society*, 234.

21. See A. O. Neville quoted in *BTH*, Part 2.

22. Katherine Ellinghaus, "Biological Absorption and Genocide: A Comparison of Indigenous Assimilation Policies in the United States and Australia," *Genocide Studies and Prevention* 4, no. 1 (Spring 2009): 66.

23. Alan Charlton, "Conceptualising Aboriginality: Reading AO Neville's *Australia's Coloured Minority*," *Aboriginal Studies* 2 (2002): 54.

24. A. O. Neville quoted in Manne, "Aboriginal Child Removal," 232.

25. Ellinghaus, "Biological Absorption and Genocide," 67.

26. Neville confuses such terminology. He states: "Just what do we mean by absorption, assimilation and suchlike terms?" Quoted in Charlton, "Conceptualising Aboriginality," 56.

27. Neville quoted in *BTH*, Part 4.

28. Neville quoted in *BTH*, Part 2.

29. *BTH*, Part 4.

30. Colin Tatz, *Genocide in Australia: AIATSIS Research Discussion Papers No. 8*, Australian Institute of Aboriginal and Torres Strait Islander Studies no. 8 (1999), accessed 13 June 2011, http://www.aiatsis.gov.au/research/docs/dp/DP08.pdf, 6. To reiterate, Article 2(a) is killing members of the group; (b) is causing serious bodily or mental harm to members of the group; (d) is imposing measures intended to prevent births within the group; and (e) is forcibly transferring children of the group to another group. Tatz's recent work is also a valuable resource for this topic. See Colin Tatz, *With Intent to Destroy: Reflecting on Genocide* (London: Verso, 2003).

31. Bain Attwood, "The Stolen Generations and Genocide: Robert Manne's *In Denial: The Stolen Generations and the Right*," *Aboriginal History* 25 (2001): 163–172.

32. Tatz, *Genocide in Australia*, 6.

33. See Helen Fein, "Genocide: A Sociological Perspective," *Current Sociology* 38, no. 1 (1990): 19; and Helen Fein, "Genocide, Terror, Life Integrity, and War Crimes: The Case for Discrimination," in *Genocide: Conceptual and Historical Dimensions*, ed. George J. Andreopoulos (Philadelphia: University of Pennsylvania Press, 1994), 97.

34. Gigliotti, "Unspeakable Pasts as Limit Events," 171n121.

35. Ronald Wilson quoted in Patrick Carlyon, "White Lies," *Bulletin with Newsweek*, 12 June 2001, 26.

36. Carlyon, "White Lies," 26.

37. Tatz, *Genocide in Australia*, 2.

38. Manne, "Aboriginal Child Removal," 238.

39. Michael B. Smith, *Toward the Outside: Concepts and Themes in Emmanuel Levinas* (Pittsburgh: Duquesne University Press, 2005), 13.

40. Daniel Feierstein argues that Levinas borrows the concept of the Other from the Torah: "the widow, the orphan, the poor, the foreigner." The Other is not just anyone "but the Other who suffers." Daniel Feierstein, e-mail message to author, 7 April 2011.

41. Emmanuel Levinas, *Otherwise Than Being or Beyond Essence*, trans. Alphonso Lingis, 2nd ed. (The Hague: Martinus Nijhoff, 1981), 10.

42. Colin Davis, *Levinas: An Introduction* (Oxford: Polity Press, 1996), 80.

43. Neville quoted in Charlton, "Conceptualising Aboriginality," 54.

44. Neville to Molly Craig quoted in Noyce, *Rabbit-Proof Fence*, ch. 5.

45. Tony Hughes D'aeth, "Which Rabbit-Proof Fence? Empathy, Assimilation, Hollywood," *Australian Humanities Review* (September 2002), accessed 25 June 2011, http://www.australianhumanitiesreview.org/archive/Issue-September-2002/hughesdaeth.html.

46. Smith, *Toward the Outside*, 43, 44.

47. Levinas, *Otherwise Than Being*, 47.

48. Ibid., 119.

49. Davis, *Levinas*, 77.

50. Neville refers to the absorption process as the duty of all the police in the state. In speaking to the chief inspector of police, he contends, "Everyone of your men has a role as local protector." See Noyce, *Rabbit-Proof Fence*, ch. 8.

51. Genevieve Lloyd, "No One's Land: Australia and the Philosophical Imagination," *Hypatia* 15, no. 2 (2000): 36.

52. Levinas, *Otherwise Than Being*, 118.

53. Zygmunt Bauman, *Postmodern Ethics* (Oxford: Blackwell, 1993), 51.

54. Emmanuel Lévinas, *Collected Philosophical Papers*, trans. Alphonso Lingis (Dordrecht: Kluwer Academic Publishers, 1993), 59.

55. Levinas in Emmanuel Levinas and Christoph von Wolzogen, "Intention, Event, and the Other," in *Is It Righteous to Be? Interviews with Emmanuel Levinas*, ed. Jill Robbins (Stanford, CA: Stanford University Press, 1989), 145.

56. Lévinas, *Collected Philosophical Papers*, 59.

57. Bauman, *Postmodern Ethics*, 52–53.

58. Ibid., 53.

59. Noyce, *Rabbit-Proof Fence*, ch. 10.

60. Peter R. Sedgwick, *Descartes to Derrida: An Introduction to European Philosophy* (Oxford: Blackwell Publishers, 2001), 126.

61. Leonard Grob, "Emmanuel Levinas and the Primacy of Ethics in Post-Holocaust Philosophy," in *Ethics after the Holocaust: Perspectives, Critiques, and Responses*, ed. John K. Roth (St. Paul, MN: Paragon House, 1999), 7.

62. Kevin Rudd, "Apology to Australia's Indigenous Peoples," 13 February 2008, accessed 29 June 2011, http://www.aph.gov.au/house/rudd_speech.pdf.

63. See Saima Bangash, "Stolen Generation's First Successful Claim for Damages," *Law Society Journal* 45, no. 11 (December 2007): 50–51.

64. Tony Barta, "Sorry, and Not Sorry, in Australia: How the Apology to the Stolen Generations Buried a History of Genocide," *Journal of Genocide Research* 10, no. 2 (June 2008): 210.

65. A. Dirk Moses, "Moving the Genocide Debate beyond the History Wars," *Australian Journal of Politics and History* 54, no. 2 (2008): 249.

66. Davis, *Levinas*, 41.

67. See ibid., 52.

68. Lévinas, *Collected Philosophical Papers*, 53.

5

Historical Amnesia

The "Hidden Genocide" and Destruction of the Indigenous Peoples of the United States

CHRIS MATO NUNPA

Ho Mitakuyapi. Owasin cantewasteya nape ciyuzapi do! In the Dakota language, this is a greeting that means: "Hello, my relatives. With a good heart, I greet all of you with a handshake!" *Damakota*: "I am a Dakota." *Mini Sota Makoce heci-yatanhan wahi*: "I come from the land where the waters reflect the skies, or heavens" (the state of Minnesota).

I come from a people whose lands were stolen. Thus, my perspective will be considerably different from the perspective of the people who stole the lands. I come from a people whose treaties were broken. So, my view of history will vary dramatically from the people who violated the treaties. I come from a people who were the victims of genocide. Consequently, my point of view will be diametrically opposite to that of the *genocidaires*, the people who perpetrated the genocide. To be clear, I am stating that the land thieves, the treaty breakers, and the perpetrators of genocide are the United States of America, its Founding Fathers, and its U.S. Euro-American citizenry.

I represent a people, the Dakota People, one of many Indigenous Peoples, who has been militarily conquered, colonized, and Christianized by Western Europeans, U.S. Euro-Americans, and by the U.S. government. In the 520 years since Columbus stumbled onto our shores, genocide, great destruction, suffering, exploitation, and oppression have characterized the existence of the Indigenous Peoples of the United States and of the North American continent.

Since 1492, the Indigenous Peoples of the United States of America have been, generally, on full homeland security alert. This period of 520-plus years has seen the social and cultural destruction and the extermination and elimination of many Native Nations; has seen terrorism and the continuing oppression and subjugation of Native Peoples; has seen the massive land theft of approximately three billion acres; has seen the United States, the colonizing power, violating over four

96

hundred treaties it made with the Indigenous Peoples; and has seen, in general, the systematic and state-sponsored genocide of sixteen million Native People.

At the time of initial contact (1492), there were approximately sixteen million Native Peoples within "the continental United States,"[1] and four centuries later, there were only 237,196 Native People, according to the 1900 U.S. Census.[2] This represents a 98.5 percent population decline, if one says it nicely. If one says it not so nicely, then this represents a 98.5 percent extermination rate. Genocide was practiced by the Western Europeans, beginning with the Spanish, continuing with the French and British, and then, finally, with the Americans. "By the mid-19th century, U.S. policy makers and military commanders were stating—openly, frequently, and in plain English—that their objective was no less than the 'complete extermination' of any Native People who resisted being dispossessed of their lands, subordinated to federal authority, and assimilated into the colonizing culture."[3]

Frank Chalk and Kurt Jonassohn identified four common motives of genocide: to eliminate groups of people who the perpetrators imagine are threats, to spread terror among enemies, to acquire economic wealth, and to impose an ideology or a belief upon the victim group.[4] All four of these motives are evident in the U.S. and European genocide against the Indigenous Peoples of North America. Colonial settlers in Virginia and New England in the seventeenth century attempted to obliterate the "heathens" and "savages" in the name of Christianity and civilization. In Minnesota, Texas, and California, state governments offered bounties for Indian scalps in order to spread terror among these people whose lands they wanted to steal.[5] Across the United States, governors made it state policy to solve their local "Indian Problem" through forced extinction, presidents celebrated massacres of entire villages and tribes as wise and just decisions, and newspaper editorials encouraged genocide.[6]

As has been the case with so many historical genocides "rarely described if they are remembered at all," so, too, has the genocide of the Indigenous Peoples of the United States of America been rarely described as "genocide" if it is remembered or discussed at all. The United States, as a nation, and its Euro-American population, does not mind discussing the topic of genocide, especially when it deals with the Nazis, or the Serbians, or the Hutus, or the Turks. However, when it comes time to discuss genocide of the Native nations, and because the United States and its Euro-American citizenry were the perpetrators, then the United States is conspicuous by its silence, and it suppresses the truth of what really happened in its development as a nation. The United States acts as Germany does when the topic of genocide of six million Jews comes up. The United States acts like Turkey when the subject of genocide of the one and a half million Armenians arises, or like Japan when the genocide of the Chinese and Koreans is brought up.

The United States, its colleges and universities, and the U.S. Euro-American historians seem to have a severe case of historical amnesia, and thus the genocide of the Indigenous Peoples of the United States remains hidden. Even the historians who acknowledge that the United States committed mass atrocities against Indigenous Peoples find it difficult to consider it genocide.[7] As a consequence of this historical amnesia, the U.S. public does not see that its government and society was established through genocide. Instead, the Euro-American citizenry of the United States tends to view the destruction of Indigenous Peoples as a form of historical or moral progress.[8]

This essay will use the five criteria of the 1948 U.N. Genocide Convention and will provide several examples for each criterion. I will demonstrate how the United States of America fulfilled all five of the criteria in perpetrating genocide and crimes against humanity on the Indigenous Peoples of the United States, and yet this genocide remains hidden. Emphasis will be given to the genocide of the Dakota People of Minnesota, my own people, another of the many hidden genocides, of the aboriginal peoples of the United States. The social impact of genocide upon the Dakota People and upon other Indigenous Peoples of the United States will also be discussed.

The 1948 U.N. Convention on the Punishment and Prevention of the Crime of Genocide

Article 2(a) Killing Members of the Group

Ward Churchill, in talking about the American Holocaust and about the slaughter of Indigenous Peoples of the United States, writes:

> The people had died in the millions of being hacked apart with axes and swords, burned alive and trampled under horses, hunted as game and fed to dogs, shot, beaten, stabbed, scalped for bounty, hanged on meat hooks and thrown over the sides of ships at sea, worked to death as slave laborers, intentionally starved and frozen to death during a multitude of forced marches and internments, and, in an unknown number of instances, deliberately infected with epidemic diseases.[9]

According to demographic figures from Stiffarm and Lane, there were approximately sixteen million Native Peoples within the continental United States at the time of contact in 1492. By 1900, nearly all of these Native Peoples had been wiped out.[10] How did this happen? The answer is "Genocide"! This figure, sixteen million, is greater than the population totals of the cities of New York City, Los Angeles, and Chicago combined—fourteen million, according to the 2010 census. M. Annette Jaimes writes, "Surely, there can be no more monumental example of sustained genocide—certainly none involving a 'race' of people as broad and complex as this—anywhere in the annals of human history."[11]

According to David Stannard, just twenty-one years after Columbus's first landing in the Caribbean, "nearly 8,000,000 people—those Columbus chose to call Indians—had been killed by violence, disease, and despair."[12] This killing was just on the islands—Columbus never made it to the mainland. There were still approximately sixteen million Indigenous Peoples on the mainland. If the eight million Indigenous Peoples murdered are added to the sixteen million slaughtered on the mainland, we have the total figure of twenty-four million Indigenous Peoples as victims of genocide (four times the number of Jews murdered in the Holocaust). Thus, in the three centuries following contact (1600–1900), Native Peoples were systematically slaughtered and exterminated until by 1900, there were fewer than a quarter-million Native Peoples left in the United States, according to the U.S. Bureau of Census. This would be an extermination rate of 98.5 percent. This is extremely efficient killing! According to Stannard, in the late nineteenth century, "there was, at last, almost no one left to kill."[13]

Dehumanization of the Native Peoples was used as a rationale by U.S. Euro-Americans for killing Native Peoples. For example, George Washington referred to Native Peoples as "wolves, both being beasts of prey, though they differ in shape."[14] Andrew Jackson thought the same way as Washington. Jackson urged his troops to root out from their "dens" and kill Indigenous women and their "whelps."[15] The term "savage" was constantly applied to the Indigenous Peoples. The Reverend Colonel John M. Chivington said, at the massacre of some six-hundred-plus Cheyenne, primarily women, children, and elders (most of the Cheyenne men were away on a hunt), "Kill and scalp all, little and big . . . nits make lice."[16] This foreshadowed the German Nazis—Hitler, Himmler, and others—who described the extermination of another people," the Jews, as "the same thing as delousing,"[17] or of the Hutus who compared the Tutsis to vermin.

Article 2(b) Causing Serious Bodily or Mental Harm to Members of the Group

Warfare and terror characterized the Indigenous existence, especially in the first four centuries (1500–1900). For example, on May 26, 1637, a Pequot town on the Mystic River in Connecticut was attacked in the predawn and the residents killed. As many as nine hundred women, children, and helpless old men were burned alive by Captain John Mason and his militia. Those who tried to escape the blaze were cut down with swords and axes.[18]

The Bible was used in this instance to justify the killing of Indians. "Sometimes the Scripture declareth women and children must perish with their parents," quoted John Underhill.[19] William Bradford writes, "It was a fearful sight to see them thus frying in the fire and the streams of blood quenching the same, and horrible was the stink and scent thereof; but the victory seemed a sweet sacrifice, and they gave the praise thereof to God, who had wrought so wonder-fully for them."[20] This event seemed to be a form of worship, similar to the Old Testament Israelite practice of burning a ram or lamb on the altar.

A second example, among dozens of such genocidal events, occurred nearly two hundred years later, on November 29, 1864, when six hundred Cheyenne (the death toll is debated), were massacred at Sand Creek, Colorado, while fly-ing the U.S. flag over their camp, thinking they were safe. The white soldiers, under the leadership of the Reverend Colonel John M. Chivington, a Methodist minister, perpetrated this massacre. One witness writes, "They were scalped, their brains were knocked out; the men used their knives, ripped open women, clubbed little children, knocked them in the head with their guns, beat their brains out, mutilated their bodies in every sense of the word."[21]

One could scarcely believe that these horrible events occurred, except that the participants, perpetrators, and witnesses wrote down what they did or what they witnessed.

One thing that contributed to "mental harm," stress, anxiety, and just plain terror was the use of bounties. The colonies and, later, most of the states, placed bounties on Indigenous Peoples' scalps. For example, the English placed a value of forty pounds on a male native, and twenty pounds on a female native or a male native under the age of twelve years.[22] Among my own Dakota people in the state of Minnesota in 1863, there was a bounty of twenty-five dollars, ini-tially. Then, this was raised to seventy-five dollars and, finally, to two hundred dollars.[23] Gender and age made no difference. The sum of two hundred dollars was considered an annual salary in Minnesota at the time. By this time (1860s), bounties were illegal, even according to U.S. law. Yet one of the ads placed in the *Winona Republican* on "Thursday Evening, September 24, 1863" read, "The State Reward for dead Indians has been increased to $200 for every red-skin sent to Purgatory. This sum is more than the dead bodies of all the Indians east of the Red River are worth." The system of placing bounties on Dakota scalps by the state of Minnesota was thus "state"-sponsored genocide.

Article 2(c) Deliberately Inflicting on the Group Conditions of Life Calculated to Bring About Its Physical Destruction in Whole or in Part

Three conditions, among others, which were calculated to bring about the phys-ical destruction of native peoples, included concentration camps, forced remov-als ("ethnic cleansing"), and bio-warfare. For example, in the state of Minnesota in the United States there were two concentration camps for Dakota people, one at Mankato for the men and one at Fort Snelling for the women, children, and elders.[24] After viewing photographs of the concentration camp at Fort Snelling (1862–1863), Jack Weatherford commented that they offer "a strange glimpse of a form that was to haunt the twentieth century. These pictures show us the birth of an institution, the beginning of a whole new social practice of concentrating innocent civilians into an area and imprisoning them for protracted periods without charging them with any crime."[25]

After the U.S. Congress passed the Indian Removal Act in 1834, President Andrew Jackson enthusiastically implemented the removal of the Indigenous Peoples from the eastern United States to the present-day state of Oklahoma. Thousands of Indigenous Peoples (Cherokees, Choctaws, and many more) were rounded up and concentrated in certain and various areas where they were held captive. Then the U.S. military force-marched them a range of hundreds of miles up to a thousand miles, to "Indian Territory" (the present-day state of Oklahoma). This particular item of congressional legislation is an example of state-sponsored land theft and state-sanctioned genocide on the part of the U.S. government.

One particularly heinous aspect of the genocide of Native Peoples was the practice of bioterrorism, that is, of distributing smallpox-infected blankets or handkerchiefs. Lord Jeffrey Amherst, for example, instructed his subordinate to distribute "gifts" to the Ottawas under Chief Pontiac in 1763: "You will do well to [infect] the Indians by means of blankets as well as to try every other method that can serve to extirpate this [execrable] race."[26] This disease spread rapidly among the Ottawa, Mingo, Delaware, Shawnee, and other native nations, killing perhaps 100,000 people.[27]

Another example was the distribution of smallpox-infected blankets by the U.S. Army to Mandans at Fort Clark, on the Missouri River, in present-day South Dakota. This was the causative factor in the pandemic of 1836–1840 where the native death toll probably exceeded 100,000, a conservative estimate. This made the subsequent U.S. conquest of the land west of the Mississippi River far easier than it would have been.[28]

Article 2(d) Imposing Measures Intended to Prevent Births within the Group

One example, because it involves my Dakota People, is that in the concentration camp at Fort Snelling (in the area of the Twin Cities of Minnesota), the women were kept separate from the Dakota men. The Dakota men were imprisoned in the concentration camp at Mankato, Minnesota. If the men and women are kept from interacting with each other, then of course there will be no reproduction. This is genocide!

In 1863, the Dakota men in the concentration camp at Mankato, Minnesota, were transferred to a similar facility in Davenport, Iowa. Again, approximately four hundred Dakota men were kept from their women. If the men are kept separate and there is no interacting, then there is no reproduction, no live births! Dr. Waziyatawin, in her book *What Does Justice Look Like?* writes, "In the 1860s, Dakota People were experiencing enforced sub-fecundity (a diminished ability to reproduce) as a direct consequence of gender segregation."[29] This is "flatly and intentionally genocidal," to use David Stannard's words.[30] Again, this is state-sponsored genocide. For no people can survive if there is no reproduction!

In the 1960s and early 1970s, the U.S. government, through the Interior
Department's Bureau of Indian Affairs (BIA) and the Indian Health Service (IHS),
imposed upon Indigenous women a policy of involuntary surgical sterilization,
usually without their knowledge and consent. M. Annette Jaimes refers to this
policy as "grotesque" and discusses it in detail.[31] Existence of the sterilization
program was revealed through analysis of secret documents removed by American Indian Movement members from the Bureau of Indian Affair's Washington, D.C., headquarters during its occupation by the Trail of Broken Treaties in
November 1972. A resulting 1974 study by WARN (Women of All Red Nations)
concluded that as many as 42 percent of all native women of childbearing age
had by that point been sterilized without their consent.

A subsequent investigation by the General Accounting Office (GAO) of
four IHS facilities during the years 1973–1976 showed that 3,406 involuntary
sterilizations had been performed in just these four hospitals in that period.
This would be equivalent to over a half-million among the general U.S. population.[32] Who knows how many involuntary sterilizations occurred in the other
IHS hospitals?

Article 2(e) Forcibly Transferring Children of the Group to Another Group

The history of education of the Indigenous Peoples of the United States "has
been primarily the transmission of white American education, little altered, to
the native child as a one-way process."[33] The institution of the school, particularly the boarding school, operated by either the U.S. government or the Catholic or Protestant church, was the main colonizing and educating agent. This
educational form was alien, one-sided, and coercive. One of the aims of such a
school was to "kill the Indian and save the man."[34]

There was no separation of church and state. The government and church
worked hand-in-hand to educate, Christianize, civilize, and assimilate the
Indigenous children. Two outstanding examples of this are the congressional
appropriations of 1819 and 1870. In 1819, Congress established the "Civilization
Fund," with an annual appropriation of $10,000, for "education of the frontier
tribes."[35] The funds were turned over to the missionaries of the American Board
of Commissioners for Foreign Missions. In 1870, Congress authorized an annual
appropriation of $100,000 "for the support of industrial and other schools
among tribes not otherwise provided for."[36] These educational facilities were
run directly by various churches and missionary societies.[37] Again, these congressional appropriations acts were examples of state-sponsored genocide, with
the holy approval and participation of the churches.

The boarding schools for Indigenous children became little more than
labor camps dedicated to the forced assimilation of the native child into the
mainstream of the United States. Native students in these schools frequently

had their clothes and other personal possessions confiscated and burned. They were punished, often severely, for speaking their native languages or for practicing their traditional religions or other cultural customs.[38]

It was not unusual under these conditions for a child to be taken at age six or seven and never to see his or her home and family again until age seventeen or eighteen. Altogether, the whole procedure conforms to the above criteria of the forced transfer of children from a targeted racial, ethnic, national, or religious group to be reared and absorbed by a physically dominating group, which is the crime of genocide.[39]

Because of the genocidal policy of "forcibly and systematically transferring the care of Native children to non-Indians through maintenance of a compulsory boarding school system and wholesale adoptions,"[40] the U.S. Congress passed the Indian Child Welfare Act in 1978. Of course, there was no mention of the term "genocide" in the legislation.

Thinking of Native Peoples and Jews as lice or vermin and conceiving of concentration camps were not the only things that Hitler and the Nazis had in common with the United States and its policy and programs regarding the Indigenous Peoples. They also shared the expression "final solution." Note the following passage: "It is readily acknowledged that Indian children lose their natural resistance to illness by habitating so closely in these schools (residential board schools), and that they die at a much higher rate than in their villages. But this alone does not justify a change in the policy of this Department, which is geared toward the *final solution to our Indian Problem*" (emphasis added).[41] As one can readily see, the U.S. government, Department of the Interior, and BIA were years ahead of Hitler and the Nazis in coining this phrase. I encourage readers when they hear the phrase "final solution" to think of the genocide of the Indigenous Peoples, including the Dakota People of Minnesota, perpetrated by the United States and the state of Minnesota as well as that of the Jews committed by Hitler and the Nazis.

Destruction and Social Impact of Genocide

Linda Tuhiwai Smith writes in her *Decolonizing Methodologies* about the social and political conditions that result from the genocide and destruction inflicted upon Indigenous Peoples, whenever and wherever they may be found, by the various colonizing powers—England, France, Spain, United States, et cetera. Smith describes the oppressive conditions that "perpetuate extreme levels of poverty, chronic ill health, and poor educational opportunities." She continues, "Their children may be removed forcibly from their care, 'adopted' or institutionalized. The adults may be as addicted to alcohol as their children are to glue and other drugs, they may live in destructive relationships which are formed and shaped by their impoverished material conditions and structured by politically oppressive regimes."[42] As the Indigenous Peoples continue to live in these conditions, the white-supremacist general society continues to feed them messages that they are worthless, lazy, dependent, and dumb, that is, they lack higher order human qualities.[43]

These preceding statements by Linda Tuhiwai Smith certainly apply to the Indigenous Peoples within the United States of America. Most of our reservations, especially those who do not have casinos, are like third world countries. By almost any kind of social and economic indicators, our Indigenous Peoples are at the lowest and worst levels of conditions.

From *The State of Native America*, edited by M. Annette Jaimes, I will list some of these effects and conditions under which our Indigenous Peoples of the United States of America live:

In addition to our original land base being seized (approximately 98 percent), Indigenous Peoples have experienced a complete loss of control over the resources within and upon our residual territory.

Indigenous Peoples experience as a group the most extreme poverty of any sector in the present North American population.

Indigenous Peoples experience the greatest rates of malnutrition, death by exposure, infant mortality, and teen suicide of any group on the continent.

The average life span is approximately thirty years shorter than that of a U.S. Euro-American of either gender.

Our traditional forms of government have been supplanted by a form of governance imposed on us by the United States.

Our languages have been suppressed, especially, at the boarding schools operated by both the state and the church.

Our spirituality and religious ceremonies have been suppressed. At one point, the U.S. Congress passed the American Indian Religious Freedom Act in 1978. Why should this have been necessary in a country that says it was founded in religious freedom?

Our identity, our numbers, and our cultural heritage continue to be under attack and manipulated.

Our self-determination has been suppressed, and our efforts to gain self-determination are viciously repressed.

Our youth continue to be systematically miseducated that everything that has happened to us was right and inevitable.[44]

Also in Jaimes's *The State of Native America*, Churchill and LaDuke, in their "The Political Economy of Radioactive Colonialism," discuss other social impacts of historical formations such as genocide, massive land theft, and broken treaties:

We experience the highest rate of infant mortality on the continent.

We have the highest unemployment rate.

We have the lowest per capita income.

We have the highest rate of communicable or plague diseases.

We have the lowest levels of formal educational attainment.[45]

As one can see by this listing, the Indigenous Peoples of the United States "suffer virtually the full range of conditions observable in the most depressed of Third World areas."[46] The destructive social impact of genocide on the Indigenous Peoples has been traumatic and devastating.

Conclusion: Hidden Genocides

The United States was very efficient in the destruction of its Indigenous Peoples. In fact, according to Stannard, in his book *American Holocaust*, "the Fuhrer from time to time expressed admiration for the 'efficiency' of the American genocide campaign against the Indians, viewing it as a forerunner for his own plans and programs."[47] Stannard further writes, "The destruction of the Indians of the Americas was, far and away, the most massive act of genocide in the history of the world."[48] M. Annette Jaimes writes, "Not only does the rate of extermination suffered by the Indigenous Peoples of North America vastly exceed that experienced by the Jews of Europe under the Nazis, it represents a scale and scope of genocide without parallel in recorded human history."[49]

Another devastating social effect of our history and of our genocide has been this society's continuing attitude of viewing the Indigenous Peoples as less than human, as animals, and as objects. Therefore, in the U.S. media—for example, movies, television shows, and comic books—Native Peoples are still being stereotyped, caricatured, disparaged, demeaned, and generally dehumanized. We are still the object of fun and games in the United States when we are used as sports mascots and sports teams' names: Washington Redskins, Cleveland Indians, Atlanta Braves, Kansas City Chiefs, and University of North Dakota's Fighting Sioux, for example.

In his textbook, *Genocide: A Comprehensive Introduction*, Adam Jones writes about how the words Apache, Tomahawk, Cherokee, and Winnebago bring to mind U.S. military weaponry and gas-guzzling vehicles advertised for rugged excursions across the open roads of the North American continent, away from "civilization."[50] Such cultural symbols create denigrating representations of Indigenous Peoples as violent and wild people who deserved their fate. Benjamin Madley called these "post-facto justifications" of the genocide committed against Indigenous Peoples.[51] These stereotyped and caricatured images help historians and the U.S. public to justify genocide. They also help to hide the genocide. As Donna-Lee Frieze and Elisa von Joeden-Forgey argue in their chapters of this book, genocides become hidden genocides when people believe they are forms of benevolent progress. The public intellectual Christopher Hitchens, for example, deemed a protest staged by Native Peoples and Americans against Christopher Columbus to be nothing more than "an ignorant celebration of stasis and backwardness, with an unpleasant tinge of self-hatred." The "politico-military victories" of Europeans in the Americas, he wrote, left "humanity on a slightly higher plane than it knew before" and "deserves to be celebrated with great vim and gusto" because it "inaugurated a nearly boundless epoch of opportunity and innovation."[52]

Things need to change. The great mass of U.S. Euro-Americans needs to know the facts, needs to know what happened in American history. Genocide scholars of the world need to write about the "holocaust" of the Indigenous Peoples of the United States because the multitudes do not listen to Indigenous academics as they most certainly would to their fellow white man. As Jaimes writes, "Alternatively, we are mutually confronted with the specter not of simply a present determined by the unrelenting horrors of the U.S. past, but a future dictated by the never-quite-acknowledged ugliness of a U.S. present. In a word, we face the consummation of U.S. American Nazism, with all that implies in terms of racism, sexism, militarism, environmental devastation through rampant industrialism, and the final consolidation of the U.S. police state."[53]

Genocide is a painful and unpleasant topic to face and discuss. No country, including the United States, wishes to confront the genocide in its history. The United States is in denial, is suffering from historical amnesia, and the U.S. Indigenous Holocaust continues to remain hidden. However, we must open our eyes to the lessons of the past if we do not wish to see history continue to be repeated.

In the year 2012, the Sesquicentennial of the Dakota–U.S. War of 1862, we find the state of Minnesota, its colonial institutions (for example, the Minnesota Historical Society), and its Euro-Minnesotan citizenry reluctant to acknowledge the "hidden genocide" of the Dakota People of Minnesota. Waziyatawin states that the state of Minnesota and its colonial institutions do not acknowledge the broad context "in which whites invaded Dakota homeland, frequently before any legal land cessions, with the expectation that they would dispossess Dakota people of our lands."[54] The state does not wish to recognize what happened between the state of Minnesota and the Dakota People. The state does not wish to admit to the bounties, the forced marches, the mass executions, the concentration camps, the forced removal of the Dakota from their ancient homelands ("ethnic cleansing"), the suppression of Indigenous spirituality and ceremonies, the suppression of Native languages, the boarding schools, and on and on.

It is time not only for the state of Minnesota and its Euro-Minnesotan citizenry but also for the United States and its Euro-American citizenry to acknowledge their respective "hidden genocides." It is time for Minnesota and the United States to begin telling the truth!

NOTES

1. Lenore Stiffarm and Phil Lane Jr., "The Demography of Native North America: A Question of American Indian Survival," in *The State of Native America: Genocide, Colonization, and Resistance*, ed. M. Annette Jaimes (Boston: South End Press, 1992), 27.
2. Ibid., 37.
3. Ibid., 34.
4. Frank Chalk and Kurt Jonassohn, *The History and Sociology of Genocide* (New Haven, CT: Yale University Press, 1990), 29.
5. Alfred A. Cave, "Genocide in the Americas," in *The Historiography of Genocide*, ed. Dan Stone (London: Palgrave, 2010), 283. On the way in which the pursuit of agricultural lands motivated the U.S. and European genocide against Native Peoples, see Ben Kiernan, *Blood and Soil* (New Haven, CT: Yale University Press, 2007).
6. See Benjamin Madley, "Patterns of Frontier Genocide 1803–1910: The Aboriginal Tasmanians, the Yuki of California, and the Herero of Namibia," *Journal of Genocide Research* 6 (2004): 16–192; T. G. Dyer, *Theodore Roosevelt and the Idea of Race* (Baton Rouge: Louisiana State University Press, 1980).
7. Cave, "Genocide in the Americas," 273–296.
8. Ibid., 276.
9. Ward Churchill, *A Little Matter of Genocide, Holocaust, and Denial in the Americas 1492 to the Present* (San Francisco: City Light Books, 1997), 1.
10. Stiffarm and Lane, "The Demography of Native North America," 37.
11. Ibid.
12. David E. Stannard, *American Holocaust: The Conquest of the New World* (New York: Oxford University Press, 1992), x.
13. Ibid., 146.
14. Letter of George Washington to James Duane, September 7, 1783, in Richard Drinnon, *Facing West: The Metaphysics of Indian-Hating and Empire-Building* (New York: New American Library, 1980), 65.
15. Stannard, *American Holocaust*, 240.
16. Churchill, *A Little Matter of Genocide*, 129.
17. Stannard, *American Holocaust*, 131.
18. Churchill, *A Little Matter of Genocide*, 172.
19. Stannard, *American Holocaust*, 114.
20. Ibid.
21. Foster Rhea Dulles, *The United States since 1865* (Ann Arbor: University of Michigan Press, 1959), 41.
22. Vine Deloria Jr., *Custer Died for Your Sins: An Indian Manifesto* (Norman: University of Oklahoma Press, 1988), 6.
23. Roy W. Meyer, *History of the Santee Sioux: United States Indian Policy on Trial* (Lincoln: University of Nebraska Press, 1993), 135.
24. Ibid., 136–137.

25. Jack Weatherford, *Native Roots: How the Indians Enriched America* (New York: Crown Publishers, 1991), 78.

26. Churchill, *A Little Matter of Genocide*, 154

27. Stiffarm and Lane, "Demography of Native North America," 32.

28. Ibid., 33

29. Waziyatawin, *What Does Justice Look Like? The Struggle for Liberation in Dakota Homeland* (St. Paul, MN: Living Justice Press, 2008), 57.

30. Stannard, *American Holocaust*, 119.

31. M. Annette Jaimes and Theresa Halsey, "American Indian Women at the Center of Indigenous Resistance in Contemporary North America," in Jaimes, *State of Native America*, 326.

32. Ibid.

33. Estelle Fuchs and Robert J. Havighurst, *To Live on This Earth: American Indian Education* (Garden City, NY: Anchor Books, 1973), 2.

34. Wayne Stein, "American Indian Education," in *American Indian Studies: An Interdisciplinary Approach to Contemporary Issues*, ed. Dane Morrison (New York: Peter Lang, 1997), 76.

35. Jorge Noriega, "American Indian Education in the United States: Indoctrination for Subordination to Colonialism," in Jaimes, *State of Native America*, 377.

36. Ibid., 380.

37. Ibid.

38. Stein, "American Indian Education," 76.

39. Noriega, "American Indian Education," 381.

40. Ward Churchill and Glenn T. Morris, "Key Indian Laws and Cases," in Jaimes, *State of Native America*, 17.

41. Department of Indian Affairs, Superintendent D. C. Scott to Indian Agent General Major D. McKay, DIA Archives, RG 10 Series, 12 April 1910.

42. Linda Tuhiwai Smith, *Decolonizing Methodologies: Research and Indigenous Peoples* (New York: Zed Books, 1999), 19

43. Ibid. Digression: I often say, both facetiously and seriously, that I learned when I was a teenager that "God-Damn Indian" was not one word. Growing up in southwestern Minnesota, I often heard such phrases as "God-damn lazy Indian," "God-damn welfare Indian," "God-damn dumb Indian," and so on. The colonizing governments, states, and other societies and institutions continue to deny the historical formations of these levels of poverty, and they continue to deny that genocide occurred, and so this genocide of the Indigenous Peoples remains hidden. In so doing, then, they deny Indigenous Peoples their identity, their history, and their humanity.

44. M. Annette Jaimes, "Introduction: Sand Creek," in Jaimes, *State of Native America*, 8.

45. Ward Churchill and Winona LaDuke, "The Political Economy of Radioactive Colonialism," in Jaimes, *State of Native America*, 246.

46. Ibid.

47. Stannard, *American Holocaust*, 153.

48. Ibid., x.

49. Jaimes, "Introduction: Sand Creek," 7.

50. Adam Jones, *Genocide: A Comprehensive Introduction* (London: Routledge, 2006), 82.

51. Quoted in Jones, *Genocide*, 82.

52. Christopher Hitchens, "Minority Report," *The Nation*, October 19, 1992. Quoted in Jones, *Genocide*, 82.

53. Jaimes, "Introduction: Sand Creek," 9.

54. Waziyatawin, *What Does Justice Look Like?* 78.

6

Circassia

A Small Nation Lost to the Great Game

WALTER RICHMOND

In recent years, genocide scholars and an aggressive international press have uncovered, publicized, and analyzed numerous mass murders that might have remained outside the public view in earlier times. Indeed, the well-known Serbian atrocities in Bosnia and Kosovo were only the latest in a series of ethnic cleansings of Muslims in the Balkans that began with Russia's brutal annihilation of Muslim communities in the Russo-Turkish War of 1877–1878, an ethnic cleansing that was never exposed and has been forgotten.[1] The further back in time we go, the more we see the narrative of colonial, and frequently genocidal, regimes controlled by historians whose loyalties were with the conquering regime. As a result, although a genocide might be known to the academic community or even the general public, it is not recognized as such because the actual events have been concealed or distorted by a false narrative. On occasion, international politics shine a light directly on such a genocide, and it is finally revealed after a long period of neglect. Such is the case with the Circassian genocide of 1864. Unfortunately, the genocide against the Circassian Kabardian tribe in the 1820s remains hidden even to many Circassians themselves. This chapter will analyze these two separate genocides and the reasons why one has gained attention while the other is still hidden.

The Circassians are an indigenous people of the northwestern Caucasus whose roots there go back four thousand years.[2] Although frequently described as Muslim, the Circassians only adopted Islam in the eighteenth century and practiced a syncretic religion primarily based on their pagan beliefs.[3] Over the centuries, they dealt with the Genoese, Ottomans, and Crimeans, although due to frequent devastating raids by their more powerful neighbors they were unable to develop a unified state. Instead, Circassia consisted of about a dozen tribes, the most stable of which was the Qabartay, known in the West as the Kabardians.

In 1557, the Russians and Kabardians became allies and frequently entered the battlefield together, but in 1763, Russian construction of Fort Maikop in Kabardia triggered a war that quickly escalated. By the 1820s, brutal Russian raids and massacres left Kabardia nearly completely depopulated.[4] In western Circassia, Russia's interference in a civil war in 1796 earned them the hatred of the largest tribe, the Shapsugs, and hostilities escalated there as well. When the Ottomans relinquished control of the Black Sea coast in the 1829 Treaty of Adrianople, the Russians attacked Circassia but were unable to complete their conquest until after the Crimean War. With an invasion force of seventy thousand men, the Russians burned villages, food, and supplies throughout Circassia in order to starve the people into submission.[5] The Circassians were supposedly given an ultimatum: move to the swampy lowlands north of the Kuban River or leave for the Ottoman Empire. In fact, no choice was given to the vast majority, who were driven to the Black Sea coast in winter 1863, where tens of thousands died from exposure, starvation, typhus, and animal attacks while the Russians did nothing to assist them.[6] Thousands more died in the ships en route to Turkey and shortly after arriving there.[7] Based upon my research, my conservative estimate is that at least 625,000 people died out of a total population of 1.25–1.5 million.[8]

While Circassia was well known outside the Caucasus, it played no role in international politics until it became a pawn in the geopolitical calculations of Russia, Turkey, Britain, and France in the 1830s. Russia's competition with the Ottomans for control of the Caucasus had already led to the Kabardian genocide, while Russia's determination to incorporate all of the Caucasus into the empire no matter the cost resulted in the genocide of 1864. When Russia and Great Britain started the Great Game—a competition for control of South Asia—the Black Sea became a focus of attention and the British aided the Circassians against the Russians. However, after Britain and France neutralized Russian naval power in the Crimean War, the Europeans abandoned the Circassians to face the Russians alone. The Great Game moved east to Afghanistan, and the Circassian genocide was forgotten. The Russians were free to construct a false narrative about the conquest of Circassia that effectively hid the genocide from future generations. At the same time, the enormity of the genocide of 1864 overshadowed the Kabardian genocide, and it became hidden from even the Circassians themselves.

Genocide in Kabardia

Until the early eighteenth century, the Russians considered the Kabardians a trusted ally. The two nations had fought side by side against common enemies for more than 150 years. However, the Ottoman Empire had allies among the Kabardian aristocracy as well, and Kabardia quickly fragmented into the pro-Russian Lesser Kabardia and the politically torn Greater Kabardia. Once St. Petersburg began to colonize the North Caucasus, and its goal of controlling the northern shores of the Black Sea became apparent, the Ottoman Empire began to exert pressure on its allies within Kabardia to pledge allegiance to the Porte. A "tug of war" ensued, culminating in the Russo-Turkish War of 1735–1739. According to the 1739 Treaty of Belgrade, Kabardia was declared a neutral "barrier" between the two empires, effectively leaving it defenseless.[9] By 1763, Russia was appropriating Kabardian land and building forts, disrupting centuries-old pasturing routes. After attempting to negotiate, the Kabardians took up arms. In 1801, St. Petersburg began construction of a line of forts directly through the heart of Kabardia in order to build a military road through the Daryal Pass in the Caucasus Mountains. This action inflamed tensions even more, and the war escalated. In the first decade of the nineteenth century, General Sergei Bulgakov carried out a brutal campaign of destruction and murder against the Kabardians that finally resulted in his dismissal from the army.[10] A few years of peaceful coexistence followed, but after the appointment of General Alexei Ermolov as commander-in-chief of the Caucasus in 1816, the Kabardians suffered a blow that nearly resulted in their complete annihilation.

Ermolov's first incursion into Kabardia occurred in May 1818, when five fugitive Kabardians took refuge in the *aul* (village) of Tram. The villagers were ordered to turn over the party, an impossible demand: it would have violated an ancient custom that held the guest to be sacred regardless of his legal status.[11] The Russians surrounded the village at night, drove all the inhabitants out, burned the village, and took all of the livestock. Afterward, Ermolov warned the Kabardians that "in the future I will show no mercy to convicted bandits: their villages will be annihilated, their property taken, their wives and children slaughtered."[12] The entire Kabardian nation began to migrate into western Circassia while Ermolov returned to Chechnya and placed General Karl Stahl in charge of Kabardian affairs. Stahl arrived in early 1819 and immediately began a campaign against the residents of Lesser Kabardia, who had been consistently loyal to Russia since the sixteenth century.[13] All of Kabardia had already been devastated by two decades of plague, and so the population had no ability to resist. Stahl launched his invasion in 1820, annihilating all the auls he came across. Most of the Lesser Kabardian aristocrats signed a pledge of loyalty, but shortly afterward Major Taranovsky demanded at gunpoint that the Kabardians move from their fertile valleys to the highlands.[14]

Hostilities increased, and by 1821 the Russians had lost control of the situation.[15] Ermolov returned in September and developed a plan to "pacify" Kabardia: the Russians would rustle all the Kabardians' cattle, thereby threatening them with starvation, and destroy all their auls to leave them without shelter in the winter.[16] Russian forces went through Kabardia in December and January, stealing thousands of head of cattle and horses and burning all the auls. Ermo-lov ordered that "the punishment is to be carried out against armed men only,"[17] but troops led by Colonel Kotsyrev destroyed every aul they came across, "throw-ing several thousand elderly, women, and children out of their homes"[18] and on at least one occasion attacked an aul and "bayoneted anyone who wasn't hiding—men, women, and children."[19] The survivors were forced to migrate to the lowlands during what turned out to be a very harsh winter and were given no assistance in building shelter. Ermolov's response was that "the winter isn't so harsh or enduring in this land that it will be painful for the people to live in the open air for two months."[20] Prisoners were either forced into military service or given to the Cossacks as slaves, as were villagers who returned to the destroyed auls to look for anything of value the Russians didn't steal.[21]

As brutal as this campaign was, it was only a preparation for Ermolov's own assault in the spring. Numerous forces armed with heavy artillery crossed into Kabardia on May 22. The Russians followed the river valleys, burning auls and rustling livestock.[22] Once again, little organized resistance was met (there were very few Kabardians left), and the majority of the survivors fled to western Circassia. On July 24, the Russians stopped their advance.[23] The Kabardians had been completely devastated: in 1790 the combined population of Greater and Lesser Kabardia was between 200,000 and 300,000, but in 1830 there were fewer than 30,000 in Greater Kabardia, while all the people of Lesser Kabardia either died or had fled.[24]

Launching a comprehensive campaign that did not spare the elderly, women, or children, and leaving thousands of people without shelter in a par-ticularly harsh winter after Kabardia had been severely crippled by a plague (which Ermolov referred to in his memoirs as his "ally"),[25] was undoubtedly designed to deal a deathblow to the Kabardian nation. Ermolov's rapid coloniza-tion of Lesser Kabardia with Cossacks and Ossetians was clear evidence that he had no intention to allow the Kabardians to recover from their losses;[26] the fact that the Kabardians survived at all can only be described as a miracle. Unfortu-nately, as Kabardia was so far removed from the concerns of post-Napoleonic Europe, their plight received no attention. Even today, this chapter of history has been forgotten by most Circassians, both because it was never properly recorded when it happened and because of the far greater tragedy of the geno-cide of 1864. In academic studies of the genocide by Circassian scholars, the Kabardian episode is either hardly mentioned or ignored completely.[27] Of all the Circassians I have spoken with, looking for stories about the genocide, only one—a descendant of one of the most respected Kabardian families—was able to relate a piece of oral history concerning the events of the 1820s. It seems the genocide of 1864 was such a traumatic event for the entire Circassian nation that Ermolov's destruction of Kabardia has assumed the role of precursor to the

Circassian genocide within the Circassian scholarly community and has been completely forgotten by the Circassian people.

The Destruction of Circassia

While it was the national tragedy that caused the Circassians themselves to remember only the genocide of 1864, it was the geopolitical significance of Russo-Ottoman competition in the Black Sea that focused Europe's attention on Circassia at all. The Treaty of Belgrade not only changed Kabardia's status from ally to buffer state, it also created a ticking time bomb through its de facto assignment of the rest of Circassia to the Ottoman Empire. In this regard, the treaty was fantasy. The Jane tribe in the far west paid tribute to the Ottomans, but by the eighteenth century most of them had joined the "free" mountain tribes, the Shapsugs and the Abzakhs, who vociferously opposed allegiance to any foreign power. When Cossack colonies appeared north of the Kuban River in the late eighteenth century, the Circassians had strained but fairly stable relations with them. After St. Petersburg interfered in a Circassian civil war in the 1790s, many Circassians turned against St. Petersburg.[28] In 1800, Tsar Paul I gave Cossack bands permission to raid Circassian villages, and hostilities escalated. After the Turks relinquished their (fictitious) control of the northeastern Black Sea coast in the 1829 Treaty of Adrianople, the Russians launched a full-scale invasion of Circassia.

It was at this same time that Russia's increasingly influential role in Europe and its military strength became worrisome to some segments of European society, and it was only in this broader context that the fate of the Circassians entered into the consciousness of European politicians. The British objected (correctly) that Russia's acquisition of Circassia was a violation of the 1827 Treaty of London, in which the signatories (England, Russia, and France) agreed not to seek "any augmentation of territory" as a result of the Greek War for Independence. An anti-Russian movement in England began to influence British foreign policy for a time, particularly after the Russo-Turkish alliance at Unkiar Skelesi in 1833.[29] Circassia entered the debate when a young diplomat named David Urquhart warned that once the Russians controlled the Caucasus, they would be able to launch campaigns into Iran, Central Asia, and India. In 1834, the British sent Urquhart to the Caucasus, and he quickly took upon himself the task of urging the Circassians to create a unified government; then he returned to Constantinople and published a series of pamphlets designed to justify British intervention. After failing to gain support for war in the Parliament, he attempted to incite war himself by violating the Russian blockade of the Black Sea coast in 1836.[30] Meanwhile, the British press continued to publicize the Circassian cause.[31]

For the next several years, the British infiltrated the North Caucasus with other agents to encourage the Circassians in their war against the Russians, promising them material support.[32] However, the actual level of assistance given to the Circassians was far less than what would have been required for success against the Russian army. The fact of the matter was that the British were promising the Circassians a level of military support they were in no position to provide while encouraging the Circassians to escalate hostilities. The most influential agent was James Bell, who lived in Circassia for extended periods between 1837 and 1839. Bell attempted to create a unified leadership from the Circassian aristocracy and encouraged the Circassians to reject offers from the Russians. He also thwarted the attempts of some Circassian leaders to encourage compromise with the Russians at the very time that British resolve for sustained support of the Circassians was faltering. While there is little doubt that the Russo-Circassian War would have escalated in any event, Bell's intervention in Circassia was part of a geopolitical gamble by Great Britain in which the Circassians bore the full burden of the risks of failure.[33]

The little British support that continued during the 1840s would be even more severely curtailed by debates among the European powers over the focus of what would become the Crimean War. Prime Minister Lord Palmerston had hopes of using the war as a means of driving Russia from the west Caucasus entirely, but after the fall of Sevastopol on September 8, 1855, French Emperor Napoleon III wanted to take the war into eastern Europe.[34] However, the French were financially crippled, and since the Ottomans were militarily exhausted, the British faced the choice of concluding peace or fighting Russia alone.[35] Napoleon delivered a peace proposal to St. Petersburg and after conferring with his ministers, Russian Emperor Alexander II decided to seek a way out of the war in January 1856.[36] The subsequent Treaty of Paris sealed the Circassians' fate. Although the British representative Lord Clarendon vigorously argued that the Kuban River should be the border between Russia and Turkey, France and Turkey both agreed with the Russian representative Filip Brunnov that according to the Treaty of Adrianople, the area south of the Kuban (i.e., Circassia) was Russian territory. Clarendon then tried to stipulate that Russia would not be allowed to rebuild fortresses on the Black Sea coast, but again France supported Russia.[37] An amnesty was granted for nationals who fought on the side of the enemy, but it was extended only to nations Russia had previously controlled, and as the Circassians had never been under Russian control, they were excluded.[38] The Circassians were effectively turned into a stateless people, foreigners in their own land.

With the surrender of Imam Shamil and the fall of Chechnya and Dagestan in 1859, Caucasus Commander-in-Chief Prince Baryatinsky placed Nikolai Evdokimov in command of the Right Wing of the Caucasus line, north of Circassia.[39]

Evdokimov proposed the same strategy he used against Shamil: the rapid construction of roads and fortifications linked by crossroads, and a canvassing of the mountains to search for auls, burning the Circassians' food supplies, and seizing their livestock. The Circassians would be hemmed in and, left without food or shelter, would ultimately die of starvation and exposure if they didn't surrender. However, Evdokimov proposed one other measure that was not taken in Chechnya: the Circassians would be deported en masse from their homeland and forced either to settle north of the Kuban River or to immigrate to Turkey, and Circassia would be colonized by Cossacks. However, it turned out differently.

In June 1860, Russian forces surrounded the Besleney tribe and forcibly drove out four thousand families, purportedly to new homes in the Urup River valley. While Russian historians reported that the majority subsequently voluntarily migrated to the Ottoman Empire, Reserve Commander General Milenty Olshevsky commented that they "were sent to Turkey by the force of our arms in spring 1861."[40] Evdokimov's intentions reached the other Circassian tribes even before the Besleneys were deported, and on June 13 they held a *hase* (congress) in Sochi where the representatives decided to create a unified government and petition the European powers one last time. They built a *mejlis* (parliament), but Russian troops came almost immediately and destroyed it.[41]

On July 20, Evdokimov began the invasion of the rest of Circassia. Elders representing the Abzakh tribe came to him and asked him to stop building on their land, promising to live in peace and accept Russian suzerainty. In response, Evdokimov occupied their auls, accused them of violating their previous oath of allegiance, and demanded they either move to the lowlands or leave for Turkey. The Abzakhs asked if a deputation could be sent to St. Petersburg, but Evdokimov only allowed them to petition Baryatinsky. When the deputation arrived in Tbilisi, Baryatinsky's adjutant Grigol Orbeliani recommended that they petition Emperor Alexander himself, as he was planning a trip to the region in the fall. Once he found out about the planned meeting, Defense Minister Dmitry Milyutin worked to convince the emperor to reject any proposal the Circassians made. In a letter to Alexander of September 2, Milyutin dismissed the deputation as a trick and a last resort by a defeated people, stating that "we must persistently continue to settle the region with Cossacks, for I cannot withdraw my longstanding view that, once the Cossacks have squeezed the natives from the mountains, we can permanently rule the region, create peace there and no longer be in danger of losing the Caucasus at the first break with the naval powers."[42] Meanwhile, Evdokimov continued the conquest of Circassia unabated, rapidly constructing roads, forts, and settlements while burning auls and destroying food supplies.[43]

When Alexander met the official Circassian deputation in September, he demanded that the Circassians surrender and leave their homeland, for either the lowlands beyond the Kuban River or the Ottoman Empire.[44] The Circassians knew full well that the lowlands being offered to them were uninhabitable; as Olshevsky frankly stated, the Russians never expected them to accept the offer:

> It was impossible to believe that . . . the entire mass of the population would agree to migrate to the places to which they were directed. . . . Didn't exchanging their cherished mountains and forests, full of health, freedom, and independence for the noxious Black Sea plains and the swampy lowlands of the Bolshaya Laba mean giving themselves up as victims of the fever? And, really, if the Cossacks, who were born in the miasmas or migrated there from the steppes, fell ill in terrible numbers there, then what sort of effect would the miasmas have on the inhabitants of the mountains, who had always breathed fresh, healthy air?[45]

In his official correspondence, Evdokimov expressed surprise at the number of Circassians who chose emigration, but it was general knowledge among the administration and the troops that he knew how large the emigration would be.[46] Furthermore, the Caucasus officer M. I. Venyukov claimed Evdokimov made no secret of his intention to send all the Circassians to Turkey:

> I can't help but remember a conversation with Count Evdokimov . . . he took me to task for indicating the Bjeduhs on an ethnographical map of the Kuban region in 1862.
> "When do you plan to publish this map?" he asked me.
> "I don't know; that will depend on the Geographical Society; most likely at the end of next year (1863)."
> "Well, you should know, most respected sir (this was the Count's usual epithet for a subordinate), that if you wish to make your map of current interest, then rub out the Bjeduhs. There, in Petersburg, they talk about humaneness, interpreting it falsely. I consider humaneness to be love for one's country, for Russia, her deliverance from enemies. So what are the Bjeduhs to us? I will expel them, like all the remaining mountaineers, to Turkey."[47]

As for the Circassians who remained, Venyukov reported that Evdokimov treated them as an unwanted element: "[Evdokimov's] firm conviction was that the best consequence of the years-long, expensive war was the expulsion of all the mountaineers across the sea. Therefore, even though those who remained beyond the Kuban were peaceful and had submitted to Russian rule, he looked upon them exclusively as an inescapable evil and did everything he could to reduce their numbers and restrict their ability to live comfortably."[48] Furthermore, considering the enormous security precautions the Russians took when a few thousand Chechens were resettled to the lowlands, the notion of more than one million of the most anti-Russian Circassians moving north of the Kuban River could not possibly have been proposed in earnest.[49]

In November 1861, a Russian force of 40,000 moved into the heart of Circassia to drive all the inhabitants over the ridge and down toward the coast of the Black Sea while a second force moved out from Anapa along the coast to trap them there.[50] By spring 1862, the Circassians had been completely driven from the north face and had fled over the main Caucasus ridge.[51] The Anapa contingent drove the Natuhay tribe, who had agreed to Alexander's terms in September, out of their lands and toward one of the proposed deportation points.[52] Throughout the year, the Russians drove the Circassians farther into the mountains from all directions, building fortifications to make it impossible for them to return. A Russian officer and eyewitness, I. Drozdov, reported that a large number took refuge in Kurj Canyon, and so his regiment bombarded it with grapeshot in early June.[53] Shortly afterward, the Russians killed hundreds of Circassians who were without ammunition.[54] Drozdov witnessed other massacres as well: in June 1862, his detachment bombarded a forest where Circassian families were hiding with cannon fire, after which hundreds of Circassians sacrificed themselves to the cannons to allow their families to escape.[55] Three months later, Evdokimov blindly bombarded an aul in the woods for six hours before night fell and the surviving villagers were able to escape.[56]

As the Russians pushed ahead, they burned everything that could keep the Circassians alive. On June 1, 1863, the last major battle took place, in which a Circassian force of around five thousand was routed by Russian cannon fire.[57] After this, some Circassians began coming to the Russian camp to surrender, while others stopped fighting and hid in the thickets. The Russians would destroy all the dwellings and food in a valley, wait a week, then move back through the region and destroy the temporary dwellings the Circassians had built in the meantime. Many surrendered, but certainly many more, especially children and the elderly, fell victim to hunger, disease, the elements, and wolves.[58] A French covert agent named A. Fonvielle reported that the Circassians were reduced to eating tree leaves and that typhus wiped out the majority of those hiding in the thickets.[59]

By December 1863, the Russians had driven large numbers of Circassians into the Sochi River valley. The winter was particularly brutal, but nevertheless the Russians continued to move through the southern reaches of Circassia "in order to supervise the expulsion of the mountaineers and, if need be, to expel them by force." Drozdov described the scene: "On the road our eyes were met with a staggering image: corpses of women, children, elderly persons, torn to pieces and half-eaten by dogs; deportees emaciated by hunger and disease, almost too weak to move their legs, collapsing from exhaustion and becoming prey to dogs while still alive."[60] Reporting on the refugees awaiting deportation

to Turkey in late winter 1863, Olshevsky noted similarly horrific scenes: "[C]ondi-
tions worsened daily for the Abzakhs and Shapsugs awaiting deportation to Turkey. At last their situation reached a desperate state, when everyone living along
the coast of the Black Sea as well as between the main ridge and the Kuban
were crammed into the mouth of the Tuapse River, the only point designated
for departure to Turkey."[61] Just as the worst of the winter storms began to hit,
the coastal Shapsugs and the Abzakhs from the north ridge were forced down
to the mouth of the Tuapse as well. Thousands of people were pressed together
around Fort Velyaminovskaya, "in the open air, constantly pierced by a cold
wind, flooded by frequent rains, suffering from lack of provisions and lacking
hot food." Olshevsky watched as "children, women and the elderly fell seriously
ill and died, primarily of typhus and dysentery." The entire shore was covered
with graves.[62]

Both Drozdov and Olshevsky reported that the skippers overloaded their
boats and that many died from the crowded conditions and the foul weather.[63]
Olshevsky placed the blame for the massive number of deaths on the shore
squarely on the shoulders of Evdokimov: "Why did it happen that . . . the Abzakhs
and Shapsugs, who were being driven from their homeland, suffer such horrific
sufferings and deaths? It was exclusively because of the hurried and premature
movement of our troops to the sea prior to the spring equinox. Had the Dak-
hovsky Detachment moved a month or two weeks later, this would not have
happened."[64] Evdokimov was repeatedly told of the disaster but continued to
drive Circassians to the shore and was even reported to have written: "I wrote to
Count Sumarokov as to why he keeps reminding me in every report concerning
the frozen bodies which cover the roads. Don't the Grand Duke and I know this?
But really, does it depend on anyone to avert this tragedy[?]"[65] The entire deportation process was only finished in spring 1865, although most were deported
by summer 1864.

How was such a crime concealed from the international community, whose
eyes were focused on it as it happened? Once British attention turned to Afghanistan, the reports of Circassian suffering ceased entirely. The Circassians kept the
oral history of the genocide alive, but they also deliberately segregated themselves from the nations where they settled in order to fight assimilation. Even
the Russian administration was kept in the dark about the extent of the tragedy.
The brutality of the deportation process was concealed by the Russian military,
even from their own leadership in St. Petersburg: in the reports of 1864, details
of the horrific conditions faced by the deportees are conspicuously absent.[66] In
his official report, Evdokimov notably omits the period January–March 1864,
which is precisely when the majority of the deaths occurred.[67] Thanks to the British ambassador to Constantinople, news of the fate of the Circassians became
public knowledge as it happened, but London took no steps to stop it despite

having overwhelming naval superiority in the Black Sea.[68] Britian's failure to live up to its commitments to the Circassian people was a major contributor to the "hiding" of the genocide of 1864. Had Britain gone to war as it had promised the Circassians, not only would the genocide quite possibly not have happened, but the world's attention would have been drawn to the events transpiring in the Caucasus. Even if their intervention had failed, a war between Russia and Great Britain would have enshrined the Circassian genocide in the history of western Europe. Instead, its distance from London and Paris has hidden it from view.

The Circassian genocide was a result of a geopolitical struggle over the people's strategically placed homeland. The Russian Caucasus command decided that because of their large numbers and refusal to submit to Russian rule, the people had to be removed one way or another and Circassia itself eliminated. In the words of General Rostislav Fadeev: "[T]he Circassians, owing to their position along the coast, could never be firmly consolidated into Russia as long as they remained in their homeland."[69]

For Evdokimov, there was no question of coexisting with the Circassians:

I have had the honor to report to Your Excellency about the value and necessity of uninhibited dispatching of the natives of Kuban *Oblast* for settlement in Turkey. . . . By force of arms, of course, they will finally submit to our demands and settle where we direct them, but after settling in their new locations they won't soon forget their former way of life . . . as soon as some pretext appears for foreign interference, naturally the intriguers in Constantinople will continue to keep the large native population here under observation and will direct all their efforts toward inciting them in a more or less hostile manner toward us.[70]

The Circassians, by their very presence, were a security risk and had to be expelled to Turkey. As Evdokimov was in command of the expulsion and operated virtually autonomously, the notion that the Circassians were given a real opportunity to resettle north of the Kuban must be looked at with a great deal of skepticism.

The British viewed Circassia as a barrier to keep Russia from controlling the Black Sea, while the French were primarily concerned about Russian expansion into Eastern Europe. Under these conditions, a serious fight on behalf of the Circassians could never be undertaken, and despite the good intentions of a handful of British citizens, the European powers abandoned the Circassians, allowing the Russians to commit genocide against them. While there was some interest in British diplomatic circles in helping the Circassians regain their homeland shortly after the Bolshevik Revolution, this idea was ultimately scrapped.[71] Public knowledge of the genocide virtually disappeared, and the Circassian diaspora began to be assimilated in the nations where they settled: Turkey, Jordan, Israel,

Egypt, Libya, and many other places. It was only with Paul B. Henze's seminal work on the Circassian resistance in 1992 and Stephen Shenfield's 1999 article "The Circassians: A Forgotten Genocide?" that serious scholarship on the subject began.[72] Still, there were very few documents to draw from, and most of them were decidely pro-Russian. It was only with the Russian Federation's establishment of the site runivers.ru in 2009 and the government of Georgia's decision in 2010 to open its state archive to foreign scholars that a large volume of source material has become available to scholars.

Apart from one brief period of openness, the Russian and Soviet governments have continued to conceal the genocide from its citizens. The Soviets briefly attempted to present a full account in the 1920s,[73] but by the 1960s the official narrative repeated tsarist assertions: the Circassians began the hostilities, the Russians offered them fertile lands, the emigration to Turkey was a voluntary choice, and the huge numbers of deaths were a tragic accident. These assertions have been undermined by the recent publication of archival materials, although well-known Russian scholars still repeat them.[74] After fifteen years of relative quiescence following the fall of the Soviet Union, Circassians petitioned the Russian Duma to recognize the Circassian genocide in 2005, to which Moscow responded by announcing a farcical 450th anniversary of the "peaceful unification" of Circassia and Russia, based upon a mutual-defense treaty several Kabardian princes signed in 1557.[75] This act, which would imply that the entire Russo-Circassian War was nothing more than a rebellion, incensed Circassians around the world. However, it was the International Olympic Committee's selection of Sochi as the site of the 2014 Winter Games in 2007 that galvanized Circassian activists. The outrage expressed by the Circassians at the prospect of the Olympic stadium being built on the site of the last massacre of Circassians on the 150th anniversary of their final defeat, and the disingenuous efforts of Moscow to conceal and distort these facts, are ironically bringing the Circassian genocide to the attention of the world once again.[76]

Although both genocides occurred long ago, uncovering them reveals processes that repeat themselves in future tragedies and makes it clear that the process of revealing hidden genocides is an important part of studying more recent crimes. First of all, the primary tactic used in both cases—starvation—chillingly presaged Stalin's forced starvation of Ukrainians, Kazakhs, Belorusians, and Moldovans in the Holodomor genocide of the 1930s. Ermolov's actions against the Kabardians, although nearly forgotten, may in fact have been the first modern genocide in that Ermolov, in his attempt to destroy the Kabardian nation, was applying the principles of Decembrist theoretician Pavel Pestel, who believed in assimilation of all non-Russian subjects, with annihilation as the only other alternative.[77] Ermolov, a sympathizer with the Decembrists' goals, repeatedly applied this theory to his conquest of the Caucasus, most devastatingly in Kabardia. If genocide is a perverse outgrowth of modern nationalism, then Ermolov stands as the first example of its practitioners.

The 1864 genocide, on the other hand, was the first great ethnic cleansing of the modern era. Again, Stalin learned a lesson from his tsarist predecessors and deported the populace of a dozen Caucasus nations to Central Asia as slave labor, forcing upon them conditions that would have led to their destruction had Nikita Khrushchev not repealed the order.[78] Likewise, such forced deportations became an ugly feature of twentieth-century ethnic conflicts, and the Circassian genocide appears to be the first case in modern Europe. Just a few decades later, both Muslims and Christians incurred massive suffering as the Ottoman Empire disintegrated, subjecting multiple populations to forced migration.[79] By the early twentieth century, the world witnessed the Armenian genocide, which was followed by multiple genocides, most significantly the Holocaust. As Paul B. Henze has correctly stated, "none of these ethnic disasters is entirely unrelated to the others."[80] Perhaps the most-remembered aspects of the Circassian genocide are the model that it provided for future ethnic cleansings and genocides and the fact that the perpetrators went unpunished as the world watched. Thus, the Circassian genocide of 1864 should be studied as not only the predecessor but also a major influence upon subsequent crimes against humanity. As a result, uncovering the genocide will not only complete the historical record of the Circassian nation but also contribute to our understanding of genocide in the future.

Despite its scale and significance, and London's failure to uphold its promises, the 1864 genocide was not only forgotten by the British but even denied. After the Bolshevik Revolution, the Circassians of Turkey approached the British for help to return to the Caucasus. The British response was to adopt the Russian justification for the genocide, since Circassian interests now ran counter to British goals in the region: "The moment when Turks are endeavouring to create an Islamic movement in the Caucasus seems ill-chosen for favouring return to that country of an unknown number of perhaps the most warlike of all Ottoman subjects, whose original immigration into Turkey is believed here to have been due rather to reluctance to remain under the rule of a Christian power than to alleged Russian oppression."[81] The only interest the British had in Circassians was, as the Polish agent Mihail Czaikowski put it, as "a tool . . . through which they distress and frighten the Russians."[82] When their usefulness was over, their only patron in the international arena abandoned them too. By the twentieth century, the only mention of Circassia in the press was a luxury liner by that name.

Ironically, the current Russian government has inadvertently placed the spotlight on the Circassian genocide by hosting the 2014 Olympic Winter Games in the resort town of Sochi. *Time* magazine, Reuters, and other sources have described the Circassians' efforts to gain the right to repatriation. While still a little-known event, as the Olympics approach and the Circassians' anti-Sochi campaign escalates, the Circassian genocide may not be hidden much longer.

NOTES

1. For documents pertaining to the ethnic cleansing of Muslims during the War of 1877–1878, see Bilâl N. Şimşir, *Rumeli'den Türk Göçleri: Belgeler; Cilt I, Doksanüç Muhacereti 1877–1878*, 2 vols. (Ankara: Türk Kültürünü Araştırma Enstitütüsü, 1968).

2. A. G. Gadzhiev, *Drevnee Naselenie Dagestana* (Moscow: Nauka, 1975), 65.

3. For an analysis of Circassian religious beliefs, see S. A. Lausheva, *Evoliutsiia Religioznykh Verovanii Adygov: Istoriia i Sovremennost'* (Rostov-na-Donu: SKNTs VSh, 2001).

4. Walter Richmond, *The Northwest Caucasus: Past, Present, Future* (London: Routledge Press, 2008), 61–62.

5. Milentii Ol'shevskii, *Kavkaz c 1841 po 1866 god* (St. Petersburg: Zvezda, 2003), 516; Georgian State Archive, f. 416, op. 3, doc. 1177, 100–199.

6. A. Fonvill', *Poslednii God Voiny Cherkesii za Nezavisimost' 1863–1864 gg.* (Nal'chik: Izdanie zhurnala Adygi, 1991), accessed 16 July 2011, http://www.aheku.org/page-id-1012.html; I. Drozdov, "Posledniaia Bor'ba s Gortsami na Zapodnom Kavkaze," *Kavkazskii Sbornik* 2 (1877): 456–457; Ol'shevskii, *Kavkaz*, 549–550.

7. Adol'f Berzhe, *Vyselenie Gortsev s Kavkaza* (Nal'chik: M. i V. Kotliarovykh, 2010), 31–35.

8. Ibid.; Kemal Karpat, *Ottoman Population 1830–1914: Demographic and Social Characteristics* (Madison: University of Wisconsin Press, 1985), 68–69. For a discussion of the disparities in estimates, see Sarah A. S. Isla Rosser-Owen, "The First 'Circassian Exodus' to the Ottoman Empire (1858–1867) and the Ottoman Response, Based on the Accounts of Contemporary British Observers" (master's thesis, University of London, 2007), 21–22; "The Circassian Exodus," *Times* (London), 12 May 1864, 10.

9. Boris Mal'bakhov, *Kabarda v Period ot Petra I do Ermolova* (Nal'chik: Kniga, 1998), 26–27.

10. Ibid., 186.

11. Sultan Khan-Girey, *Zapiski o Cherkesii* (Nal'chik: Knizhnoe Izdatel'stvo "El'brus," 1978), 300–301.

12. Vasilii Potto, *Kavkazskaia Voina v 5i Tomakh* (Moscow: Tsentrpoligraf, 2006), 2:210.

13. Georgii Kokiev, "Raspad Kabardy na Bol'shuiu I Maluiu I Ustanovivshiesia Otnosheniia s Sosednimi Narodami," in *Istoriia Kabardino-Balkarii v Trudakh G. A. Kokieva*, ed. G. Kh. Mabetov (Nal'chik: El'-Fa, 2005), 200–201; Adol'f Berzhe, ed., *Akty, Sobrannye Kavakzskoiu Arkheograficheskoiu Kommissieiu* (Tiflis: Arkhiv Glavnago Upravleniia Namestnika Kavkaza, 1866–1904), 1:91.

14. Mal'bakhov, *Kabarda*, 222–224.

15. Potto, *Kavkazskaa Voina*, 2:212–213.

16. Berzhe, *Akty*, 6.2:468–469.

17. Ibid.

18. Safarbi Beituganov, *Kabarda i Ermolov: Ocherki Istorii* (Nal'chik: El'brus, 1993), 80.

19. Potto, *Kavkazskaia Voina*, 2:219.

20. Berzhe, *Akty*, 6.2:468–469.

21. Mal'bakhov, *Kabarda*, 227–231; Beituganov, *Kabarda i Ermolov*, 76–82; Vladimir Kudashev, *Istoricheskie Svedeniia o Kabardinskom Narode* (Kiev: Tipo-Litografiia S. V. Kul'zhenko, 1913), 116.

22. V. A. Fedorov, ed., *Zapiski A. P. Ermolova* (Moscow: Vysshaia Shkola, 1991), 377–379.

23. Mal'bakhov, *Kabarda*, 240; Fedorov, *Zapiski*, 379.

24. A. Kh. Kasumov and Kh. A. Kasumov, *Genotsid Cherkessov: Iz Istorii Bor'by Cherkesov za Nezavisimost' v XIX Veke* (Nal'chik: Logos, 1992), 14; Kasbolat Fitsevich Dzamikhov, *Adygi v Politike Rossii na Kavkaze (1550-e—Nachalo 1770-x gg.)* (Nal'chik: Izdatel'skii Tsentr El'-Fa, 2001), 75.

25. Fedorov, *Zapiski*, 283.

26. Mal'bakhov, *Kabarda*, 240–241.

27. See, for example, Kasumov and Kasumov, *Genotsid Cherkessov*; Tugan Kumykov, ed., *Arkhivnye Materialy o Kavkazskoi Voine i Vyselenii Cherkesov (Adygov) v Turtsiiu* (Nal'chik: El'-Fa, 2003); Ramazan Traho, *Circassians* (Munich: R. Traho, 1956); and R. U. Tuganov, *Tragicheskie Posledstviia Kavkazskoi Voiny dlia Adygov. Vtoraia Polovina XIX–Nachalo XX Veka: Sbornik Dokumentov* (Nal'chik: El'-Fa, 2000).

28. Khan-Girey, *Zapiski o Cherkesii*, 191–192; Khan-Girey, *Besl'nii Abat*, accessed 24 May 2011, http://www.circassianlibrary.org/lib/00018/text_1_5_1.html; Askhad Chirg, *Razvitie Obshchestvenno-Politicheskogo Stroia Adygov Severo-Zapadnogo Kavkaza (Konets XVIII-60-e gg. XIX v.* (Maikop: Kabardino-Balkarskii Nauchnyi Tsentr Rossiiskoi Akademii Nauk/ Agygeiskii Respublikanskii Institu Gumanitarnykh Issledovanii, 2002), 51–53.

29. John Howes Gleason, *The Genesis of Russophobia in Great Britain: A Study in the Interaction of Policy and Opinion* (New York: Octagon Books, 1972), 135.

30. Ibid., 164–204.

31. See, for example, *Times* (London), 25 September 1835, 2; 20 February 1836, 1; 5 March 1836, 1; 3 June 1836, 5; 27 January 1837, 5; 1 August 1837, 7; 28 May 1841, 5.

32. Vladimir Degoev, *Bol'shaia Igra na Kavkaze: Istoriia i Sovremennost'* (Moscow: Russkaia Panorama, 2001), 54–60.

33. Richmond, *The Northwest Caucasus*, 61–62; Degoev, *Bol'shaia Igra*, 117–156.

34. Winfried Baumgart, *The Peace of Paris 1856: Studies in War, Diplomacy, and Peacemaking*, trans. Ann Pottinger Saab (Santa Barbara, CA: ABC-Clio, 1981), 25.

35. Ibid., 25–37.

36. E. V. Varle, *Krymskaia Voina* (Moscow/Leningrad: Izdatel'stvo Akademiia Nauk SSSR, 1950), 2:546–550.

37. Baumgart, *Peace*, 111–112; J. B. Conacher, *Britain and the Crimea, 1855–56: Problems of War and Peace* (New York: St. Martin's Press, 1987), 195–196.

38. Conacher, *Britain and the Crimea*, 203, 215.

39. Ol'shevskii, *Kavkaz*, 476.

40. Semen Esadze, *Pokorenie Kavkaza i Okonchanie Kavkazskoi Voiny* (Moscow: Gosudarstvennaia Publichnaia Istoricheskaia Biblioteka Rossii, 2004), 351; Kumykov, *Arkhivnye Materialy*, 2:60–61, 66; Ol'shevskii, *Kavkaz*, 518.

41. Esadze, *Pokorenie*, 352.

42. Berzhe, *Akty*, 12:932–933.

43. Esadze, *Pokorenie*, 352–353.

44. Ibid., 354–357.

45. Ol'shevskii, *Kavkaz*, 532.

46. Berzhe, *Vyselenie Gortsev*, 27–28.

47. M. I. Veniukov, "Kavkazskie Vospominaniia," *Russkii Arkhiv* 1 (1880): 433.

48. Ibid., 436.

49. See Berzhe, *Akty*, 12:664–678.

50. Ol'shevskii, *Kavkaz*, 517.

51. Esadze, *Pokorenie*, 62.

52. Ol'shevskii, *Kavkaz*, 542–543; Richmond, *The Northwest Caucasus*, 75.

53. Drozdov, "Posledniaia Bor'ba," 432.

54. Ibid., 433.

55. Ibid., 434–437.

56. Ibid., 441–442.

57. Ibid., 450–451.

58. Georgian State Archive, f. 416, op. 3, doc. 1177, pp. 110–199.

59. Fonvill', *Poslednii God*.

60. Drozdov, "Posledniaia Bor'ba," 456–457.

61. Ol'shevskii, *Kavkaz*, 549.

62. Ibid., 549–550.

63. Drozdov, "Posledniaia Bor'ba," 457; Ol'shevskii, *Kavkaz*, 550–551.

64. Ol'shevskii, *Kavkaz*, 551.

65. Rostislav Fadeev, *Kavkazskaia Voina* (Moscow: Algoritm, 2005), 187.

66. See, for example, Kumykov, *Arkhinvye Materialy*, 149–281; Georgian State Archive, f. 416, op. 3, doc. 16.

67. Kumykov, *Arkhivnye Materialy*, 212–213.

68. See, for example, "The Circassian Exodus," *Times* (London), 21 May 1864, 11; "The Circassian Exodus," *Times* (London), 11 June 1864, 1; "The Circassian Exodus," *Times* (London), 17 June 1864, 1; "The Circassian Exodus," *Times* (London), 26 July 1864, 4.

69. Fadeev, *Kavkazskaia Voina*, 152.

70. Georgian State Archive, f. 416, op. 3, doc. 139, 2–3.

71. See, for example, FO 196842, telegram of Admiral Webb, 26 November 1918, and FO 196482, telegram of Foreign Office, 30 November 1918.

72. Paul B. Henze, "Circassian Resistance to Russia," in *The North Caucasus Barrier: The Russian Advance towards the Muslim World*, ed. Abdurakhman Avtorkhanov and Marie Bennigsen Broxup (New York: St. Martin's Press, 1992), 62–111; Stephen D. Shenfield, "The Circassians: A Forgotten Genocide?" in *The Massacre in History*, ed. Mark Levene and Penny Roberts (New York: Berghan Books, 1999), 149–162.

73. See, for example, reissues of nineteenth-century works by the Obshchestva Izucheniia Adygeiskoi Avtonomnoi Oblasti in Krasnodar in 1927, e.g, Ya. Abramov, *Kavkazskie Gortsy*; N. Dubrovin, *Cherkesy (Adyge)*; L. Liul'e, *O Natukhaitsakh, Shapsugakh i Abadzekhakh* (Adygeisk: Vozrozhdenie, 1990), and others.

74. Kumykov, *Arkhivnye Materialy*; Tuganov, *Tragicheskie Posledvstviia*. For an example of current scholarly work that echoes tsarist apologetics, see Mark Bliev, *Rossiia i Gortsy Bol'shogo Kavkaza: Na Puti k Tsivilizatsii* (Moscow: Mysl', 2004).

75. "Outrage at 'Fake' Circassian Anniversary," *Institute for War and Peace Reporting*, 15 October 2007, accessed 31 July 2011, http://iwpr.net/report-news/outrage-%E2%80%9Cfake%E2%80%9D-circassian-anniversary-0.

76. See Valery Dzutsev, "The Circassian Question May Acquire a Tangible European Dimension," *Jamestown Foundation North Caucasus Analysis* 12, no. 15 (2011), accessed 31 July 2011, http://www.jamestown.org/single/?no_cache=1&tx_ttnews%5Bswords%5D=8fd5893941d69d0be3f37857626Iae3e&tx_ttnews%5Bany_of_the_words%5D=circassian&tx_ttnews%5Btt_news%5D=38224&tx_ttnews%5BbackPid%5D=7&cHash=f49fa27dc528bf835b9f2305aead9a48.

77. Patrick O'Meara, *The Decembrist Pavel Pestel: Russia's First Republican* (New York: Palgrave Macmillan, 2003), 82–83.

78. See J. Otto Pohl, ed., *Journal of Muslim Minority Affairs* 22, no. 1 (2002), for a comprehensive study of the Stalinist deportations.

79. See Justin McCarthy, *Death and Exile: The Ethnic Cleansing of Ottoman Muslims 1821–1922* (Princeton, NJ: Darwin Press, 1995).

80. Henze, "Circassian Resistance," III.

81. Unsigned cipher telegram to Admiral Webb, 30 November 1918, F.O. 608/196/482.

82. Quoted in T. Kh. Kumykov, ed., *Arkhivnye Materialy O Kavkazskoi Voine i Vyselenii Cherkesov (Adygov) v Turtsiiu (1848–1874), Chast' II* (Nal'chik: El'-Fa, 2003), 77.

THREE

Forgetting, Remembering, and Hidden Genocides

7

The Great Lakes Genocides

Hidden Histories, Hidden Precedents

ADAM JONES

This chapter explores a range of hidden and little-known genocides in the modern history of the African Great Lakes region and the implications of incorporating them into our comparative understanding of genocide, both in a regional context and beyond it. These implications are at once conceptual/theoretical, pedagogical/practical, and moral/ethical. They touch upon central, sometimes incendiary debates in genocide studies and the wider public sphere. They also typify what genocide studies is partly about: the "salvaging" and comparative integration of genocides that have been ignored or effaced from the record, often because a reckoning with them would challenge the power of dominant myths and their guardians.

I begin by outlining the specific "hidden" genocidal events that should be incorporated if the beginnings of a coherent portrait are to be drawn of modern "Great Lakes genocides" (1959 to the present). I then discuss the tendency to reframe and resituate genocides in comparative genocide studies, extending the analysis to a broader "Great Lakes" contextualizing of the "Hutu Power" genocide of Tutsis in 1994.

Genocidal Events

The only genocide in the African Great Lakes region to have commanded the consistent, indeed canonical, attention of genocide scholars and activists is the holocaust of at least half a million Rwandan Tutsis, together with tens of thousands of oppositionist Hutu, between April and July 1994. The numerous genocidal events preceding and following the 1994 watershed may all be classed as hidden genocides. In addition to meriting study on their own terms, all are essential to understanding the apocalyptic events in Rwanda in 1994. In

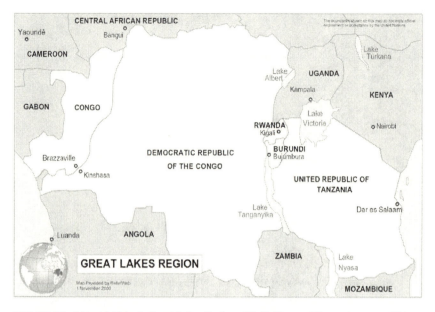

FIGURE 7.1. Map of Africa's Great Lakes Region. (Definitions of the region vary. This one excludes Uganda, as does the present chapter, which focuses on Rwanda, Burundi, and the eastern Democratic Republic of the Congo.)

(Courtesy ReliefWeb)

chronological order, the major landmarks are: the "independence massacres" of Tutsis, beginning in 1959–1960 and reaching a crescendo in 1963–1964; the 1972 genocide/eliticide in Burundi; the renewed massacres of Rwandan Tutsis in 1990–1993, as well as killings of a smaller but unknown number of Hutu civilians by the Tutsi-dominated RPF (Rwandan Patriotic Front) in zones of Rwanda under its occupation; the reciprocal genocidal killing in Burundi in 1993; the subsidiary but substantial genocidal killing of Hutus by RPF forces during the genocide of Rwandan Tutsis in April–July 1994; and the Congolese catastrophe following the Rwandan genocide, including both the "genocide of the camps" (my term) inflicted by RPF forces and their allies in 1996–1997 and the wider, more decentralized genocidal killing since then by military and paramilitary forces under diverse sponsorship (Rwandan in particular).

It is my contention that the "hidden" aspect of these genocides is a consequence of political and methodological factors. Politically, at least since the ebbing of the early post-independence crises, the Great Lakes region of Africa has been consigned to the margins of international affairs and social-scientific scholarship. There could be no more vivid indicator of this marginal status than the almost-unanimous decision by key international actors to flee the Rwandan scene in April 1994, thereby allowing the genocide of the Tutsis to unfold unmolested. Since that time—fueled by a pervasive sense of shame that the post-genocide government of Rwanda has dexterously manipulated and by Western powers' designation of the "new Rwanda" as a model for all Africa—the tendency has been to focus *exclusively* on the Tutsi genocide of 1994. This has the effect of constructing a crude moral dichotomy around the Hutu-Tutsi divide (Hutu = bad/genocidal/perpetrators; Tutsi = good/victims/rescuers). This mapping of the Hutu-Tutsi relationship is further limited to Rwanda alone, thereby obfuscating (1) the similar conflict configurations in Burundi and the Democratic Republic of the Congo (DR Congo), and (2) the role of Tutsi agents, in particular the present Rwandan government and its affiliated Congolese militias, in perpetrating acts of mass violence, including genocide, both before and after the 1994 watershed.

There is a more "neutral" methodological process at work here as well, however. It comprises the tendency of comparative genocide scholarship, first, to orient itself around an "anchoring" genocide, generally but not always one occurring on a vast scale, and second, once anchored, to begin explorations of contiguous analytical and geopolitical territory, including genocidal events that are usually classed as secondary or subsidiary to the anchoring genocide and analyzed in relation to it. As study deepens, the tendency is for the anchoring genocide to gradually lose its overwhelming primacy, and for events and processes related to it increasingly to become subjects of analysis in their own right, rather than for their instrumental utility in understanding the anchoring genocide. A more searchingly contextualized and usually *regionalized* understanding of genocidal processes tends to result. Such a regional framing may be nowhere more vital than with regard to mass violence and genocide in the Great Lakes region of Africa.

I return to these subjects later in the chapter, but for now, let us sketch some key events relevant to a consideration of genocide and hidden genocides in the Great Lakes region since the late colonial period. I begin with the region's first large-scale outbreak of interethnic violence on the twentieth-century record.

Massacres and Forcible Expulsions of Tutsis, 1959–1964

When Belgium abandoned its patron-client relationship with Rwandan Tutsis and transferred its support to the insurgent Hutu majority in the late 1950s, the stage was set for the first substantial eruption of interethnic killing in Rwanda's recorded history. While there was generalized conflict in some areas and atrocities on both sides, the focus of "the harshest violence," in Gérard Prunier's summary,

> was in the north-west, where the Hutu principalities had made their last stand against the Belgian-Tutsi forces in the 1920s and where hatred of the *Banyanduga* ran high. Although it was the area with the smallest Tutsi population, it was where the Tutsi were most relentlessly hunted down. Starting in early 1960, the colonial government began to replace most of

the Tutsi chiefs with new Hutu ones. These immediately organised the persecution of the Tutsi on the hills they now controlled, which started a mass exodus of refugees abroad, which eventually took some 130,000 Rwandese Tutsi to the Belgian Congo, Burundi, Tanganyika and Uganda by late 1963.[1]

Perhaps one thousand Tutsis were murdered in this initial onslaught. Much worse was to come in 1963–1964, when, responding to an abortive invasion by Tutsi exiles from Burundi, the most severe and sustained massacres of the pre-1994 period occurred. "The government used the occasion [of the failed revolt] to launch a massive wave of repression in which an estimated 10,000 Tutsi were slaughtered between 1963 and January 1964." In Gikongoro prefecture alone, according to Nigel Eltringham, "it was estimated that in the period 24–28 December 1963, between 5,000 and 8,000 Tutsi were killed," some "10–20 percent of the Tutsi population of that prefecture."[2] According to Prunier, "Foreign reactions to these killings, which had no East-West dimension, were muted,"[3] although the philosopher Bertrand Russell denounced them in *Le Monde* as "the most horrible and systematic massacre we have had occasion to witness since the extermination of the Jews by the Nazis."[4] By the time the massacres ebbed, perhaps twenty thousand Tutsis had been murdered and another three hundred thousand expelled from Rwanda.[5]

Though these mass atrocities were little known even at the time, and are all but forgotten today, their consequences were profound. This period marked the birth of the Tutsi exile movement which, beginning in 1960, formed "small commandos of exiled Tutsi"; these "were ineffective and behaved more like terrorists than like guerrilla fighters, apparently not caring about the violent reprisals on the Tutsi civilian population which their attacks provoked"[6]—most massively in 1963–1964. The trend would again prevail in the early 1990s, as the RPF launched an invasion from Rwanda that heightened the sense of crisis and threat in the Hutu-dominated regime, encouraging the rise of extremist elements and the formation of militias that inflicted genocidal massacres even before the 1994 holocaust. For Eltringham, "the horrifying events of late 1963/early 1964 . . . must be seen as the true precursor to the genocide [of Tutsis] of 1994."[7]

Renewed atrocities against Rwandan Tutsis occurred in 1967 and again in 1972–1973, during Juvénal Habyarimana's ascension to power. For space reasons, and because their scale and their wider reverberations in our narrative were limited, I do not consider them here.

Genocide in Burundi, 1972

The genocide of Hutus, especially educated Hutus, at the hands of Burundi's Tutsi-controlled army in 1972 was preceded by an abortive Hutu coup and the selective killing of thousands of Tutsis. Up to two hundred thousand Hutus were then murdered in a Tutsi army bloodbath. According to Peter Uvin, "These events constitute the defining moments in independent Burundi's history. They crystallized Hutu and Tutsi identities and created a climate of permanent mutual fear."[8]

Time magazine depicted the genocidal campaign while it was under way:

> The primary targets of the government's continuing "pacification drive" are the Hutu "elite"—meaning not merely the five Hutu cabinet ministers who were summarily executed at the beginning of the rebellion but practically anybody who can write his own name or afford a hut with a corrugated-iron roof instead of a thatched one. At one school, 140 Hutu boys and girls were shot or hacked to death by soldiers. Though the rate of killings had diminished by last week, troops were still descending on isolated villages at night and murdering the local leaders. . . . With their devastating pogrom, the Tutsi overlords have unquestionably bought themselves a few more years in power.[9]

There were striking parallels between the mass killing of Hutus in Burundi in 1972 and the slaughter of Tutsis in neighboring Rwanda in 1994. An atmosphere of existential fear pervaded the ranks of principal perpetrators: "Many Tutsi perceived the Hutu attacks [associated with the failed coup attempt] as posing a mortal threat to their survival . . . many Tutsi saw the wholesale elimination of Hutu elites as the only way of effectively dealing with this clear and present danger—in short, it was a kind of 'final solution' to a situation that threatened their very existence as a group."[10] Consequently, levels of popular participation in the genocide were high and decisive: "The killing of Hutu seemed to have become part of the civic duty expected of every Tutsi citizen," according to René Lemarchand. In the first of several distinct historical echoes and influences that bind the genocide of the African Great Lakes region, this mortal fear derived directly from "the demonstration effect of the Rwanda Revolution" of 1959.[11] And as would prove true on at least two further occasions (Rwanda in 1994 and DR Congo thereafter), displaced populations fleeing persecution and vengeance (from Burundi and Rwanda, respectively) provided some of the most enthusiastic *génocidaires* in subsequent rounds of mass murder.[12]

But there were also significant differences between Burundi in 1972 and Rwanda in 1994. Rather than a full-scale root-and-branch genocide such as evolved in Rwanda, Burundi's genocide was a classic (perhaps *the* classic) *eliticide*—aimed at stripping the targeted group of its educated elements. Though many Hutu females also died, it was also a classic *gendercide* against (educated) Hutu males. So intensive was the targeting of Hutus on grounds of gender, age, and imputed educated or "elite" status that in the contemporary (June 1972) assessment of Michael Hoyt, "In area after area no educated male Hutu is believed to be alive. This is particularly true in the south where we have word from [a] growing number of villages that no Hutu males remain at all."[13] In Rwanda in 1994, despite pronounced gendercidal overtones at certain times and in many places (producing, it appears, a substantial demographic deficit of males in the post-genocide period), the mass killing, particularly in the most gargantuan massacres, was utterly indiscriminate and "root-and-branch."[14]

Apart from providing an iconic case of eliticide and of Tutsi genocide of Hutus—the latter aspect being one that would reverberate throughout the region until the cataclysm of 1994—the 1972 genocide was notable on a couple of additional counts. The lack of interest that accompanied it set a pattern for the 1994 events. Whether the perpetrators in 1994 were directly conscious of it or not, it provided one of the most vivid exemplars of genocide occurring without significant outside opposition and intervention—or even attention. As with Rwanda in 1994, the fact was that Burundi in 1972 was "too remote . . . too poor, too little, and probably too black to be worthwhile," in Alison Des Forges's merciless assessment.[15] In both cases, the genocidal regimes clearly felt they had carte blanche to conduct systematic killing of political and ethnic opponents, in the (merited) expectation that the outside world would dismiss it as nothing more than "tribal violence in Africa." Finally, the 1972 genocide, and the memory of its "success" in quelling Hutu popular mobilization, directly influenced the behavior of the Burundian army during a renewed round of genocidal killing in 1988—in which massacres of some three thousand Tutsis were followed by the slaughter of about twenty thousand Hutus[16]—and again in 1993, during events that receive closer attention below.

Renewed Massacres of Rwandan Tutsis, 1990–1993, and Killings of Hutus by the RPF

According to the Report of the International Panel of Eminent Personalities to Investigate the 1994 Genocide in Rwanda and the Surrounding Events, "Massacres of the Tutsi began at the very outset" of the civil war that erupted with the RPF invasion of Rwanda in October 1990. And "in a real sense, [the massacres] did not end until the RPF victory of July 1994." Such massacres were punctuated by "a reign of terror" in which "murder, rape, harassment or imprisonment could befall any Tutsi at any time."[17] According to Alison Des Forges, some two thousand Tutsis were killed in these massacres.[18]

Representatives of four human-rights NGOs (nongovernmental organizations) "issued a well-documented report that came close to declaring that genocide was a serious future possibility," while the U.N. special rapporteur on Summary, Arbitrary, and Extrajudicial Executions "largely confirmed the conclusions" and "concluded that the massacres that had already taken place seemed to conform to the Genocide Convention's definition of genocide." Tutsis, wrote the special rapporteur, constituted "the overwhelming majority" of

victims of the massacres, and were "targeted solely because of their membership in a certain ethnic group and for no other objective reason." According
to the International Panel, "On virtually each occasion, [the massacres] were
carefully organized. On each occasion, scores of Tutsi were slaughtered by mobs
and militiamen associated with different political parties, sometimes with the
involvement of the police and army, incited by the media, directed by local government officials, and encouraged by some national politicians."[19] The reaction
of the outside world was typically muted: only the Swiss government called for
an investigation of the slaughter.

The implications of these genocidal massacres are plain. They were a "trial
run" for a full-scale holocaust, even if the timing of a decision for a "final solution" of the Tutsi "problem" remains a subject of considerable controversy. The
experts of the International Panel discerned "a pattern emerging through these
successive slaughters" in 1991–1992: "It appears that the radicals and military
worked together trying out different techniques of killing. As the experiments
progressed, their leaders learned two lessons: that they could massacre large
numbers of people quickly . . . and that, based on the reactions they had elicited
to date, they could get away with it."[20]

It was also at this time, according to Alison Des Forges, that the Rwandan
authorities learned "how easily foreigners accepted explanations of 'ancient,
tribal hatred'" and thereafter "repeatedly underlined the 'tribal' nature of the
killings . . . insist[ing] that they had been simply unable to control the outburst
of spontaneous, popular rage."[21] This was a trope that would be deployed with
considerable success after the outbreak of the holocaust of 1994.

Mention must also be made of the "numerous reports of human rights abuses
committed by the RPA [Rwandan Patriotic Army, the military wing of the RPF]" in
Rwanda after its October 1990 invasion, with "hundreds of deliberate and arbitrary killings" as well as "'disappearances' of captured combatants and unarmed
civilians suspected of supporting the [Habyarimana] government," in Amnesty
International's evaluation. The United Nations Commission of Inquiry that vis-
ited Rwanda in 1993 spoke of "substantial grounds" for concluding that the RPA
was guilty of crimes against humanity.[22] The RPF seemed to have learned from this
as well: that it could successfully keep a lid on its own crimes and exempt its officials from international efforts to prosecute the perpetrators of mass atrocities.

"Reciprocal Genocide" in Burundi, 1993

The mass violence that erupted in Burundi following the murder of the Hutu president Ndadaye by operatives of the Tutsi-monopolized army (October 21, 1993) may
stand as one of those instances—not uncommon—in which multiple ethnic groups
adopt genocidal strategies against each other, albeit on differing scales. According to René Lemarchand, "The sudden eruption of anti-Tutsi violence only hours

following the news of Ndadaye's death, resulting in countless atrocities and random killings of Tutsi civilians [by Hutus], was the triggering factor behind an equally devastating display of anti-Hutu violence by the army," murdering anywhere between thirty thousand and a hundred thousand people, by Lemarchand's estimate.[23]

As well as being both horrific and largely hidden from the historical record, the 1993 genocide of Hutus in Burundi directly prepared the ground for the genocide of Tutsis in Rwanda in 1994. Burundian Hutu refugees—350,000 of whom fled to Rwanda after the Tutsi-dominated army went on the rampage—appear to have been significant as agents and supporters of the mass killing of Tutsis in April-July 1994.[24] The refugees brought tales of mass atrocity at Tutsi hands, giving "a powerful stimulus to the crystallization of Hutu Power in Rwanda and thus contribut[ing] significantly to the radicalization of Hutu politics on the eve of the carnage," Lemarchand notes.[25] They also helped to make the resulting propaganda assault on Rwandan Tutsis—painting them as spies and saboteurs, as a "fifth column" poised to join with the RPF invaders to exterminate Hutus—persuasive to most Hutus. Studies of ordinary genocidal perpetrators and accomplices since the 1994 genocide, above all Scott Straus's, have consistently reported that these messages were widely believed and generated a sense of mortal fear among Rwandan Hutus.[26]

Mass Killings of Rwandan Hutus by the RPA, April–July 1994

Accompanying the mass slaughter of Tutsis and oppositionist Hutus by "Hutu Power" elements were massacres on a genocidal scale (claiming tens of thousands of victims in total) and of a genocidal character (mass killings of unarmed Hutus) by the RPF, though the degree of central direction and explicit license from above remains uncertain in many instances. These massacres were first detailed in the "Gersony Report" of the United Nations. Deniers of the Rwandan genocide have made much of the fact that the report was effectively suppressed by the United Nations, but much of the information Gersony had unearthed was quickly and prominently published, in the section of Alison Des Forges's *Leave None to Tell the Story* (1998) dealing with RPF/RPA crimes.

Were these crimes genocidal? Gersony's and Des Forges's assessments, supplemented by expert commentary, suggest that they were—on a substantially smaller scale than "Hutu Power's" extermination campaign of Tutsis, but eminently prosecutable nonetheless. According to Gérard Prunier, in his magnum opus *Africa's World War* (2009), the RPF in 1994 waged "a massive campaign of killings, which could not be considered simply as uncontrolled revenge killings even if some of the murders belonged to that category." He described "frequent stories of people who had been called to a meeting by the RPF and who, when they expected in typically Rwandese fashion to be told what the new power wanted them to do, would be slaughtered indiscriminately." The large number of victims, together with the fact that "the RPF did not wish to attract attention," meant that "disposal areas were set up in a variety of places to incinerate the corpses." All these considerations factored in Prunier's assessment of whether the killings were "systematically organized": "Given the size of Rwanda, [and] the discipline of the RPA, it is almost impossible that they were not." He added mordantly: "Work parties to bury bodies and the use of crematoria in several areas hardly suggest improvisation."[27]

The resonance of these genocidal massacres is limited at this point. Though this is no more than speculation, it is likely that the killing is submerged in Hutu collective memory by the wider upheavals, forced exile, and mass mortality by starvation and disease later in 1994—and probably also by the traumas of the "genocide of the camps" and attendant genocidal killing of Hutus in 1996–1997. The significance of the Tutsi-on-Hutu killing during the genocide of 1994 perhaps will increase in coming years, as it is more closely investigated, and (unfortunately) as it is exploited by those who deny the genocide of the Tutsis—a subject examined further below. The idea of "double genocides" is extremely attractive to those seeking to establish a moral equivalence between the RPF and Hutu Power in the barbarity of their 1994 actions (or even, in the case of Herman and Peterson's *The Politics of Genocide* examined below, to deny Hutu-organized genocide and to allege that the RPF was the only organized force capable of mass killing in 1994!).[28]

Genocide in Eastern Zaire (Subsequently DR Congo)

The most murderous phase of the Congolese conflict began with the 1994 spillover of Hutu refugees and génocidaires from Rwanda into Goma and surrounding territories. This phase can be examined from two distinct perspectives: as a systematic genocidal campaign that is part of a large-scale, centrally directed military strategy (the "genocide of the camps" in 1996–1997), and as an accompanying and enduring series of smaller-scale, more decentralized genocidal massacres (1994 to the present). Generally these have been perpetrated by paramilitary militias, frequently with foreign support (e.g., the AFDL/APR militias sponsored by the RPF, discussed below), or by more temporary and freelance formations (gangs, vigilante groups, and so on).

The 1996–1997 "genocide of the camps" has already been touched upon. It remains intensively little-studied, if such a thing is possible: the United Nations report of 2010, first leaked and then published in slightly bowdlerized form, is the first comprehensive source available in English. As Prunier noted in *Africa's World War*, "there seems to have been an unspoken compact among the various Western actors not to prevent the Rwandese from carrying out their revenge since it was the West's lack of reaction during the genocide that had made it possible in the first place. . . . The RPF calculated that guilt, ineptitude, and the hope that things would work out would cause the West to literally let them get away with murder. The calculation was correct."[29] This inertia long prevented outside observers from gaining an accurate understanding of exactly what occurred during the genocide—though precious few evinced an interest in the subject. More than any other case discussed in this chapter, the DR Congo killings constitute a *deliberately* hidden genocide. Their obfuscation is the product, not just of the standard distance and uninterest, but of influential actors' determination to keep the subject off the international agenda and out of the international courts.

The 2010 U.N. report may finally end this conspiracy of silence. Its language was uncompromising, for instance, in describing the RPF-backed AFDL/APR militias' rampages during the "genocide of the camps" and its aftermath, an account that merits extended quotation:

> The majority of the victims were children, women, elderly people and the sick, who posed no threat to the attacking forces. . . . Very large numbers of victims were forced to flee and travel long distances to escape their pursuers, who were trying to kill them. The hunt lasted for months, resulting in the deaths of an unknown number of people subjected to cruel, inhuman and degrading living conditions, without access to food or medication. On several occasions, the humanitarian aid intended for them was deliberately blocked, . . . depriving them of assistance essential to their survival. . . . It is therefore possible to assert that, even if only a part of the Hutu population in Zaire was targeted and destroyed, it could nonetheless constitute a crime of genocide, if this was the intention of the perpetrators. . . . Several incidents listed in this report point to circumstances and facts from which a court could infer the intention to destroy the Hutu ethnic group in the DRC in part, if these were established beyond all reasonable doubt. Firstly, the scale of the crimes and the large number of victims are illustrated by the numerous incidents described above. The extensive use of edged weapons (primarily hammers) and the systematic massacre of survivors, including women and children, after the camps had been taken show that the numerous deaths cannot be attributed to the hazards of war or seen as equating to collateral damage. . . . Particularly in North Kivu and South Kivu but also in other provinces, the massacres often began with a trick by elements of the AFDL/APR, who summoned the victims to meetings on the pretext either of discussing their repatriation to Rwanda in the case of the refugees, or of introducing them to the new authorities in the case of Hutus settled in the region, or of distributing food. Afterwards, those present were systematically killed. . . . Such acts certainly suggest premeditation and a precise methodology. . . . Furthermore, no effort was made to make a distinction between Hutus who were members of the ex-FAR/Interahamwe [the genocidal militia in Rwanda in 1994] and Hutu civilians, whether

or not they were refugees. This tendency to put all Hutus together and "tar them with the same brush" is also illustrated by the declarations made during the "awareness-raising speeches" made by the AFDL/APR in certain places, according to which any Hutu still present in Zaire must necessarily be a perpetrator of genocide, since the "real" refugees had already returned to Rwanda. These "awareness-raising speeches" made in North Kivu also incited the population to look for, kill or help to kill Rwandan Hutu refugees, whom they called "pigs."[30]

In its most condemnatory passage, the report's authors wrote that "the systematic and widespread attacks described in this report, which targeted very large numbers of Rwandan Hutu refugees and members of the Hutu civilian population, resulting in their death, reveal a number of damning elements that, if they were proven before a competent court, could be classified as crimes of genocide." It was this summation, and the deployment of a genocide framework throughout, that most infuriated Rwandan officials. Their protests, and perhaps an autonomous reconsideration by the U.N. High Commissioner for Refugees (UNHCR) panelists, led to the language being slightly watered down in the final report. For example, "a number of damning elements" in the statement just cited was altered to "a number of inculpatory elements." Remaining, however, was the reference to "crimes of genocide" that had so riled the Rwandans.[31] It was notable that none of the threatened retaliation (e.g., withdrawal of U.N. peacekeepers) in fact resulted.

As for the broader context of genocide in the Democratic Republic of the Congo, it is impossible to do meaningful justice to the subject here, given the dizzying array of actors and the still-cloudy nature of much of the mortality inflicted. For our purposes, most relevant are the role of the Hutu paramilitary formations escaping to Zaire at the end of the 1994 genocide and the role of the militias, particularly that led by the Tutsi Laurent Nkundabagenzie (known as Nkunda), supported by Rwanda's RPF regime as a means of countering the threat of Hutu exiles and expanding Rwandan influence in eastern Congo. Nkunda's "record of violence in eastern Congo includes destroying entire villages, committing mass rapes, and causing hundreds of thousands of Congolese to flee their homes," according to Howard French.[32] International criticism of Rwanda's support for Nkunda appears to have been an important factor in the militia leader's arrest by Rwandan authorities in January 2009, though in 2012, renewed accusations circulated of Rwandan complicity in militia funding and training, this time of the predominantly Tutsi "M23" rebels. The response of key Rwandan backers—like the United States, Great Britain, Germany, and the Netherlands, all of whom suspended at least some aid deliveries—suggested that for the RPF's foreign friends, the bloom was at last off the rose.

"Discovering" Genocides, Reframing Genocides

How can one explain the pervasive absence of attention to the broad range of mass-atrocity events in the Great Lakes outlined above? Why have they remained hidden from understanding, not only as far as public discussion and understanding are concerned, but even for genocide students and scholars who are well familiar with what took place in Rwanda in 1994?

In the introduction to this volume, the editors have ably outlined the *political* factors that lead to some genocides becoming recognized and even "canonical" while others are ignored, downplayed, blatantly misrepresented—or even celebrated! Many of these factors are also evident in the Great Lakes case.

First, no part of the world is more frequently depicted in hegemonic discourses as "marginal," "underdeveloped," and dependent than Africa. And on the African continent, no region has been constructed as such a savage and incomprehensible "heart of darkness" as the Great Lakes region. (Indeed, it was DR Congo, in its previous Belgian colonial incarnation, that gave rise to Joseph Conrad's famous—and implicitly condescending—phrase.[33]) This offers a convenient capsule explanation for why the "outside world" (read: the West) ignored or downplayed *all* outbreaks of genocide and other mass violence in the Great Lakes region. Patterns of such violence, usually designated as "tribal," were deemed too barbaric to be accessible to "civilized" observers. As anonymous Africans in states no longer directly controlled by Western interests, the victims of such violence were deemed irrelevant and unworthy of attention. To the extent that violence in Africa assumed significance in the international order, it was *only* insofar as external actors and rivalries were directly affected—for example, with the superpower struggles over Angola and Mozambique in the 1970s and 1980s, or conflict in the one sub-Saharan African country that claimed membership in the Western "club," that is, South Africa.[34] In this light, the Western involvement in the Rwandan conflict of the early 1990s stands as somewhat anomalous and predictably halfhearted. The precipitous withdrawal of the foreign troops that could have suppressed the 1994 genocide, and the abandonment of Tutsis and Hutu moderates to their fate at Hutu Power's hands, is entirely in keeping with postcolonial mindsets and practices.

The objectively catastrophic consequences of those 1994 decisions transformed the hegemonic discourse of violence and genocide in Rwanda and the Great Lakes region. For reasons of its immense scale and brutality, as well as the unusually prominent role of "ordinary people" in the slaughter, the Rwandan genocide was quickly absorbed into the core canon of twentieth-century genocides (see the introduction to this volume). And much as the Israeli government's claim to "inherit" and incarnate the suffering of the Jewish Shoah, set against a backdrop of Western guilt, tended to shield Israel from criticism for its violent treatment of Palestinians and others, so did the post-genocide Rwandan government's claim to have "ended" the 1994 genocide (when the West would not), and to have advanced a "progressive" model of development and reconciliation for post-genocide Rwanda, tend to obfuscate the RPF's role in violence before, during, and after the 1994 events.

As with the Israeli case, too, Rwanda's incorporation into a Western-dominated security and alliance structure served to grant the Rwandan government an exemption from criticism and intervention, with regard to both its domestic policies (including pervasive authoritarianism and murderous repression) and its genocidal actions in DRC in 1996–1997 (and probably since). With regard to the Congolese violence, just as many Israeli attacks can be explained and excused as "defensive" responses to acts of terrorism against Israelis, so could the "genocide of the camps" be presented as a response to violent Hutu-militant incursions from Congo. In both cases, there was an empirical buttress for such claims. But what is notable for our purposes is that the viability of a "self-defense" framing depends largely on whether one is in the good books, or the pockets, of the hegemonic powers.

This combination of willful ignorance, feelings of guilt, and strategic favoritism goes far to explain both why the Rwandan genocide of 1994 was allowed to unfold and why that genocide ever since has sucked the air out of discussions of all other post-1959 genocides in the Great Lakes region of Africa. A final, more objective factor should be proposed: the *diffuse, generalized, and often reciprocal nature* of mass atrocity in the region. If violence in Rwanda since 1959 overwhelmingly assumed an anti-Tutsi character, genocidal outbreaks in Burundi (in 1993) and in Zaire/DRC were more reciprocal and tit-for-tat in nature. The Western, and perhaps human, preference for clear perpetrators and victims rarely was satisfied. Likewise, the preference for discrete and bounded historical "events," with clear causal agents and consequences, is undermined when genocide takes on a "slow-motion" character as in the DRC, with much of the mortality produced indirectly through starvation and disease, rather than directly with guns, grenades, and machetes. Genocide scholars, no less than ordinary publics, are still trying to wrap their minds around such ambiguous-seeming violence.

While politics is central to an understanding of why most Great Lakes genocides have remained hidden, this element of diffuseness/ambiguity reminds us that a political explanation is necessary but not sufficient. In closing this section, I want to consider one further aspect: the methodology by which genocide scholarship has sought to approach and encompass its subject.

I suggested earlier that comparative genocide research tends to alight first on an anchoring genocide in a national or regional context. Such a genocide is denoted by its objective scale and severity—but also by the resources available to launch public-education campaigns, fund fellowships and endowed chairs, and so on; and by wider geostrategic or international-political aspects (so that the occurrence of the Balkans genocide on European soil, or the shameful abandonment of distant Rwanda by the Western powers in 1994, also influenced the prevailing paradigm). A typical pattern is for this combination of factors to produce, at first, a somewhat monolithic focus on an anchoring genocide (the Jewish Holocaust, the Armenian genocide, the Rwandan Tutsi genocide). Over time—reflecting the "inkblot" pattern of academic investigation, in which research spreads out from central foci; reflecting, too, perceptions that attention to anchoring genocides has occluded attention to others—the hidden genocides begin to be investigated and reclaimed. They attract material and scholarly attention and resources. As they accumulate, they challenge the existing paradigm and generally prompt it to shift.

The process is quite similar to the process studied by Thomas Kuhn in *The Structure of Scientific Revolutions*, with an important difference. Whereas in the natural-scientific realm, paradigms tend to be radically displaced and transcended by their successors (as Newtonian physics was displaced by an Einsteinian paradigm), in genocide studies the dominance of anchoring genocides tends to diminish only somewhat, and in relative rather than absolute terms. Even the most dramatic erosion of a dominant paradigm in genocide studies—the "relativizing" of the Jewish Holocaust and the decline of Holocaust exceptionalism—led only to the Holocaust being studied as *one* of the most severe and destructive genocides of all time, rather than a *uniquely* severe and destructive one. In absolute terms, of course, Holocaust studies (including in a comparative-genocide context) has never been more vital and fertile an enterprise, even in the wake of this paradigmatic reframing.

In its relatively brief history, comparative genocide studies itself has undergone a number of defining paradigm shifts. The first was probably its foundational one: the emergence, from the field of Holocaust studies, of a comparative field that applied Holocaust-derived frameworks and lessons to other genocides. Initially the framework was still Holocaust-centric, or at least Holocaust-exceptionalist. Quite quickly, however, the field settled on a research agenda in which no one genocide is privileged above all others.[35]

The field has also gradually moved away from black-and-white depictions of genocide to more nuanced and contextualized ones. In particular, notions of "good guys versus bad guys" tend to give way to analyses that are less bound by time and space, and amenable to epochal, regional, and civilizational framings. Thus, for example, the Jewish Holocaust is increasingly analyzed *both* in terms of "the Nazis' other victims" and against a backdrop of macro-historical processes (e.g., as a late form of Western colonialism). The Armenian genocide has been reconceptualized as one facet of an "Ottoman destruction of Christian minorities" during the First World War,[36] as well as in the light of the macro-historical decline of the Ottoman Empire (and the vast suffering inflicted on Muslim as well as Christian populations in the process of Ottoman imperial "unweaving").[37]

The growing theoretical sophistication of a young field like genocide studies is evident here. The shift from a mechanistic, top-down, ideology-fueled model of genocide to a more sophisticated one emphasizing *dynamism, contingency,* and *evolution* in genocidal events and processes naturally leads to a broadening of scope and the opening of a range of new subjects for intellectual inquiry. And since we have devoted extended attention to hegemonic discourses, it is crucial to emphasize the role of *counter-hegemonic* actors and theories in undermining established paradigms. The increased attention to indigenous peoples or slavery in the genocide-studies literature, for example, must be seen as reflecting the countercultural initiatives launched in the West in the 1960s, the growing activism of indigenous people and people of color, and a mounting skepticism toward received wisdom and established political authorities. The introduction to this book makes it clear how far we have yet to travel, as genocide scholars and activists, in expanding our agendas beyond our blinkered, predominantly privileged backgrounds. But we should not overlook how far the field of comparative genocide studies has progressed, and how notably its analyses have deepened, during a relatively brief period.

Studying Hidden Genocides: Benefits for Understanding and Advocacy

What are some of the theoretical and ethical advantages of revealing the hidden genocides, and incorporating them into a reconfigured and expanded framework?

Perhaps the most significant benefit of incorporating hidden genocides into a regionwide framing is that it helps us understand *connections, continuities, and spillover effects* in mass violence. This is nowhere clearer than in the context of the countries of Africa's Great Lakes region. At a national level, the connections and continuities between the events of 1963–1964 in Rwanda and the violence of the early 1990s, culminating in the 1994 holocaust, are so direct and significant that the latter events are simply incomprehensible without a grasp of the former. Much the same could be said of genocide in Burundi in 1972 and 1993. International connections and spillovers are no less significant: for example, between Burundi in 1993 and Rwanda in 1994, or between Rwanda in 1994 and DR Congo since that time.

Incorporating hidden genocides and their spillover effects can also assist us in understanding why "ordinary men," and sometimes women, commit genocide. In the Rwandan case, Hutus who were internally displaced, traumatized, and pushed to the margins of subsistence by RPF attacks in the north of the country were frequently eager recruits for the Interhamwe militia and for grassroots killing squads. Hundreds of thousands of Hutu refugees from the reciprocal genocidal killing in Burundi in 1993 fled to Rwanda, likewise swelling the pool of militiamen and génocidaires. The epic displacement of Hutus to Zaire/DR Congo in the aftermath of the 1994 genocide has reverberated through the region ever since, providing the core personnel of Hutu-dominated militia groups and directly triggering the Tutsi-inflicted bloodbath in eastern Congo in 1996–1997.

A "hidden genocides" reframing also extends *recognition and validation* to all victims of genocide. In a Great Lakes context, it should sharply reduce the tendency to cast the Hutu/Tutsi ethnic divide in simplistic good-versus-evil terms: clearly, agents and forces on both sides of the divide have committed genocidal atrocities, whether in Rwanda, Congo, or Burundi. The hubris and "persistent appeal[s] to absolute history"[38] that haunt ethnopolitics in the Great Lakes region might diminish if the mutual or reciprocal aspect of much violence in the region were acknowledged. Narcissistic smugness in such matters can be lethal, contributing directly to new outbreaks of violence.

I believe there are grounds, nonetheless, for preserving the 1994 genocide of the Tutsis as an anchoring genocide in this expanded framework, much as the Jewish Holocaust continues legitimately to serve this purpose for the Nazis' multifarious genocides. No Nazi genocide was as systematic, all-encompassing, and intricately programmed as the Jewish one. Likewise, no communal attack in the Great Lakes region was so totalizing and systematic as the Tutsi holocaust, or perpetrated so directly and intentionally. (As noted, though the death toll in Congo is much larger, most of the deaths there have been inflicted by indirect/structural means, mainly starvation and disease, rather than direct murder.)

This point is relevant to an engagement with one of the conundrums of a hidden genocides framework, sadly relevant for Africa's Great Lakes region. How can we prevent these hidden genocides from being exploited by agents of genocide denial, particularly those who challenge the significance or actuality of the anchoring genocides? Is a boundary discernible between responsible revisionism and what I have called "egregious genocide denial"?

This issue has two key elements in the Great Lakes context. The first concerns the ugly campaign of outright denial of the 1994 Tutsi genocide in Rwanda, centered on Rwandan Hutu exiles and a small coterie of legal, academic, and media advocates based mostly in North America. Their denialist discourse—claims either that there was an equivalence in the mass killings of Tutsis and Hutus in 1994 or that *no systematic killing of Tutsis occurred at all*—has bubbled beneath the surface of public discourse since 1994, its most prominent spokespeople being accused Hutu génocidaires and their lawyers. But it took a sharp and unexpected turn toward academic respectability in mid-2010, with the publication of Edward S. Herman and David Peterson's denialist tract, *The Politics of Genocide*.[39] Herman and Peterson's interpretation of Rwanda (pp. 51–68 of their book) situates itself at the outer edge of denialist rhetoric, alleging that the Tutsi-dominated RPF was the "only organized force" in Rwanda capable of inflicting mass killing, denying thereby that systematic mass killing of Tutsis occurred, and depicting the diverse agents of Hutu Power as discombobulated and victimized throughout. The RPF's mass killings in Rwanda in 1994 and Zaire/DR Congo in 1996–1997, which appear clearly to qualify as genocidal, are of course crucial elements in this denialist discourse. Unaccompanied by an account of the vastly greater killing of Tutsis and opposition Hutus by agents of Hutu Power, this is a borderline deranged effort, cherry-picking a few useful factoids from legitimate scholars who would not touch Herman and Peterson's denialist enterprise with a ten-foot pole.[40]

On the other side of the genocide-denial equation—in a palpable irony—stands the Kagame/RPF regime of Rwanda. It has sought to render itself immune to accusations that it committed genocide and crimes against humanity against Hutus, on a scale of tens of thousands of victims in Rwanda in 1994 and up to three hundred thousand in the 1996–1997 "genocide of the camps." It has likewise fended off any legal attempt to confront those crimes—not that any significant international authority has actually proposed prosecutions. The RPF vision of a Rwanda at peace and undergoing reconciliation between ethnic groups was, however, dealt a harsh blow by the U.N. findings leaked and published in 2010—as evidenced by the Rwandan government's furious and multifaceted response to the UNHCR report.

Serious and sustained investigation by scholars and human-rights advocates of mass RPF atrocities, including genocide, in Rwanda and DR Congo will certainly undermine the Rwandan government's shameful posturing. Such investigations are necessary if hidden genocides are to be uncovered, and some justice for them rendered, in both intellectual and legal/restitutive terms. There is no reason this project cannot proceed responsibly, without skirting the abyss of denying the 1994 genocide of Rwandan Tutsis, let alone diving headlong into it. Indeed, any scholar or other analyst would be irresponsible to pronounce on Great Lakes genocides without familiarizing herself or himself with the extraordinarily rich range of testimony, documentation, and scholarly analysis of the 1994 Tutsi genocide. For comparative genocide scholars, it is a trove that entrenches Rwanda as a "canonical" twentieth-century case of genocide along with the Armenian genocide and the Jewish Holocaust. This status reflects not only the scale, systematization, and human horror of each of the events but also the way it has generated a detailed and complex primary and secondary literature that is of enormous use in crafting comparative frameworks for genocide studies.

Conclusion: The Rwandan Genocide in Regional Context

Much as the Nazi slaughter of European Jews was long analyzed apart from the genocidal campaigns that accompanied and even preceded it, so the 1994 Rwandan genocide of "Tutsis and oppositionist Hutus," as it is usually described, has tended to be studied in isolation. The reasons for this are perhaps similar to those which kept the Jewish Holocaust preserved from comparison and contextualization for so long. They include

- widespread ignorance of historical context (in the Rwandan case) or preceding/accompanying genocidal campaigns (in the case of the Holocaust);
- an entrenching of a given narrative of genocidal events/victim groups as iconic, reflecting the strategic preferences of hegemonic actors, powerful diasporic lobbies, and relative disparities of access to resources for education and outreach; and
- concern that attention to wider context might relativize the atrocities in a way that could be seen to downplay the slaughter of Jews/Tutsis, even playing into the hands of genocide deniers.

In many other cases, substantial historiographical and theoretical advances have been made by reframing and recontextualizing genocidal events, including supplementing the analysis with attention to hidden genocides that are closely connected to the anchoring one—whether in time and space, conceptually, or both. Fears that attention to overarching Nazi strategies would overshadow the specifically *Jewish* Holocaust are belied by the unprecedented vigor and sophistication of Holocaust studies today. There is no reason that research into genocide in the Great Lakes region of Africa should not proceed along similar lines. It should be eclectic and fair-minded, skeptical of received wisdoms, and open to reconfigurations and paradigm shifts—while not losing sight of objective realities, including substantial disparities in the character and outcome of genocidal campaigns. If hidden genocides can be explored and incorporated in an intellectually and ethically responsible fashion, they should contribute to a more informative and nourishing discussion. They should also help to guide the efforts of genocide scholars and activists, making them more adept at analyzing past genocides, and better equipped to predict and confront future genocidal outbreaks.

NOTES

1. Gérard Prunier, *The Rwanda Crisis: History of a Genocide* (New York: Columbia University Press, 1995), 51.
2. Nigel Eltringham, *Accounting for Horror: Post-Genocide Debates in Rwanda* (London: Pluto Press, 2004), 43.
3. Prunier, *Rwanda Crisis*, 56.
4. Russell quoted in Eltringham, *Accounting for Horror*, 43.

5. Alison Des Forges, *Leave None to Tell the Story: Genocide in Rwanda* (New York: Human Rights Watch, 1999), 40.

6. Prunier, *Rwanda Crisis*, 54.

7. Eltringham, *Accounting for Horror*, 180.

8. Peter Uvin, "Ethnicity and Power in Burundi and Rwanda: Different Paths to Mass Violence," *Comparative Politics* 31, no. 3 (1999): 258.

9. "Burundi: Double Genocide," *Time*, 26 June 1972. See also Romain Forscher, "The Burundi Massacres: Tribalism in Black Africa," *International Journal of Politics* 4, no. 4 (1974–75): 77–87; and Warren Weinstein, "Ethnicity and Conflict Regulation: The 1972 Burundi Revolt," *Africa Spectrum* 9, no. 1 (1974): 42–49.

10. René Lemarchand, *Burundi: Ethnic Conflict and Genocide* (Cambridge: Cambridge University Press, 1994), 101.

11. René Lemarchand, "The Burundi Genocide," in *Century of Genocide: Eyewitness Accounts and Critical Views*, ed. Samuel Totten, William S. Parsons, and Israel W. Charny (New York: Garland, 1997), 317–333.

12. Lemarchand writes: "Particularly in the northern region, where refugee camps [for Hutus] were located, much of the killing was done by Tutsi refugees, perhaps as much out of revenge as out of fear that they might once again be the target of Hutu violence" ("The Burundi Genocide," 325).

13. Hoyt quoted in Lemarchand, *Burundi*, 103.

14. For a detailed analysis, see Adam Jones, "Gender and Genocide in Rwanda," in *Gendercide and Genocide*, ed. Adam Jones (Nashville, TN: Vanderbilt University Press, 2004), 98–137.

15. Des Forges quoted in *Chronicle of a Genocide Foretold, Part 2: "We Were Cowards"* (Ottawa: National Film Board of Canada, 1997).

16. Ravi Bhavnani and David Backer, "Localized Ethnic Conflict and Genocide: Accounting for Differences in Rwanda and Burundi," *Journal of Conflict Resolution* 44, no. 3 (June 2000): 285. See also Uvin, "Ethnicity and Power," 258.

17. *Rwanda: The Preventable Genocide*, Report of the International Panel of Eminent Personalities to Investigate the 1994 Genocide in Rwanda and the Surrounding Events (Addis Ababa: IPEP/OAU, 2000), 45, 48.

18. Des Forges, *Leave None to Tell the Story*, 87.

19. *Rwanda: The Preventable Genocide*, 47–48.

20. Ibid., 48.

21. Des Forges, *Leave None to Tell the Story*, 91.

22. Amnesty International report quoted in Eltringham, *Accounting for Horror*, 101.

23. René Lemarchand, *The Dynamics of Violence in Central Africa* (Philadelphia: University of Pennsylvania Press, 2009), 146.

24. On the role of Burundian refugees as perpetrators in 1994, see Lee Ann Fujii, *Killing Neighbors: Webs of Violence in Rwanda* (Ithaca, NY: Cornell University Press, 2009), 86; Lemarchand, *Dynamics of Violence*, 20, 58.

25. Lemarchand, *Dynamics of Violence*, 58.

26. Straus found "that most [Hutu] perpetrators participated in violence because they feared the consequences of not doing so. . . . What comes through [in interviews with perpetrators] . . . is a sense of acute insecurity, even panic." Scott Straus, *The Order of Genocide: Race, Power, and War in Rwanda* (Ithaca, NY: Cornell University Press, 2006), 157.

27. Gérard Prunier, *Africa's World War: Congo, the Rwandan Genocide, and the Making of a Continental Catastrophe* (Oxford: Oxford University Press, 2009), 15–17, 21.

28. For a quantitative and qualitative examination of the "double genocide" argument, see Philip Verwimp, "Testing the Double-Genocide Thesis for Central and Southern Rwanda," *Journal of Conflict Resolution* 47, no. 4 (2003): 423–442.

29. Prunier, *Africa's World War,* 147, 23.

30. "Key Excerpts from UN Report on Rwandan Army Genocide in DR Congo," BBC Online, 27 August 2010, available at http://www.congoplanet.com/article.jsp?id=45261725. The full title of the report is *Democratic Republic of the Congo, 1993–2003: Report of the Mapping Exercise Documenting the Most Serious Violations of Human Rights and International Humanitarian Law Committed within the Territory of the Democratic Republic of the Congo between March 1993 and June 2003* (Geneva: Office of the High Commissioner of Human Rights, 2010). The full text as published in October 2010, with minor wording changes in some sensitive passages, is available online at http://www.ohchr.org/Documents/Countries/ZR/DRC_MAPPING_REPORT_FINAL_EN.pdf; the quoted passages are from sections 512–517.

31. Jeffrey Gettleman and Josh Kron, "UN Report on Congo Massacres Draws Anger," *New York Times,* 1 October 2010.

32. Howard W. French, "Kagame's Hidden War in the Congo," *New York Review of Books,* 24 September 2009, http://www.nybooks.com/articles/23054. See also Filip Reyntjens and René Lemarchand, "Mass Murder in Eastern Congo, 1996–1997," in *Forgotten Genocides: Oblivion, Denial, and Memory*, ed. René Lemarchand (Philadelphia: University of Pennsylvania Press, 2011), 20–36.

33. As Nigel Eltringham notes, "the phrase 'Heart of Darkness' evokes opaqueness, incomprehensibility, the inability to grasp meaning" (*Accounting for Horror,* 63).

34. An exception might be cited for the humanitarian response to famine crimes in Ethiopia in the mid-1980s, or to the plight of Hutu refugees in Zaire following the 1994 Rwandan genocide. In both cases, however, the context of violent conflict was submerged to the point of invisibility by the wider discursive framing.

35. For an excellent example of the new comparativist perspective on the Holocaust, see Donald Bloxham, *The Final Solution: A Genocide* (Oxford: Oxford University Press, 2009).

36. "The Ottoman Destruction of Christian Minorities" is the title I chose when revising and reframing the chapter on "The Armenian Genocide" for the second edition of my *Genocide: A Comprehensive Introduction* (London: Routledge, 2010), chap. 4. It may be worth noting that for the third edition, I plan a similar treatment for the Rwandan genocide, making it a central component of a reframed chapter titled "Genocide in the Great Lakes Region of Africa since 1959."

37. One senses, as well, that the gradual canonization of the Guatemalan genocide of the 1970s and 1980s was critical to expanding the understanding of indigenous peoples' genocides around the western hemisphere, even though indigenous activists had deployed the genocide framework much earlier. The clear element of Western (especially U.S.) complicity in the Guatemalan genocide may also have prompted or facilitated attention to more sensitive and inconvenient cases of genocide against native populations in the United States and other Western-colonized territories.

38. Eltringham, *Accounting for Horror,* 178.

39. Edward S. Herman and David Peterson, *The Politics of Genocide* (New York: Monthly Review Press, 2010).

40. Adam Jones, "Denying Rwanda: A Response to Herman and Peterson," 16 November 2010, http://jonestream.blogspot.com/2010/11/denying-rwanda-response-to-herman.html.

8

Genocide and the Politics of Memory in Cambodia

ALEXANDER LABAN HINTON

When Cambodians talk about Democratic Kampuchea (DK), the genocidal period of Khmer Rouge rule in Cambodia when up to two million of Cambodia's eight million inhabitants perished from April 1975 to January 1979, they recall many paths of ruin, the memories breaking light into this time of shadows, when memory itself became a crime.

Chlat, a low-ranking provincial government official who was a student prior to DK, recalled one such path: the death of his brother Sruon. Sharp and pensive, Chlat was one of those people who might have gone far if the trajectory of his life had not been broken by the Khmer Rouge revolution. His smile echoed his life, struggling to blossom and always taut, as if about to recoil. We spoke many times about his life, including the period when memory itself became a crime.

For, in their radical experiment in social engineering, the Khmer Rouge launched an assault on the past, seeking to obliterate everything that smacked of capitalism, "privatism," and class oppression.[1] This attack ranged far and wide. Broadly, the Khmer Rouge targeted Buddhism, the family, village structure, economic activity, and public education—key sociocultural institutions through which memory was ritually, formally, and informally transmitted. More specifically, they assaulted social memory by burning books and destroying libraries; banning popular music, movies, media, and styles; destroying temples; truncating communication; terminating traditional holidays and ritual events; separating family members; homogenizing clothing; and eliminating private property, including photos, memorabilia, and other mementos.

This onslaught on the past was dramatically signified by the first significant act the Khmer Rouge took upon attaining power: rusticating the entire urban population. Ordered to evacuate their homes with little notice, hundreds of thousands of people clogged the arteries leading out of Phnom Penh and the other provincial capitals. As they shuffled toward an unknown beginning, past the pagodas, schools, cinemas, restaurants, parks, streets, and homes that landscaped their past, the urbanites discarded a trail of memories: wads of now-worthless bank notes blowing in the wind, luxury sedans that had run out of fuel, food that had rotted in the blazing heat, books too heavy to carry, and, most tragically, the bodies of the old and the infirm unable to survive the journey. And still they would bear the stain of their past.

In the new revolutionary society, each person had to be reworked, like hot iron, in the flames of the revolution. The Khmer Rouge called this "tempering" people (*luat dam*, literally "to harden by pounding"). One urban evacuee explained, "The dreaded phrase was *lut-dom. Lut* is the part of metal processing in which a rod of metal is placed in a fire until it is red-hot and pliable. *Dom* means the hammering—when the hot metal is put on the anvil and pounded into shape. *Lut-dom* described the way people were expected to be molded by Angka ("the Organization") into the pure Communists of the future."[2]

Memory was to be reshaped during this process until it aligned with the party line, which colored the past in revolutionary red. Borrowing a Maoist metaphor that resonated with Buddhist conceptions of the wheel of life and the two wheels of dhamma, the Khmer Rouge spoke of "the Wheel of History" (*kang brâ-vattesas*)[3] that, powered by natural laws that had been discerned by the "science" of Marxist-Leninism, had and continued to move Cambodia inexorably toward communism, crushing everything in its path.

This vision of the past was clearly laid out in a landmark speech given by Pol Pot on September 29, 1977, to celebrate the seventeenth anniversary of the founding of the Communist Party of Kampuchea (CPK). Not only did the speech announce publicly for the first time the very existence of the CPK and Pol Pot's leadership of it, but it also laid out the history of revolutionary struggle in Cambodia, which had faltered in "slave," "feudal," and "feudo-capitalist" stages because of the lack of a proper "political line."[4] This line only began to be ascertained, Pol Pot proclaimed, at the CPK's First Party Congress, held from September 28–30, 1960, by twenty-one revolutionaries who locked themselves into a secret room in the rail yard of Phnom Penh.

Having discerned through "scientific analysis" the key contradictions in Cambodian society (between "the Kampuchean nation and imperialism, especially U.S. imperialism" and between classes, especially "the capitalists and the landlords"[5]), the party was able to light the flames of revolution that, "like dry straw in the rice fields" during the hot season, "needs only a small spark to set it on fire."[6] From that point on, Pol Pot stated, the fire spread throughout the country, enabling the revolutionary movement to defeat not just the Khmer Republic but the United States as well. Just as the party line had enabled the

Khmer Rouge to win victory, so too would it lead Cambodia toward communist utopia faster than ever before.

Achieving this goal required the creation of a country filled with a new sort of revolutionary being who, after being "tempered" by hard peasant labor, criticism and self-criticism sessions, political meetings, and constant indoctrination, developed a progressive political consciousness that accorded with the party line and history. Those showing signs of being unable to rid themselves of vestiges of the "corrupt" past—for example, as evinced by dwelling too much on one's former life, complaining about the difficult conditions of life, failing to display appropriate enthusiasm for the revolution, making mistakes in one's duties, or missing work—were sometimes said to have "memory sickness" (*comngii satiaramma*).[7] If the sickness was chronic or did not heal rapidly, it was "cured" by execution. Indeed, execution served as the most direct and thorough means of obliterating counterrevolutionary memories of the past.

Chlat smoked as he told me these stories of how his family trekked out of Phnom Penh in the blazing sun, at times moving only a meter in two hours; how the Khmer Rouge requisitioned his watch, diploma, and clothes; how his brother-in-law, a former military officer, was identified and led away, never to return; and how his grandfather died and was buried on the side of the road in a grave marked only by incense. The first time Chlat offered me a cigarette, which I declined, he smiled tightly and told me how he had begun smoking during DK when he was assigned to transport human excrement from the latrines so that it could be used for fertilizer. He explained, "The smell was overwhelming and the cigarettes cut the stench. After I stopped working there, I continued to smoke because of hunger. I was never full but when I smoked my hunger would diminish." Another time he told me that he smoked because his head was so busy. If he ruminated on some difficult matter like DK, smoking would ease his heart. As Chlat recalled these events, he'd take a drag of his cigarette, embers briefly aglow like his memories, then ash.

We usually met in the evening at the home of a mutual friend, after Chlat had finished work at the provincial government office. The electricity would often fail and we would sit around a table dimly illuminated by a single candle and the lit end of his cigarette, which traced his profile and cast shadows against the walls. It was on one of these nights that he first told me of how his brother's path turned toward the Pagoda at the Hill of Men in 1977, in the midst of a major purge. Chlat's family had returned to his parents' birth village, where people knew the family's suspect urban background and that his older brother Sruon had worked in the import-export business there. Speaking in a low monotone, punctuated by long pauses and sudden thumps of his cigarette against the ashtray, Chlat recalled how Sruon was taken to the pagoda, which had been transformed into an extermination center:

> First we heard that trucks had been coming to take people from neighboring cooperatives to a "new village." Rumors spread that the people were taken to be killed. The trucks arrived at my village without warning. No one had been informed. People began to be taken away at noon. You could see that it was primarily 1975 people, particularly those who were lazy or unable to work hard, who were ordered to go to the "new village." . . . When [my elder brother] Sruon's name wasn't called out—he had been sick and unable to work much lately, so we were worried—he couldn't believe his good fortune. He kept telling me and my father, "I'm really lucky. I must have done good deeds in the past to escape death, because those people are not going to a 'new place,' they're going to be killed and discarded."
>
> Sruon's name still hadn't been called by 8:00 that evening. He had just finished saying "I'm out of danger. I'm not going to die," when Sieng, the village head, tapped on our door and told Sruon, "Gather your things. The trucks are going to take you to a new village." Sruon stopped speaking and slowly sat down on the bed, terrified, thinking about what he suspected was going to happen to his family. Finally, he said, "So, my name is on the list, too." Someone, I suspect it might have been a distant relative of mine who spied for the Khmer Rouge, must have gotten them to replace his name with that of my brother at the last moment. Sruon instructed his wife and children to get ready to go. He told me, "Take care of father and our siblings. As for me, don't believe that they are taking me to a new place. There isn't one. They are taking us to be killed." Everything was still; no one spoke. All you could hear was the patter of the rain.
>
> The people whose names were called were ordered to gather at a nearby pagoda. Sruon picked up his youngest child, protecting him from the rain and mud, and took his family there. It was getting late, so the Khmer Rouge ordered everyone to sleep in the pagoda that night. Guards prevented the people from leaving the premises. Children were crying from hunger because they weren't given food. The next day, at first light, the Khmer Rouge loaded everyone on the trucks and drove off. My brother and his entire family were executed at the Pagoda at the Hill of Men. . . . A few days later, clothes were distributed to people in our village. They were the garments of the people who had been loaded into the trucks. I saw them give out my brother's clothes.

Chlat's memory of his brother's death is chilling, more so when one considers that, throughout Cambodia, millions of people endured similar moments of death, suffering, and terror during DK. Such memories, and the powerful emotions they evoke, have proven to be a powerful dynamic in Cambodia, as different groups have rewritten the horizon of the DK past to meet the needs of the present, asserting their legitimacy and moral authority in the process even as they depict—or even obfuscate—the genocidal past.

This essay explores several dimensions of this politics of memory, particularly that of the People's Republic of Kampuchea (PRK), the Vietnamese-backed successor of DK, which tied its legitimacy closely to a set of discursive narratives about the genocidal past. In addition, we can discern another broad shift in the politics of memory in Cambodia around the time of the 1993 U.N.-backed elections in Cambodia. At this time, nongovernmental organizations proliferated in Cambodia, and discourses of reconciliation, human rights, and justice were localized, often in Buddhist terms, in another reworking of the memory of the genocidal past. Yet another shift in the politics of memory, in which the Khmer Rouge atrocities came to be viewed through the lens of human rights and justice, can be discerned in the negotiations for and ultimate launch of a U.N.-backed trial of former Khmer Rouge leaders.

After discussing the PRK's apparatus of truth, knowledge, power, and memory, I turn to a consideration of Buddhism, which has operated in both conjunction and disjunction with the state-level narratives, as have other local-level and international discourses. More broadly, this essay grapples with the theme of hidden genocide in several ways. On the one hand, it explores how truth claims about genocide are linked to the intersection of power and knowledge. On the other, the essay illustrates how complicated histories are contested and depicted in reductive ways, including ones that obfuscate or even deny mass murder.

Legitimacy and Liberation

In January 1979, when a Vietnamese-backed army invaded Cambodia, routing the Khmer Rouge, the sands of memory shifted once again. Cambodia's roads began to swell with people, some returning to lost lives and homes, others seeking new ones, still others heading toward the border and unknown places. It was a time of remembrance, as friends and family long separated came together and shared their stories of where they had been, what they had endured, and who had been lost. Then they began to rebuild their lives.

Many, like Chlat, had nothing and had to confront the immediate problem of how to survive and make a living. Eventually Chlat found a job as a teacher. At Banyan, the village located near the Pagoda at the Hill of Men in Kompong Cham that had remained empty during DK, former residents trickled back home. Amidst their greetings, they found horrific reminders of the recent past: dozens of mass graves, village wells filled with corpses, and the reek of death when the winds blew from the direction of the pagoda. They returned to what they knew best, farming the land, though now their rice fields adjoined killing fields and their plows sometimes churned up the bones and clothes of the dead.

In Phnom Penh, two Vietnamese photographers who had accompanied the invading army were drawn by a stench to the grounds of a former high school.[8] What they found inside echoed the gruesome scenes Banyan villagers had discovered: recently executed men whose throats had been cut, some still chained to iron beds and lying in pools of blood; shackles, whips, and other instruments of torture; and the prison cells of the condemned. Within days, search crews discovered an enormous cache of documentation, ranging from photographs to confessions.

In the midst of this upheaval, the newly established People's Republic of Kampuchea faced numerous problems, ranging from an economy and infrastructure in shambles to potential famine.[9] Almost immediately, however, the new regime was beset by problems of legitimacy. On the one hand, the PRK government, headed by Heng Samrin, was closely linked to Vietnam, which had supplied roughly 150,000 troops for the invasion and wielded obvious influence over the government.

While initially welcoming Vietnam's help in overthrowing the Khmer Rouge, many Cambodians remained deeply suspicious of a country frequently viewed as a historical enemy that they believed had long secretly desired to "swallow" Cambodian land. Many also viewed the new regime with suspicion both because, like DK, it was socialist and because a number of PRK officials—including Heng Samrin and his foreign minister, Hun Sen, who would be prime minister by 1985—were themselves former Khmer Rouge who had fled DK during purges of their factions. These suspicions were heightened by PRK propaganda, which at times eerily echoed that of the regime's socialist predecessor.[10] Finally, the PRK government was to be increasingly threatened by new resistance groups and a resurgent Khmer Rouge army, which after arriving in tatters on the Thai border, was propped back up by foreign powers concerned more with cold war politics than with genocidal criminality.

Memory mixed with politics as the PRK regime set out to establish a narrative of the recent past that would buttress their legitimacy both domestically and abroad.[11] Genocide stood at the center of this story. The new political narrative centered on the theme of a magnificent revolution subverted by a small group of evildoers, led by the Pol Pot, Pol Pot–Ieng Sary, or Pol Pot–Ieng Sary–Khieu Samphan "clique."[12] Inspired by a deviant Maoist strain of socialism, the narrative went, this clique had misled or coerced lower-ranking cadres (including, by implication, PRK leaders who were former Khmer Rouge) into unwittingly participating in a misdirected campaign of genocide. As a result, most former Khmer Rouge cadres, including, by implication, PRK officials, were not ultimately responsible for the events that had transpired during DK. Indeed, they and their Vietnamese allies had "liberated" Cambodia from the scourge of the Pol Pot clique.

Socialist discourses remained central to this narrative, as the PRK regime could still speak of how the revolutionary movement had "won the glorious victory of April 17, 1975, totally liberating our country" from "the yoke of colonialism, imperialism, and feudalism."[13] A December 3 declaration establishing the precursor of the PRK, the Kampuchea United Front for National Salvation (KUFNS), made just prior to the invasion, described how "the reactionary Pol Pot–Ieng Sary gang" had "usurped power" and taken Cambodia down the wrong direction soon after liberation through policies such as the rustication of the urban centers, forced collectivization, the "abolition of money and markets" and religion, forced marriage, social reclassification, the undermining of family and village life, and the creation of conditions that led people to live "in misery as slaves." These acts foreshadowed "massacres, more atrocious, more barbarous, than those committed in the Middle Ages or perpetrated by the Hitlerite fascists."

The PRK regime, in turn, staked its claim to legitimacy as the true bearers of the revolutionary mantle and, crucially, as the ones who, with the help of their Vietnamese "brothers," had liberated the people from this hell on earth that had "nothing to do with socialism!" In the PRK narrative, the regime remained the people's protector, a "back" (*khnang*) upon which they could rely to ensure that the horrors of the DK past were not repeated. With a growing Khmer Rouge insurgency on the border, this role was of enormous importance to the populace.

While every government defines itself in terms of an imagined past and future, new regimes, particularly ones like the PRK that ascend to power with questionable legitimacy, devote enormous effort in asserting such visions. Their mechanisms for the production of truth are varied, ranging from the codification of law to educational instruction to the creation of memorials. By bringing a number of seemingly heterogeneous institutions together, a government is able to create a functionally overdetermined "apparatus" to further its strategic goals, such as the popular interpellation of discursive narratives that enhance the regime's legitimacy and control.[14]

We can see just such a process at work during the PRK, as the government used multiple institutions, discursive structures, and symbols to assert its legitimacy. One key nexus was education. On the one hand, education served as a reminder of the brutality of the DK regime, since they had largely abandoned formal instruction and turned many schools into prisons or storage areas.[15] While there was some primary education during DK,[16] the Khmer Rouge believed that the former education system corrupted the minds of the young and that the best education was political indoctrination and learning through "struggle" on the economic "front lines." Thus, drawing on Maoist discourses, the Khmer Rouge proclaimed: "The spade is your pen, the rice field your paper" and "If you want to pass your Baccaulareate exams, you must build dams and canals."[17]

Teaching about the Genocidal Past

The devastation of the past was also marked physically, both in the deteriorated condition of the schools and teaching materials (symbolically marking the deterioration of Cambodia under the Khmer Rouge) and, in many cases, walls marred by bullet holes (symbolically marking the violence of the past and danger of the present). On the other hand, education represented one of the great achievements of the PRK regime, which rapidly rebuilt the school system. In a September 24, 1979, speech commemorating the reopening of schools for the 1979–1980 year, Heng Samrin invoked these themes, stressing how under the "barbaric genocidal regime of the Pol Pot–Ieng Sary clique" the country's "infrastructure in the domain of education and of teaching [has been] completely shattered," with the educated, including students and teachers, singled out for slaughter.[18]

These sorts of discourses were explicitly incorporated into teaching materials. Thus, by 1983, a first-grade writing book included a poem titled "The Suffering of the Kampuchean People in the Pol Pot–Ieng Sary Period," which was adorned with a graphic showing a couple being executed while a child watched in horror and a man was being hanged in the background.[19] Likewise, a first-grade moral education (*selathoa*) book included lessons named "The [New] Revolution Has Given Happiness to the People" (with a graphic showing happy citizens cheering soldiers) and "The Pol Pot–Ieng Sary Clique's Criminal Plan to Destroy [Our] Race" (with a graphic that showed people being executed at a mass grave by cadres with studded clubs and bloody hoes).[20] Essays were followed by questions for class discussion, such as three that appeared in the tract "The Pol Pot–Ieng Sary Clique's Criminal Plan to Destroy [Our] Race":

1. What types of criminal acts did the Pol Pot–Ieng Sary clique inflict upon the Cambodian people who were ethnic Khmer like you?
2. These despicable ones killed Khmer in what sorts of ways?
3. What sort of intention did these despicable ones have that led them to kill your fellow members of the Khmer race?

The lesson book provided unsparing answers to the five- and six-year-olds, describing "the most savage acts of killing," such as when "these despicable ones" (*vea*) dug "enormous, deep ditches" into which they dumped their victims "dead or alive" after striking them with hoes, axes, and clubs. Women and children, the text notes, were not spared: "Their intention was to kill and destroy

Kampucheans so that they would be extinguished."[21] Such texts emphasize the difference of the Pol Pot–Ieng Sary clique, marking them as non-Khmer, a dangerous enemy plotting the annihilation of the Cambodian race, and, by implication, as a deviant communist sect.

Reading through such school texts, we find most of the discursive narratives—which were supplemented by related photos and posters—central to the PRK's regime of truth: repeated descriptions of the "savage" and "criminal acts" committed by the "Pol Pot–Ieng Sary clique" and of the enormous suffering of the people, assertions of the clique's lack of Khmerness and its deviant socialism, proclamations of the everlasting friendship between Kampuchea and Vietnam, glorification of the "great liberation" on January 7, 1979, panegyrics to the rapid progress the PRK was achieving, and tributes to the PRK army and militias that protected the people from a return of the DK past. One fourth-grade writing text I came across, published in 1988, focused on all of these themes and more (in fact, the majority of the articles touched upon these issues), including two consecutive articles on Tuol Sleng, one ("Torture at Tuol Sleng") with a graphic of a dead prisoner shackled to an iron above a pool of blood and instruments of torture.[22]

Memorializing the Genocidal Past

Here we find one of a number of cross-linkages to other parts of the PRK apparatus of truth and memory. In contrast to the verbal focus (albeit with powerful graphics) of the school texts, PRK memorials like Tuol Sleng and Choeung Ek place emphasis on nonverbal symbolism.[23]

Opened on July 13, 1980, the Tuol Sleng Museum of Genocidal Crimes is constructed to create a sense of authenticity, as if providing a glimpse of the prison just moments after it had ceased operation.[24] This sense is most immediately and forcefully connoted by the first of four buildings a visitor encounters, where one enters the seemingly intact interrogation rooms where the last prisoners were hastily killed, bloodstains faintly visible on some floors. Not leaving anything to the imagination, each room includes an enlarged photograph of an executed prisoner taken just after the Khmer Rouge had abandoned the prison. The second building contains wall after wall of mug shots that were taken when prisoners arrived at the security center. The faces in the pictures show all sorts of expressions, but all are haunting, as the visitor, who has already seen Building One, knows in graphic detail what their fate was.

In the third building, the visitor finds classrooms divided into small brick cells in which the prisoners were shackled next to a small ammunition canister into which they relieved themselves. A list of Khmer Rouge prison rules—the only written text of note in the building—states that a prisoner had to ask

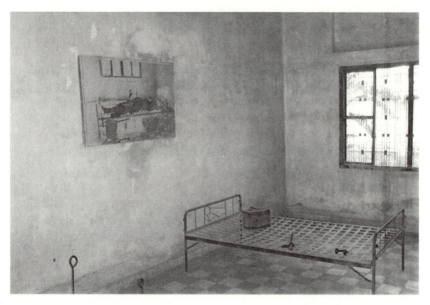

FIGURE 8.1. Photograph of Executed Prisoner and Cell, Tuol Sleng Genocide Museum
Photo by Alexander Laban Hinton

FIGURE 8.2. Barbed-Wire Exterior of Building C, Tuol Sleng Genocide Museum
Photo by Alexander Laban Hinton

permission before doing so. The last building is somewhat more reminiscent of a traditional museum, featuring glass cases with Khmer Rouge artifacts ranging from devices of torture to busts of Pol Pot that were being built on the premises. This building contains more written text than the other buildings but is still visually dominated by the artifacts and pictures of Khmer Rouge atrocities painted by Vann Nath, a former prisoner. Until recently, though, perhaps the most impressive exhibit sat in the last room, a twelve-square-meter map of Cambodia made out of 300 skulls, taken from provinces throughout Cambodia,[25] with waterways painted blood-red.

Such skulls have become iconic of DK, serving as the focus of memorials at the "Genocidal Center at Choeung Ek," which opened in 1980, and local memorials throughout Cambodia—including one at the site of the killing field of the Pagoda at the Hill of Men—that were constructed following a 1983 PRK directive.[26] The skulls condense an array of referents linked to the PRK discourses of legitimacy, ranging from the death, destruction, and brutality of DK to the danger of a return of the "Pol Pot–Ieng Sary clique." The photos at Tuol Sleng serve a similar purpose, as Cambodians know the fate of the people portrayed and can project themselves back into the DK past when they, too, suffered greatly and faced death on a daily basis. Tuol Sleng and the memorials are also evidence, proof of the "criminal acts" that Pol Pot's group committed.

Along these lines, (lack of) vision is a prominent metaphor in these memorials, particularly the blindfolded skull, with all of its powerful significations.[27] Most immediately, it associates DK with a loss of memory and sensory perception. Many survivors recall DK as a time when people retreated into themselves, speaking when necessary but living in silence much of the time. Many people whispered to each other, "Plant a kapok tree" (dam daem kor) a phrase that had a secondary connotation of muteness and thus also meant "Remain mute." Along these lines, the lack of sight is also linked to incapacitation, as people lost their freedom and agency on a daily basis. More ominously, DK was linked to incapacitation through death, both literally—the blindfolded skulls say it all in one sense—and more figuratively through narratives of the disappeared and how the Khmer Rouge sometimes consumed their victim's livers, a potent act in a society where liver is linked to vitality. And then, of course, the DK regime is linked to social death and the erasure of memory.

While the victims lost their sight, the Khmer Rouge claimed to be "all-seeing." The DK regime was in many ways panoptic, as a network of spies kept track of what people said and did. In political tracts, the regime was described as "all-seeing" and "clairvoyant." On the local level, people whispered, "Angkar has the eyes of a pineapple." In such ways, the theme of vision cut across PRK propaganda, suggesting the terror, incapacitation, and ignorance associated with DK.

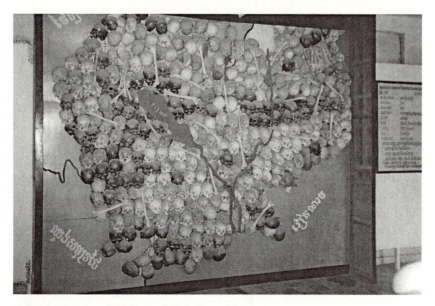

FIGURE 8.3. Map of Skulls, Tuol Sleng Genocide Museum

Photo by Alexander Laban Hinton

Such sites and images interface with other dimensions of the PRK apparatus of truth and memory: holidays such as the January 7 commemoration of
the "liberation," the May 20 "Day to Remain Tied in Hatred," the PRK subsidy of
publications and films about DK, the 1979 trial of Pol Pot and Ieng Sary in absen-
tia, PRK laws on the Khmer Rouge, and so forth.

Despite the power of these redundant PRK narratives and institutions,
such apparatuses are never monolithic. Instead, they are always challenged
from outside and within because of the mismatch between the regime's more
homogeneous discourse of truth and the more heterogeneous beliefs and
understandings of the populace. All the propaganda in the world about the
"Friendship of Kampuchea and Vietnam," for example, could never assuage
Chlat's animosity toward the Vietnamese, a sentiment shared by some Cambodians who feel that the Vietnamese look down upon Cambodians and
have sought, both in the past and the present, to seize Cambodian territory.
"I hate them," he would tell me again and again, "I don't have words to tell
you how much I hate them." And then he would launch into a diatribe about
the malicious and scheming nature of the Vietnamese. Vietnam also figured
prominently for many Cambodians living abroad, who, while sharing the PRK's
horror of DK, viewed the PRK as a front for Vietnamese control and believed
Cambodia must be liberated from the PRK and the Vietnamese archenemy
with which it was allied.

Hiding Genocide

Geopolitics and political expediency also provided an opportunity for the obfuscation, minimization, or even denial that mass atrocities had taken place in Cambodia during DK. On an international level, the United States and its cold war allies viewed Vietnam's invasion of Cambodia as a further Soviet bloc expansion into Southeast Asia, one that also violated the principle of state sovereignty. This alarmed ASEAN countries as well, particularly Thailand, which confronted a massive influx of Cambodian refugees and Vietnamese troops on its border. China, the longtime supporter of the Khmer Rouge, also viewed Vietnam's invasion as a threat, particularly given China's historical tensions with Vietnam and frosty relationship with the Soviet Union. In February 1979, China even invaded Vietnam in retaliation for its occupation of Cambodia and role in deposing the Khmer Rouge.

Cambodia became a key proxy site in which all of these tensions would play out. The United States, China, Thailand, and a number of Western powers joined together not just to rearm and revitalize the Khmer Rouge, who had been soundly defeated by the Vietnamese troops, but to provide them with international legitimacy. This new policy of supporting the Khmer Rouge culminated in the September 21, 1979, vote to allow Democratic Kampuchea to retain Cambodia's seat at the United Nations.[28]

Two months later, the U.N. General Assembly passed a resolution calling for states not to intervene in Cambodian affairs and for all "foreign forces" to withdraw from Cambodia. These countries faced a quandary, as they effectively were granting international legitimacy to a genocidal regime, whose mass human rights violations were often hidden by euphemisms, a practice that continued all the way up until the 1991 Paris Peace Accords, which referred vaguely to preventing a recurrence of the "politics and practices of the past."[29]

The Khmer Rouge used this newfound legitimacy and the geopolitical situation to make claims of its own about the past. These claims echoed those of the PRK regime in odd ways. If the PRK regime condemned the genocidal actions of the "Pol Pot–Ieng Sary clique," the Khmer Rouge claimed that it was the "Vietnamese Le Duan clique" that was engaging in a "war of genocide" against Cambodians. Echoing DK rhetoric that Vietnam had always "had the ambition to annex and swallow Kampuchea,"[30] the Khmer Rouge claimed that the Le Duan clique was engaging in mass slaughter, toxic warfare, looting, destruction, and starvation in "a war more ferocious and savage than Hitler's war of genocide."[31] As a result of its "criminal policy of genocide," the Vietnamese had already "killed over 2 million Kampucheans" even as "the entire Kampuchean race [was] on the verge of extinction." Playing on geopolitical fears, the Khmer Rouge warned that this campaign was but one step in a war that threatened to spread "to Southeast Asia, Asia, and the Pacific region," originating from "the global strategy of Soviet international expansionism."

Like much of the international community, the Khmer Rouge avoided mention of the genocide, an elision all the more glaring given that they now accused the Vietnamese of genocide. When questioned by the media about the increasing number of reports of mass human rights violations during DK, the Khmer Rouge took things one step further, denying what had taken place. While admitting that local authorizes had committed some excesses, they claimed that "not many" had been killed, "in all of Cambodia perhaps some thousands."[32]

As for the PRK evidence, including the exhibitions at Tuol Sleng, the Khmer Rouge dismissed it as a fabrication. A December 16, 1994, radio broadcast stated:

> Concerning those skeletons at Tuol Sleng, they are purely and simply part of the psychological war waged by Vietnam in its aggression against Cambodia. The communist Vietnamese collected skulls and bones from graveyards all over north and south Vietnam, brought them by truck to Cambodia, and displayed them in an exhibition at Tuol Sleng as part of a psychological propaganda campaign to legalize their aggression against and occupation of Cambodia.

Some of the Khmer Rouge continued these denials to the very end. When asked in 1997, shortly before his death, about the mass deaths during DK, Pol Pot replied, "Look at me, am I a savage person? My conscience is clear."[33] He denied that he had ever heard about Tuol Sleng prior to 1979.

For a time in the mid-1990s, the political successor of the PRK regime, the Cambodian People's Party (CPP), also helped divert attention away from the Khmer Rouge genocide. With the signing of the 1991 Paris Peace Accords and subsequent U.N.-sponsored elections in 1993, the new Cambodian government, which would increasingly be dominated by the CPP, began to focus on reconciliation, in part because of a campaign to entice Khmer Rouge soldiers, who were still fighting a guerrilla war against the government, to defect. The school curriculum was completely revamped so that almost all mention of the atrocities committed by the Khmer Rouge was removed.

In the new post–cold war political situation, the Khmer Rouge lost most of the international support they had enjoyed during the 1980s. The Cambodian government's defection campaign enjoyed success, as large groups of Khmer Rouge soldiers began to defect in the mid-1990s. After he defected in 1996, Ieng Sary was allowed to travel freely and even reside at times in Phnom Penh.

When Khieu Samphan and Nuon Chea defected two years later, Prime Minister Hun Sen stated that they should be greeted "with bouquets of flowers, not with prisons and handcuffs." Moreover the country should "dig a hole and bury the past and look ahead to the 21st century with a clean slate."[34] For their part, the two Khmer Rouge leaders offered seemingly half-hearted apologies, with Khieu Samphan urging people to "let bygones be bygones . . . it is the only way to reach national reconciliation. It is the sine qua non condition for peace and stability in our country."[35] Nuon Chea, in turn, said, "Actually, we are very sorry not only for the lives of the people of Cambodia, but even for the lives of all animals that suffered because of the war."[36] While Hun Sen was heavily critiqued for his comments, this reconciliation phase of the political memory in Cambodia illustrates how, in the name of peace, attempts may be made to push genocidal acts of the past out of view.

If the CPP's broad orientation to the Khmer Rouge at this time stands in stark contrast to the PRK period, it was by no means hegemonic. Hun Sen's statements about "burying the past" were critiqued by a variety of opposition parties and members of civil society, many of whom based their criticisms on conceptions of human rights and the rule of law that had been heavily promoted by the international community during and after the 1993 United Nations Transitional Authority in Cambodia (UNTAC) elections.

Meanwhile, with the shifting sands of time and politics, countries that had long downplayed the genocide during the PRK period, including the United States, now began to advocate for a tribunal. In 1994, for example, the U.S. government passed legislation leading to the creation of the Cambodian Genocide Program, whose objective was, in part, to gather documentation that could be used in a trial. And, even as Hun Sen ostensibly welcomed the former Khmer Rouge leaders, he was in the initial stages of negotiations that would lead to the establishment of the Extraordinary Chambers in the Courts of Cambodia, which began operation in 2006. The launch of the court was in part linked to a new juridical framing of politics and memory that would view the Khmer Rouge atrocities from the lens of human rights, criminal law, and justice.[37]

Buddhist Understandings

State-level narratives of the past, of course, are never hegemonic. Groups and individuals remember and cope with the past in a variety of ways that may contradict, diverge from, marginally intersect, or simply differ from state discourses. In Cambodia, Buddhism has played an interesting role in this regard.

When Buddhism was resurrected, with restrictions, by the PRK regime, Cambodians throughout the country began rebuilding temples and reconstituting their ritual life. The PRK government saw Buddhism as an institution through which party ideals could be disseminated, and its destruction under the Khmer Rouge served as another useful symbol of the abuses of DK. However, Buddhism also provided a set of understandings about the events that had occurred through notions of karma, merit, and action. It also provided a way of coping with the past through meditation and concepts of forgiveness and letting go of anger.

Thus, when speaking of the villager who was responsible for sending Sruon to his death, Chlat drew upon state-level, Buddhist, and non-state-level discourses:

> I continue to think of revenge. But this thought of revenge, it doesn't know how to stop. And we should not have this thought or the matter will grow and keep going on and on for a long time. We should be a person who thinks and acts in accordance with dhamma. [A person who seeks revenge] only creates misery for our society. It is a germ in society. But I continue to think of revenge. . . . The people who killed my brother, who put down his name to get into the truck, are all alive, living in my village. To this day, I still really want revenge. I keep observing them. But, I don't know what to do. . . . The government forbids it.

To understand Chlat's remarks, and thus to begin to understand his response to the violence of the past, one must also unpack other local idioms that structured his response—in particular, the ontological resonances that give them power and force.[38]

Buddhist understandings are often central to such responses. Thus, Cambodians sometimes say that Khmer Rouge perpetrators will "suffer from their kamma." Many invoke a Buddhist saying: "Do good, receive good. Do bad, receive bad." Buddhist doctrine provides an explicit ontology that explains how violence originates in ignorance and desire. If the consequences of violence are manifest in overt signs, such actions also have long-term consequences. On the one hand, violence may lead others to seek vengeance against you. On the other hand, harming others is considered a Buddhist sin resulting in a loss of merit and, most likely, diminished status in the next life.

Moreover, becoming bound in such cycles of violence and anger upsets the equilibrium that is so crucial to well-being for Cambodians, in terms of both social relations and bodily health, the two being highly interrelated in Cambodian ethnopsychology. Emotions such as anger constitute a potential disruption of this balance, signaling a disturbance in the social fabric in which a person is embedded and producing "felt" somatic manifestations, such as pain (*chheu*), discomfort (*min sruol khluon*), dizziness (*vil*), or heat (*kdav*), symptoms of which Cambodians constantly scan.[39] The "choking heat" of anger, then, metaphorically references the felt "pressure" of an animating yet potentially disruptive psychosocial process that strongly "moves a person's heart" to act.[40] Chlat's invocation of heat and anger, then, indexes a culturally meaningful state of imbalance associated with the past, one that is not just an "inner disturbance" but is a signifier of social suffering with its political and moral implications.[41]

Besides providing an etiology of violence and its consequences, Buddhism offers a remedy for this toxic state of being—the middle path. On the local level, Cambodians are enjoined to follow five moral precepts (*seyl bram*), the first of which is the injunction not to kill. Monks preach that one must learn to control and extinguish one's anger, which arises from ignorance and desire and leads to violence and suffering. In Buddhism, the mindful way of dealing with anger is to recognize its source and to let it disappear, since anger, like everything else in the world, is impermanent. Those who continue to act in ignorance will suffer from the consequences of their actions, with their deeds following like a shadow, as one suffers through the countless cycles of birth and rebirth.

If Buddhism provides a sort of ontological justice for victims, it also suggests that their suffering is a cosmic consequence of their own (or the Cambodian collective's) bad actions in the past.[42] Some viewed what was going on as the fulfillment of Buddhist millenarian prophesies, such as the well-known Buddhist predictions (*put tumneay*). Many of these foretold a time when demons or members of the lowest rungs of Khmer society would take over and invert the social order, leading to an assault on Buddhism and widespread famine and death.[43] In fact, a popular DK metaphor for the need to remain silent, "plant a kapok tree," seems to have been taken from just such a prophesy, as Pin Yathay explains,

> Puth was a nineteenth-century sage who prophesied that the country would undergo a total reversal of traditional values, that the houses and the streets would be emptied, that the illiterate would condemn the educated, that infidels—*thmils*—would hold absolute power and persecute the priests. But people would be saved if they planted a kapok tree—*kor*, in Cambodian. Kor also means 'mute.' The usual interpretation of this enigmatic message was that only the deaf-mutes would be saved during this period of calamity. Remain deaf and mute. Therein, I now realized, lay the means of survival. Pretend to be deaf and dumb! Say nothing, hear nothing, understand nothing![44]

On a cosmological level, such prophesies played upon Khmer understandings of purity and contamination, which are in part structured in terms of the opposition between the Buddha and demons, dhamma and adhamma, order and disorder, coherence and fragmentation.[45]

To fully understand the politics of memory in Cambodia, then, we must look not just at the larger state-level discursive structures but at their points of articulation with and divergence from more local-level discourses and counter-discourses. In many instances, there is convergence. But, there are also important points of divergence, such as more local-level Buddhist discourses during the PRK.

This reemergence was signified dramatically by Maha Ghosananda's peace marches in the early 1990s, which symbolically asserted the revival of the sangha and dhamma (for example, by planting trees and through the composition of the march itself), the importance of cleansing Cambodia and oneself of anger (for example, by sprinkling holy water on the crowds), and the need to make peace (symbolized by the path of the march, which connected different parts of the country, including past and present war zones).[46]

More recently, these Buddhist discourses have come into tension with global human rights discourses often associated with another mode of remembering the past: holding a tribunal. While Buddhism promotes mindful understanding of the past, which is one Buddhist argument for holding the tribunal, it also asserts the importance of letting go of the past and freeing oneself of anger and attachment. Depending on how they are invoked, these notions may clash with assertions that the trial will enable Cambodians to attain "justice," to finally be able to "heal themselves," and to impose the "rule of law." Such discourses are linked to Western juridical models, Christian notions of forgiveness, and assumptions about the universality of psychodynamic process.

The Politics of Memory in the Present

This story is being written today as Cambodia continues to struggle with the complexities of the past as the trial of a handful of senior leaders of the Khmer Rouge is taking place. Is this the appropriate way, at this point in Cambodian history, to deal with the past? Should the tribunal be supplemented by modalities of justice and remembering, such as a truth commission or Buddhist rituals? Or should people just let go of their anger, forget about the past, and move on?

As I think about such questions, I wonder how people like Chlat might reply. I wish I could ask him. The last time I saw Chlat, in the summer of 2003, he was emaciated and had been sick for some time. He explained with a thin smile that he had a parasite that was resistant to medication, emphasizing the point by clenching an open hand to demonstrate how the parasite closed up whenever he took medicine. We talked for a while about his past before having dinner with a mutual friend and Chlat's son. Several months later, I received a message from that friend saying that Chlat was in the hospital on the brink of death. He had been diagnosed with AIDS—the disease that was perhaps the most devastating legacy of Cambodia's reengagement with the outside world after the Cold War. Chlat died a few days later.

I think that Chlat would have wanted a tribunal, though I have no doubt that he would have been critical of the corruption of the Cambodian judiciary, the hypocrisy of the international community, and the failure of the process to reach people like the cadre who sent his brother to his death at the Pagoda at the Hill of Men. I picture the answers he might have given in that darkness, with his face silhouetted by billows of smoke and the embers of his cigarette aglow like memory, then ash.

ACKNOWLEDGMENTS

This essay is a revision of a chapter was originally published in *People of Virtue: Reconfiguring Religion, Power, and Morality in Cambodia Today*, edited by Alexandra Kent and David Chandler (Copenhagen: NIAS Press, 2008), 62–81.

I would like to thank Alexandra Kent, Thomas LaPointe, Douglas Irvin-Erickson, and Nicole Cooley for their comments and suggestions. This essay is dedicated to Chlat.

NOTES

1. David Chandler, *Voices from S-21: Terror and History in Pol Pot's Secret Prison* (Berkeley: University of California Press, 1999); Alexander Laban Hinton, *Why Did They Kill? Cambodia in the Shadow of Genocide* (Berkeley: University of California Press, 2005); Ben Kiernan, *The Pol Pot Regime: Race, Power, and Genocide in Cambodia under the Khmer Rouge, 1975–79* (New Haven, CT: Yale University Press, 1996).

2. Joan D. Criddle and Teeda Butt Mam, *To Destroy You Is No Loss: The Odyssey of a Cambodian Family* (New York: Anchor, 1987). See also Henri Locard, *Pol Pot's Little Red Book: The Sayings of Angkar* (Chiang Mai, Thailand: Silkworm, 2004).

3. See Locard, *Pol Pot's Little Red Book*, 211.

4. Pol Pot, *Long Live the 17th Anniversary of the Communist Party of Kampuchea: Speech by Pol Pot, Secretary of the Central Committee of the Kampuchea Communist Party Delivered on September 29, 1977* (Phnom Penh: Ministry of Foreign Affairs, 1977).

5. Ibid., 25–26.

6. Ibid., 38.

7. Criddle and Mam, *To Destroy You*, 99.

8. Chandler, *Voices from S-21*, 1f.

9. Evan Gottesman, *Cambodia after the Khmer Rouge: Inside the Politics of Nation Building* (New Haven, CT: Yale University Press, 2003).

10. Ibid., 60.

11. Ibid.; Judy Ledgerwood, "The Cambodian Tuol Sleng Museum of Genocidal Crimes: National Narrative," *Museum Anthropology* 21, no. 1 (1997): 82–98.

12. Ledgerwood, "The Cambodian Tuol Sleng Museum."

13. The following quotations are from Gottesman, *Cambodia*, 7–8; and Sapordamean Kampuchea, "Organ of the Cambodian National United Front for National Salvation," Foreign Broadcast Information Services, Asia and Pacific, H3–H8, 4 December 1978.

14. Michel Foucault, *Discipline and Punish: The Birth of the Prison*, trans. Alan Sheridan (New York: Vintage, 1979); Edward W. Said, *Orientalism* (New York: Vintage, 1999).

15. David M. Ayres, *Anatomy of a Crisis: Education, Development, and the State in Cambodia, 1953–1998* (Honolulu: University of Hawaii Press, 2000).

16. Ibid.

17. Locard, *Pol Pot's Little Red Book*, 96–97.

18. Cited in Ayres, *Anatomy of a Crisis*, 126.

19. People's Republic of Kampuchea, *Reading and Writing, First Grade* (Phnom Penh: Ministry of Education, 1983).

20. People's Republic of Kampuchea, *Morality, First Grade* (Phnom Penh: Ministry of Education, 1984).

21. Ibid., 29.

22. People's Republic of Kampuchea, *Reading and Writing, Fourth Grade* (Phnom Penh: Ministry of Education, 1988), 21.

23. Ledgerwood, "The Cambodian Tuol Sleng Museum"; Boreth Ly, "Devastated Vision(s): The Khmer Rouge Regime in Cambodia," *Art Journal* (Spring 2003): 66–81.

24. Ledgerwood, "The Cambodian Tuol Sleng Museum"; Paul Williams, "Witnessing Genocide: Vigilance and Remembrance at Tuol Sleng and Choeung Ek," *Holocaust and Genocide Studies* 18, no. 2 (2004): 234–254.

25. Ledgerwood, "The Cambodian Tuol Sleng Museum."

26. Rachel Hughes, "The Abject Artefacts of Memory: Photographs from Cambodia's Genocide," *Media, Culture & Society* 25 (2003): 23–44.

27. See Ly, "Devastated Vision(s)."

28. Ramses Amer, "The United Nations and Kampuchea: The Issue of Representation and Its Implications," *Bulletin of Concerned Asian Scholars* 22, no. 3 (1990); see also Tom Fawthrop and Helen Jarvis, *Getting Away with Genocide: Cambodia's Long Struggle against the Khmer Rouge* (London: Pluto, 2004).

29. Paris Peace Accords, Article 3, 15; Fawthrop and Jarvis, *Getting Away with Genocide.*

30. Democratic Kampuchea, *Black Paper: Facts and Evidences of the Acts of Aggression and Annexation of Vietnam against Kampuchea* (Phnom Penh: Department of Press and Information of the Ministry of Foreign Affairs, 1978), 1–2.

31. The remaining quotations in this paragraph are from Voice of Democratic Kampuchea, "[December 18] Statement of the Joint Congress [*maha sanibat ruom*] of the Standing Committee of the Kampuchean People's Representative Assembly, the Government of Democratic Kampuchea, Representatives of the National Army of Democratic Kampuchea and Representatives of Various Government Ministries," Foreign Broadcast and Information Services, Asia and Pacific, 26 December 1979.

32. Henry Kamm, "Aide Says Pol Pot Regime Is Ready to Join Old Foes against Vietnam," *New York Times,* 1 June 1979, A6.

33. Nate Thayer, "On the Stand," *Far Eastern Economic Review*, 30 October 1997, 17.

34. Seth Mydans, "Cambodian Leader Resists Punishing Top Khmer Rouge," *New York Times*, 29 December 1998, A1.

35. Seth Mydans, "Under Prodding, 2 Apologize for Cambodian Anguish," *New York Times*, 30 December 1998, A3.

36. Ibid.

37. For a discussion of one of the ways in which the current moment is framed in this manner—as part of a "transitional justice imaginary"—see Alexander Laban Hinton, "Transitional Justice Time: Uncle San, Aunty Yan, and Outreach at the Khmer Rouge Tribunal," in *Genocide and Mass Atrocities in Asia: Legacies and Prevention*, ed. Deborah Mayerson and Annie Pohlman (New York: Routledge, 2013), 82–94.

38. Hinton, *Why Did They Kill?*

39. Devon Hinton, Khin Um, and Phalnarith Ba, "*Kyol Goeu* ('Wind Overload') Part I: A Cultural Syndrome of Orthostatic Panic among Khmer Refugees," *Transcultural Psychiatry* 38, no. 4 (2001): 403–432; Devon Hinton, Khin Mum, and Phalnarith Ba, "*Kyol Goeu* ('Wind Overload') Part II: Prevalence, Characteristics, and Mechanisms of *Kyol*

Goeu and Near-*Kyol Goeu* Episodes in Khmer Patients Attending a Psychiatric Clinic," *Transcultural Psychiatry* 38, no. 4 (2001): 433–460.

40. *Vochânanukrâm Khmaer* [Khmer dictionary] (Phnom Penh: Buddhist Institute, 1967).

41. Arthur Kleinman, Veena Das, and Margaret Lock, eds., *Social Suffering* (Berkeley: University of California Press, 1997).

42. See, for example, Haing Ngor, *A Cambodian Odyssey* (New York: Warner Books, 1987), 157, 312.

43. See Ledgerwood, "The Cambodian Tuol Sleng Museum"; Frank Smith, "Interpretive Accounts of the Khmer Rouge Years: Personal Experience in Cambodian Peasant World View," Wisconsin Papers on Southeast Asia, Occasional Paper No. 18 (Center for Southeast Asian Studies, University of Wisconsin-Madison, 1989).

44. Pin Yathay, *Stay Alive, My Son* (New York: Touchstone, 1987), 63.

45. Alexander Laban Hinton, "Purity and Contamination in the Cambodian Genocide," in *Cambodia Emerges from the Past: Eight Essays*, ed. Judy Ledgerwood (DeKalb, IL: Center for Southeast Asian Studies, Northern Illinois University, 2002), 60–90; see also Bruce Kapferer, *Legends of People, Myths of State: Violence, Intolerance, and Political Culture in Sri Lanka and Australia* (Washington, DC: Smithsonian Institution Press, 1988).

46. Monique Skidmore, "In the Shadow of the Bodhi Tree: Dhammayietra and the Reawakening of Community in Cambodia," *Crossroads* 10, no. 1 (1997): 1–32.

9

Constructing the "Armenian Genocide"

How Scholars Unremembered the Assyrian and Greek Genocides in the Ottoman Empire

HANNIBAL TRAVIS

This chapter critically examines the scholarly and political discourse since the 1960s on the Armenian genocide. This discourse represents not simply a forgetting or continued unawareness that there were Assyrian and Greek victims of the anti-Christian massacres of the late Ottoman Empire and early Turkish republic, but sometimes an active suppression of existing historical knowledge about Assyrian and Greek experiences. From the standpoint of critical genocide studies, the "Armenian genocide," like the "Holocaust," is the culmination of a long-term campaign to establish a binary racial conflict and the exclusivity of one group's fate, a gross simplification of the broader understanding of the crime of genocide as mass murder that prevailed in the 1940s.[1]

As emphasized by the other contributions to this volume, genocides may become "hidden" as a result of national security dogmas, historical amnesia, politicized interpretations of the concept of genocide, and global power politics. A. Dirk Moses has pointed to a combination of these factors in analyzing efforts to conceal the existence of genocides other than the Jewish Holocaust in the exhibits of the Canadian Museum for Human Rights. Moses observes that a certain conception of genocide as a discontinuous event within Western history, confined to a radical regime opposed by most of the West in a far-off time, suppresses the larger pattern of crimes by Western empires and their allied states against indigenous Africans, Americans, and Asians.[2] For this reason, historical amnesia and restrictive interpretations of the crime of genocide, such as those of Stephen Katz or William Schabas, vindicate Western civilization against more fundamental charges that its politicians were complicit in centuries of imperial and ultranationalist genocides including in the Republic of Turkey.[3]

Selective legal history and the relegation of some genocides to the memory hole serves important structural imperatives of realpolitik. The countries making up the North Atlantic Treaty Organization (NATO), claiming a unique moral leadership in conflicts such as those occurring in the Balkans and the Persian Gulf in the 1990s and those occurring in Iraq, Libya, and Syria in the 2000s, utilize their ideological state apparatuses to impose a vision of genocide as a discontinuous phenomenon unconnected with imperialism and consistently opposed by the Western alliance, primarily affecting the Jews, Bosnians, and Tutsis. To view genocide, as did Raphael Lemkin, as a potentially long-term replacement of a "national pattern" by an aggressive *ethnos* or nation is to invite comparisons to such important Western projects as settler colonialism or the Vietnam or Iraq wars. In the case of Turkey, the thesis that not only the Armenians but also the Assyrians and the Greeks were victims of a long-term process of colonization, Turkification, and Kurdification—across a variety of regimes—threatens the myth of Turkey as a moderate and secular state deputized by NATO to resolve ethnic conflicts in the former Ottoman Empire, as we witness today in Syria and saw previously in the former Yugoslavia and Iraq.[4]

The ideological state apparatuses of Turkey, the United States, the United Kingdom, and France propound a view of the Armenian genocide as a discontinuous episode in an otherwise tolerant and progressive society. In Turkey, a leading role has been taken by the Institute for Turkish Studies, which contributed to the release of a number of works denying that any Armenian or Ottoman Christian genocide occurred at all. Instead, these works occasionally concede that discontinuous massacres took place in an otherwise tolerant society disrupted by British or Russian imperialism, and their authors blame the deaths on rebellious Christian populations for having sympathies with the Christian powers of Europe.

In Britain, Oxford's Professor of Contemporary Islamic Studies, Tariq Ramadan, teaches that the essence of Islamic societies is peace and diversity, as exemplified by the tolerant Ottoman Empire, so that any remaining violence must be attributable to resistance to Western oppression or to human nature itself, rather than to patterns of ethnic or religious coercion or violence. In France, the prestigious state-supported university Sciences Po elevated Jacques Semelin to its most visible position relating to genocide research, from which perch he has published work in most of the languages of Western Europe arguing that there are three "core" genocides—those of the European Jews, the Bosnian Muslims, and the Rwandan Tutsis—with two other cases worth mentioning—the Armenians and Cambodians. The remaining cases are consigned to oblivion. In the United States, state-supported universities such as the University of California at Berkeley retain and promote faculty who articulate a theory of the Armenian genocide analogous to theories endorsed by the government of Turkey.[5]

Implications of the Armenian Genocide for Critical Genocide Studies

In many political pronouncements, and in some books by genocide and area studies scholars, the "Armenian genocide" is described as the only major mass murder taking place in the early twentieth century. For example, the United Nations Sub-commission on the Prevention of Discrimination and Protection of Minorities accepted a report in 1985 stating that the "massacre of the Armenians in 1915–1916" was an example of genocide. The European Parliament resolution of 1987 recognizing the Armenian genocide, reaffirmed in 2004, identified Armenians as the only victims of the genocidal "tragic events in 1915–1917" and did not mention Assyrians or Greeks, even though it urged recognition of the unrelated "Kurdish question." The Armenian genocide resolution that passed the Foreign Relations Committee of the U.S. House of Representatives in 2010 also singled out the elimination of the Armenian presence from Turkey.[6]

A study of the political resolutions reveals distortions of their purported source material. The first European Parliament resolution, for example, relied upon the Treaty of Lausanne from 1923, but that document did not distinguish between Armenians and other non-Muslim minorities like Assyrians and Greeks.[7] The U.S. resolution referred to evidence provided by U.S. Ambassador Henry Morgenthau and the organization Near East Relief, but these sources reveal that Assyrians and Greeks were in some ways more completely destroyed than the Armenians, and with arguably much less provocation than the Armenians.[8] For example, Near East Relief described the Assyrians as suffering the worst as a share of population and reported in 1920 that there were nearly 2.8 million Armenian survivors, but only 40,000 Assyrians—less than a quarter of the prewar Assyrian population. Ambassador Morgenthau wrote in 1917 or 1918 that 150,000 Armenians survived in Constantinople alone, nearly four times Near East Relief's estimate for all Assyrians by 1920, and more than twice Turkey's estimate of Greeks remaining by 1927.[9]

Scholars of the Armenian genocide are complicit in an ongoing concealment of the Assyrian and Greek genocides. Many of them argue that the Armenian population declined by more than one million from 1914 through 1919. They often neglect to note, however, that there were between one and two million Orthodox Greeks and approximately 500,000 Assyrians living in the Ottoman Empire in 1914 but only about 258,000 Christians of all kinds remaining in Turkey by 1927, even though Turkey once included substantial Assyrian and Greek regions.[10]

This chapter reviews categories of evidence of genocide that are regarded as relevant by Armenian and Armenian American scholars, and subjects the traditional narrative of the "Armenian genocide," drawn from thirty years of those scholars' works, to the test of that evidence. After a brief introduction to the ethnonational context of the Ottoman Christian genocide, the chapter assesses whether the Assyrian and Greek genocides have been passively forgotten or purposefully hidden, and explores some promising signs that politicians and scholars are returning to the original source material.

The Ethnonational Context

About two million Armenians lived in Ottoman Turkey, according to an informal census monitored by European representatives and carried out by the Armenian dioceses in 1913 and 1914, at least in those areas where it was not impeded by Kurdish intimidation. Although the Armenian population had declined steadily from a high of perhaps six million eleven centuries ago, it was sharply cut by massacres of 100,000 to 200,000 Armenians in 1890–1896.[11]

There were one to two million adherents to the Greek Orthodox faith living in the Ottoman Empire in 1890. The Greek homeland then included the coasts of the Aegean Sea, the Black Sea, the Sea of Marmara, and parts of inland Anatolia. Long after the Ottoman conquest of Athens, Constantinople, and the outlying Greek communities, the Greek War of Independence (1821–ca. 1833) claimed approximately 70,000 Greek lives, including tens of thousands of Greeks massacred in the city of Smyrna and the island of Chios (Scio), and approximately 50,000 slain in Morea.[12]

The Assyrians, too, fought to perpetuate their autonomy under the Ottomans. European experts estimated that there were nearly 200,000 independent

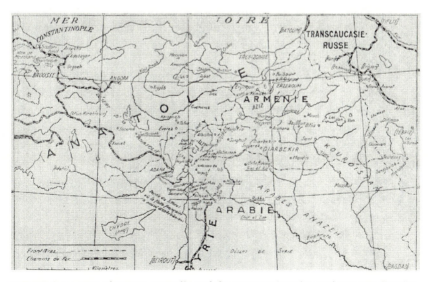

FIGURE 9.1.   Map of Eastern Anatolia and the Ottoman/Russian and Ottoman/Persian Frontiers, circa 1914.

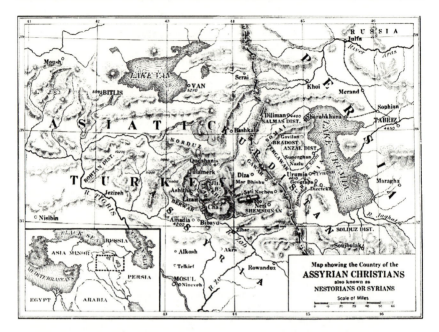

FIGURE 9.2. Map of the Hakkari Region and the Ottoman/Persian Border Area

Source: William Walter Rockwell, *The Pitiful Plight of the Assyrian Christians in Persia and Kurdistan* (New York: American Committee for Armenian and Syrian Relief, 1916).

Assyrians in upper Mesopotamia and southeastern Anatolia, and up to 500,000 Assyrians in the 1800s. There were traditionally three centers of Assyrian life: Urhay or Edessa/Urfa in the northwest, Urmia/Rezaieh in the northeast, and Nineveh/Mosul in the southwest.[13]

The Construction of the "Armenian Genocide"

One type of genocide denial is the innocent or unconscious disregard of the genocides of other groups. In 1985, a coalition of scholars published a judgment of a Permanent Peoples' Tribunal on the Armenian Genocide, concluding that there was a massacre of 1.2 million Armenians. Reading the judgment, one might well conclude that few or no Assyrians or Greeks had been killed. The scholars may have been unaware of non-Armenians' fate.[14]

In 1987, Marjorie Housepian Dobkin published a chapter on the Armenian genocide based on diplomatic traffic and newspaper reports. She supported an Armeno-centric approach by pointing to the front page of the *New York Times* on July 13, 1919, which proclaimed the death sentences of Turkey's ruling triumvirate for "crimes against Armenians" (her words). Actually, an article stated that the sentences were the culmination of "a long series of prosecutions undertaken by the officials of the new regime to clear . . . the Turkish people from blame for the Armenian, Syrian, and Greek massacres and deportations." The judgment focused on Armenians because it invoked "the crimes of massacre which occurred in Trabzon, Yozgad, and Boğazlıyan," but it also noted that "[n]on-Muslims" chafing under "despotism" were the target.[15]

In the 1990s, a number of influential works on comparative genocide studies were published, but few of them featured the Assyrian and Greek cases except in passing. Such books often declared a strictly Armenian genocide, often claiming in excess of one million or 1.5 million victims based on statistics provided by Arnold Toynbee or Johannes Lepsius. In 1995, Vahakn Dadrian published one of the first books whose source material was complete enough to support a comprehensive portrait of late Ottoman genocides. Yet he seems to have avoided quoting or paraphrasing many sources that suggest a widespread assault on non-Armenian Christians.[16] In 1996, Dadrian published a detailed analysis of the German archives and could not deny that the Greek population of Turkey was destroyed in part, but he argued that the Germans scared away the Ottomans from committing an anti-Greek genocide. Ironically, the Germans also intervened to protect the Armenians of Smyrna, yet that fact did not prevent Dadrian from concluding that the Armenian genocide had occurred. This pattern of scholarship continued until 2010, with other works claiming that 1.5 million or more Armenians were killed but ignoring or cavalierly dismissing as unworthy of analysis the systematic killing of Ottoman Assyrians and Greeks.[17]

Was an Ottoman Christian Genocide Committed between 1915 and 1925?

One explanation for why Armenian genocide scholars neglect the Assyrians and Greeks is that information might be lacking on massacres or deportations carried out against these groups. These incidents may have been forgotten, not hidden.

Prior to the 1960s, it was well established in diplomatic and scholarly communities that the Armenian genocide swept Assyrians and Greeks within a general anti-Christian persecution. The contours of this persecution, referred to at the time as "extermination," "death of a nation," "general massacre," and "holocaust," parallel the definition of genocide in international law.[18]

Ottoman and Persian documents establish that the Assyrians, along with the Armenians, were targeted as such, with local portions of these groups destroyed even as other portions of both groups fled. In 1915, the Ottoman interior minister wrote that "the Armenians of the [Ottoman] province of Diyarbekir, along with other Christians, were being massacred." Before the war, the Armenian

patriarch estimated that nearly 90,000 of the Christians of the *vilayet* of Diyarbekir were Armenian, while 55,000 were Assyrian and 5,000 were Greek.[19] In
June 1919, the grand vizier of the Ottoman Empire explained to the Paris Peace
Conference that multitudes of Christians, not restricted by him to Armenians,
had been destroyed. Ottoman documents suggest that 2,000 other Christians,
likely Assyrians, were slain in the Diyarbekir region, with their homes and busi-
nesses given to the Turkish and Kurdish population. A former Ottoman official
told the British that Hilmi Bey and another Ottoman official invaded Persia with
irregular troops and "massacred a great part of the population without distinction of race or religion." Although Persia was not part of the Ottoman Empire,
British sources described the "Nestorians" or "Syrians" and "Chaldeans" as suffering a "general exodus" from a "Turco-Kurdish" invasion in 1914–1915. A Persian official in Urmia, Persia, reported in October 1914 that the message of holy
war against Christians on behalf of the Ottoman sultan had spread among the
tribes of the Ottoman/Persian border. By early March 1915, the Persians were
reporting that Urmia had been completely plundered, leaving the population
without the means to survive. The Iranian foreign minister complained to the
Ottomans of attacks on "villages inhabited by Christians, where the population
has been violated and mercilessly massacred." These reports confirm those of
Assyrian victims who lived in Persia.[20]

The German and Austro-Hungarian allies of the Ottomans also referenced
a targeting of Christians as a whole, and not simply of Armenians. The German
ambassador in Constantinople wrote to the German imperial chancellor to
inform him that the Ottoman governor of Diyarbekir had engaged in the systematic extermination of the Christians of Diyarbekir, regardless of ethnicity or creed,
and including Assyrians. German diplomats in Mosul reported other massacres
in Assyrian areas, including in Faysh Khabour, Mardin, and Seert. German diplomats in Aleppo and Mosul reported to the ambassador that the Assyrians of
Tur Abdin, Seert and Diyarbekir were targeted. An Austro-Hungarian diplomat
co-authored a report stating that "the annihilation of the Christian element in
Turkey" was under way in 1915 as part of a "premeditated plan."[21]

Ottoman officials informed a German diplomat that they intended to clear
out their internal enemies, meaning those of the Christian faith. An Ottoman
official told an Austro-Hungarian diplomat, "We must finish with the Greeks.
I sent today battalions to kill every Greek they meet on the road." In 1917, the
Austro-Hungarian ambassador to Constantinople reported that with respect to
the Ottoman Greeks who were being deported, "The situation of the deported is
for despair. Death awaits them all." That same year, the Austrian consul in Trebizond reported that Turkish hatred for the Greeks had materialized in a campaign of extermination. Another German diplomat reported in 1918 that over
the past several years, many of the 200,000 Greek men and boys conscripted by

the Ottomans had been tortured or starved to death or had perished from the cold weather and diseases to which their superiors had exposed them.[22]

After the war, the British ambassador to the United States, James Bryce, wrote that there is "no record of massacres more unprovoked, more widespread or more terrible than those perpetrated by the Turkish Government upon the Christians of Anatolia and Armenia in 1915," including the Christians of "the Nestorian and Assyro-Chaldean churches." Half of the Assyrians died, he wrote. The British Foreign Office announced that "[i]n the latest massacres the Nestorian or Syrian Christians suffered with the Armenians," because there were "frightful massacres and deportations" in the Hakkari district of Van and in the Urmia region in 1915.[23] In 1916, a volume of documents published by Ambassador Bryce and an Oxford historian, Arnold Toynbee, described how Djevdet Bey, the military governor of Van, entered the regions of Bohtan, Bitlis, and Seert and there massacred Assyrians. Forty Assyrian villages in the vicinity of Berwar were similarly destroyed by Turkish forces and allied Kurds. When Djevdet Bey's forces reached northwestern Persia, they killed thousands of Assyrians, causing the remainder to flee, with many dying of hunger, disease, and the cold. About 8,500 deaths took place among Assyrians in the vicinity of Urmia during five months in 1915. A further 4,000 deaths occurred in a "ruthless[]" massacre of the Assyrians of Khoi, Persia in 1918. In 1919, Major E. Noel, a British political officer, reported that pro-government forces had massacred nearly the entire Christian populations of Edessa/Urfa, Faysh Khabour, Seert, Jezireh, Nisibin, and other towns. The British received the new Ottoman vizier's consent to detain and charge an Ottoman general for massacring thousands of Assyrians in Persia and Mesopotamia (Zakho). A British representative to the League of Nations reported that in 1924, Turkish forces had "destroyed" the Assyrians in the valley of the Greater Zab River. A British official in Mosul wrote that the Assyrians "have lost their former homes and more than one-third of their original numbers."[24]

The U.S. ambassador to the Ottoman Empire, Henry I. Morgenthau, noted, after describing the massacres of Armenians, that the same story could be told in modified form about "the Greeks and the Syrians." He insisted that "the same methods [of deportation and 'wholesale massacre' were applied] on a larger scale not only to the Greeks but to the Armenians, Syrians, Nestorians, and others of its subject peoples." He explained that the victims included not simply 1.5 million Armenians but two million Christians, which he identified as "Greeks, Assyrians, [and] Armenians." An American official in Edessa documented the murder of many Christian men, the rape of women and girls, and the deaths of thousands of civilians in death marches and in confinement by Ottoman forces. The U.S. consul in Aleppo reported that "from Mardin the Government deported great numbers of Syrians, Catholics, Caldeans, and Protestants."

An American official in Harput stated that the deported Assyrians suffered a "lingering . . . death." An American diplomat stationed in Urmia stated that the Assyrian refugees there were "massacred." An American missionary physician reported that Turkish and Kurdish enemies of the Assyrians "were determined to wipe them out" and received "orders . . . for the extermination of the Nestorian Christians," which "were carried out in the region of Jezireh and Sert with ruthless cruelty." U.S. Senator William King contended that because of the U.S. tilt toward Turkey (perhaps due to a combination of missionary and tobacco interests), hundreds of thousands of Assyrians and Greeks "ha[d] been slaughtered by the Turks under Kemal Pasha." The American consul-general in Smyrna reported the "methodical extermination" of multiple "Christian populations" prior to 1922.[25]

In the Assyrian case, private sources corroborate the observations of government officials. The patriarch of the ancient Syrian (Jacobite) church based in Antioch informed the British that tens of thousands of his flock had died in killings in or deportations from Diyarbekir, Mardin, Edessa, Bitlis, Harput, and Seert. About half of the Jacobite component of the "assyro Chaldean[]" nation perished, he wrote. Starting in 1919, the international press reported that more than 250,000 Assyrians and Chaldeans died in massacres and an imposed famine. In 1920, Near East Relief reported that 160,000 Assyrians had been slain, leaving relatively few survivors. Ambassador Morgenthau and genocide scholars such as Paul Bartrop, David Gaunt, Tessa Hofmann, Steven Jacobs, Adam Jones, Martin Tamcke, and Samuel Totten have credited estimates of 250,000 Assyrians slain. Unfortunately, these scholarly estimates occur in the context of rather brief case studies (in comparison with the many books and articles on the Armenian genocide), with the exception of my own works, and Gaunt's.[26]

Regarding the Greeks, Ambassador Morgenthau stated that the Ottomans had set into motion a "devilish scheme to annihilate the Armenian, Greek and Syrian Christians of Turkey." Ambassador Morgenthau declared that the Ottomans perpetrated "a violent onslaught on the whole [Greek] race." An American consul in Anatolia wrote that in 1922, Turkish nationalists invading Smyrna executed a plan to "give up the city for some days to lust and carnage," including massacres conducted in a systematic "clean up" operation, culminating in the burning of Christian areas of the city. He concluded that "the policy of the Turkish nationalists [was] to exterminate and eliminate the entire Christian element in Turkey." The U.S. high commissioner at Constantinople described the removal of all "refugees" (i.e., Greeks in Smyrna) as the Nationalists' "final . . . solution of the race problem" in Turkey. At least 100,000 people were massacred in these events, according to the U.S. consul and other sources.[27]

By 1919, Western estimates were that 400,000 Greeks had been slain in Turkey. In 1919, the Greek army landed in Smyrna to intervene against "the Turkish plan of extermination" of the Greeks, and as allowed by article 69 of the Treaty of Sèvres, signed by the grand vizier of the Ottoman Empire on behalf of the Ottoman Sultan Mehmet VI. Apparently unwilling to accept the continued survival of large concentrations of Greek civilians, Turkish nationalists organized around Mustafa Kemal and Rauf Orbay declared a national "holy war" (*cihad-ı milliye*) against the Greeks. In August 1921, the British foreign secretary described reports of Pontic Greeks experiencing "wholesale deportations and massacres differing only in scale from those of the war period," leaving "no doubt that the Angora authorities are systematically pursuing the policy of extermination." In October of that year, the British ambassador to Turkey complained to the Turkish nationalists of "wholesale executions" of Greeks. The Foreign Office had "evidence that the Angora Turks had been deporting the Christian populations of Eastern Anatolia in large masses to the coast amid every circumstance of cruelty and suffering. Their policy was indeed admitted by them to be one of deliberate extermination." In 1922, the British ambassador confirmed "a deliberate plan to get rid of minorities . . . [as the] whole Greek male population from the age of 15 upwards of Trebizond area and its hinterland is being deported apparently to labour battalions at Erzeroum, Kars and Sari Kamish." The British chargé d'affairs in Athens reported in July 1922 that: "Massacres and deportations were threatening with extermination entire Christian population of regions under Kemalists' occupation."[28]

Testimony from persons other than diplomats also confirms large-scale deportations and killings. In 1917, the chairman of the Relief Committee for Greeks of Asia Minor concluded that the "same treatment is being meted out to the Greeks as to the Armenians and Syrians." In 1921, officials with Near East Relief confirmed that the "Greeks of Anatolia" were undergoing an "extermination" or effort to "destroy" them that was "the same [as] or worse" than the anti-Armenian massacres. A representative of Near East Relief in Smyrna reported that Nationalist soldiers drove 300,000 Christians from their homes with petroleum bombs and then killed 250,000 of the displaced Christians by mass executions, burning, drowning, or starvation. Other Americans reported mass rapes of Greek women, often accompanied by executions of the victims (a pattern of conduct identified as genocide by the International Criminal Tribunal for Rwanda).[29]

Statistical Questions Going to the Existence of Genocidal Intent

Another explanation for why the Assyrian and Greek genocides may have been forgotten, rather than hidden, is the question of comprehensiveness. Vahakn Dadrian argues, for example, that to be genocidal, a "substantial ratio" of victims must be killed rather than spared, "crippling a victim group in a comprehensive and consequential way." He maintains that the Armenian genocide reflected a unique "near-total destruction."[30]

Is the distinguishing factor simply that many more Armenians than Assyrians or Greeks were slain by Ottoman forces? For example, Marjorie Housepian's important 1966 article, which was updated in 1982, reported that the Armenian genocide began in 1915 and targeted 1.2 million out of 2 million Armenians, without saying much about population declines among the Ottoman Assyrians or Greeks. It is possible that other scholars writing in the "Armenian genocide" tradition did not recognize the Assyrian and Greek experiences as genocide because they followed Housepian in focusing on the Armenian deaths, and were unaware that other populations suffered massive losses.[31]

An impartial review of the evidence, however, shows that the Ottoman Greeks and Assyrians were actually more thoroughly destroyed than the Armenians in terms of their roles in postwar Western Asian societies and their exile from their homeland. The Turkish census of 1927 showed that there were more than 77,000 Armenians remaining, but only 71,000 Assyrians and Greeks at the most, including Chaldean and Syrian Catholics, Jacobite and Church of the East Orthodox followers, and Greek and Assyrian Protestants. Although there were more Armenians than Greeks in 1927, there had been more Ottoman Greeks in 1914.[32] By 1992 there were 60,000 Armenians but only 4,000 Greeks and 20,000 Assyrians living in Turkey, according to readily available figures. In Persia/Iran, the number of Armenians rose to 190,000 in 1956 from 100,000 in 1856, while the number of Assyrians fell to only 20,000 in 1956 from 138,000 in 1856.[33]

Turning to the scale of the anti-Greek genocide, it may well have equaled or exceeded the genocide of the Armenians, depending on which set of the below-cited statistics on Armenian refugees one is inclined to credit. In mid-1914, European and American sources reported that a campaign was under way to ruthlessly cleanse the Anatolian coast of Christians, especially Greeks. During late 1914 and early 1915, the Ottomans deported between 300,000 and 500,000 Greeks from eastern Thrace. Approximately half of these deportees were murdered in their communities or during the deportations, or died of starvation, disease, the cold, or exhaustion. A Greek archbishop reported that of 160,000 Pontic Greeks deported from their homeland by the Ottomans in 1915 and 1916, only 16,000 could have survived, at the most. A report in the *New York Times* in 1917 estimated that most of the 700,000 deported Pontic Greeks died. In 1918, a Turkish parliamentarian declaimed that 500,000 Greeks had been unjustifiably killed in the northern and western coasts of Anatolia. British intelligence also estimated that 750,000 Greeks deported from Anatolia and Thrace perished.[34]

The foremost expert on genocide statistics, Rudolph Rummel, has estimated that from 1914 to 1918 the Ottomans exterminated up to 384,000 Greeks, while from 1920 to 1922 another 264,000 Greeks were killed by the Nationalists.

These figures are of the same order of magnitude as scholars' roughly contemporaneous estimate of 900,000 Ottoman Greek victims of massacre, hunger, disease, and exposure, plus 15,000 dead Greek soldiers and 45,000 missing Greek soldiers.[35]

Estimates of the number of survivors of the massive Ottoman deportations of Armenians in 1915 vary, but many estimates suggest that 0.5 to 1.2 million Ottoman Armenians outlived the war and deportations, in contrast to the Assyrians. In 1916, William Walker Rockwell, a member of the American Committee for Armenian and Syrian Relief, wrote that nearly 1.2 million Armenians survived as refugees.[36] By 1918, Armenians could point out to the United States that their nation had 3.5 million members. In 1918, the leader of the Armenian national delegation claimed that 800,000 (Anatolian) Armenians had survived. Steven T. Katz figures that there were more than one million Ottoman Armenian refugees and survivors in postwar Russia, Syria, Turkey, and other places. Both Armenian and non-Armenian scholars began in the 1970s to place the number of murdered Armenians at as few as 600,000.[37]

Scholars may have obscured the Assyrian and Greek genocides by using different techniques for estimating Armenian or Jewish versus Assyrian deaths. The typical procedure for assessing the death toll during the Armenian genocide is to start with Armenian or British estimates of the prewar Armenian population, deduct the surviving Ottoman Armenian population living in Turkey or as refugees elsewhere, and use the difference as the death toll. Similarly, Holocaust scholars often start with European census estimates of the prewar population of European Jews and deduct the number of survivors. In such estimates, the Holocaust death toll is not "discounted for deaths that would have occurred in any case [due to old age, etc.]." By contrast, when it comes to victims of anti-Assyrian persecutions, the procedure sometimes seems to be to add up death tolls of discrete massacres. This procedure ignores indirect deaths.[38]

Definitionalism in Genocide Scholarship

The Role of Non-Armenian Scholars

A perennial danger facing genocide scholarship is misguided definitionalism. Prominent Holocaust and genocide scholars such as Stephen T. Katz and Guenter Lewy have redefined genocide using a Holocaust paradigm that requires the intention be put into practice to achieve the total biological and physical destruction of a group, with no exceptions for expellees or religious converts. In response, scholars of the Armenian genocide understandably emphasize similarities between the total physical destruction of the Armenians and that of the Jews. Some scholars may not want to take on the burden of explaining how other Ottoman peoples fit into the Holocaust paradigm, especially given the number of Ottoman Greek survivors, which contemporary newspapers placed at more than a million in Greece. In addition, the Turkish census of 1927 recorded the existence of 119,822 Greek speakers. There were about 40,000 to 60,000 Ottoman Assyrians who sought a home in Iraq or Persia after 1919.[39]

The impulse to confirm that nearly every member of a group was killed before concluding that genocide occurred is ultimately misguided. It seems to ignore that in the Holocaust, often looked to as the template for genocide, the vast majority of Jews from Nazi-occupied Bulgaria and Denmark survived the war, along with 50 percent to 80 percent of Jews from Belgium, France, Hungary, and Italy, even though Belgium and France were among the first Nazi-occupied countries. Many Jews survived by armed resistance; more than 50,000 Jews fought in underground resistance movements and partisan armies. Another estimate from the postwar period suggested that two million Jews resided in European displaced-persons camps.[40]

Deportation versus Genocide

Other scholars might believe that the Assyrian or Greek experience was not a genocide because many Assyrians fled to Russia or Persia and many Greeks fled to Greece. The latter process is often euphemistically described as an "exchange" or a "population transfer," as if the Assyrians or Greeks were catching a crosstown bus. Genocide scholars must therefore explore this process in more detail.[41] As detailed above, contemporary estimates suggest that hundreds of thousands of Greeks were killed in the process of deportation and persecution. Moreover, the Armenians who were not immediately shot but who died from hunger or exposure during mass deportations are not deducted from the total death toll offered by Armenian scholars of 1, 1.2, 1.5, or even 2 million Armenian deaths. Similarly, deaths from hunger, disease, or exhaustion are not deducted from the figure of six million Jews slain in the Holocaust. Even combat deaths seemingly are not deducted from the tolls of the Armenian genocide and the Holocaust, although we know that Armenian and Jewish resistance groups fought back, particularly at Musa Dagh and Warsaw.[42]

Realpolitik and the Privileging of Present-Day Concerns

Another defensive thinking mechanism relating to genocide denial is pragmatism, in which the search for political solutions is given primacy and the assumption is that realpolitik precedes disinterested study. Common sense suggests that in a highly politicized context, it would be easier for Armenian lobbyists and sympathetic scholars to secure political recognition of one genocide than it would be to win recognition of three genocides. Their efforts in the European Parliament have, indeed, been a success. Political recognition at the federal level in the United States has also been restricted to Armenians.

Although ethnic and nationalistic realpolitik may always be with us, there are signs of change. Between 2001 and 2010, the governors of New York State have repeatedly recognized the Assyrian and Greek genocides on Armenian Genocide Remembrance Day, held each April. In 2006, the European Parliament called upon Turkey, as part of its process of accession to the European Union, to acknowledge the Assyrian and Greek genocides. Most recently, the Swedish parliament recognized the Assyrian and Pontic Greek genocides along with the Armenian genocide.[43]

Lessons for Genocide Scholarship

Studying Genocide, Not Simply the Holocaust

One explanation for the discourse on the Armenian genocide as it evolved in the period between the 1960s and 1990s is that it was motivated by a concern to draw as close an analogy as possible to the extermination of European Jewry from 1941 through 1945. This plainly drove much of the scholarship. As Raphael Lemkin himself realized, however, not every genocide must be on a par with the Holocaust to be worthy of condemnation, proceedings in an international tribunal, or commemoration in works of history and literature. Lemkin's own work suggests several analogies to the Ottoman Christian genocide other than the Holocaust, including the Mongol invasions of Western Asia, the Thirty Years' War in Europe, European conquests in the Americas, the massacres of the Herero group in German-occupied Africa, and the Russian pogroms against Jews.[44]

Remembering the Smaller Peoples

Genocide scholars have a tendency to focus on genocides in populous regions and large territories, such as Europe during World War II, Southeast Asia, the Balkans, and East Africa. But many victims of genocide studied by scholars and indigenous peoples' rights advocates belonged to very small peoples, some facing total extinction. Lemkin's work on genocide in the Americas, in the Ottoman Empire, and against the Assyrians of Iraq offers a model for studying such cases.[45]

Expanding Our Horizons

Comprehending the scale of Ottoman Christian suffering in the late Ottoman Empire requires studying sources in several languages, or recently translated from them. Many of these sources are often hard to find and quite expensive. The field of genocide studies would benefit from more collaborative efforts to share such resources, and more Web-based archives such as cjh.org, aina.org, armenocide.de, and greek-genocide.org. Without such resources, the study of Late Ottoman genocides would be considerably behind where it is today. With them, we see further into the mists of human history.

NOTES

1. A. Dirk Moses, "Revisiting a Founding Assumption of Genocide Studies," *Genocide Studies and Prevention* 6 (December 2011): 287–300, 289.

2. A. Dirk Moses, "Towards a Theory of Critical Genocide Studies," in *Online Encyclopedia of Mass Violence*, ed. Jacques Semelin (18 April 2008), http://massviolence.org/fr/IMG/ article_PDF/Toward-a-Theory-of-Critical-Genocide-Studies.pdf.

3. For an overview of this debate, see ibid.; A. Dirk Moses, "Conceptual Blockages and Definitional Dilemmas in the 'Racial Century': Genocides of Indigenous Peoples and the Holocaust," *Patterns of Prejudice* 36 (2002): 7–36, 9, 35–36, doi: 0031–322X/7–36/029696; Hannibal Travis, *Genocide, Ethnonationalism, and the United Nations* (New York: Routledge, 2012), ch. 4; Hannibal Travis, "On the Original Understanding of the Crime of Genocide," *Genocide Studies and Prevention* 7 (Spring 2012): 30–55, 31–33.

4. Moses, "Conceptual Blockages," 24–25; Taner Akçam, "Turkey's Human Rights Hypocrisy," *New York Times*, 25 June 2012, http://www.aina.org/news/20120720005216.htm.

5. On the role of the Institute for Turkish Studies, see, e.g., Speros Vryonis, *The Turkish State and History: Clio Meets the Grey Wolf* (Institute for Balkan Studies, 1991), 17, 102–123; on Britain, France, and the United States, see, e.g., Tariq Ramadan, "Islam—A Path Towards Peace" (2010), http://www.youtube.com/watch?v=nguIKiOrvaU; Jacques Semelin, *Purify and Destroy: The Political Uses of Massacre and Genocide*, trans. Stanley Hoffman (New York: Columbia University Press, 2009), 4, 179, 191–93, 227; Cihan Tugal, "Memories of Violence, Memoirs of Nation: 1915 and the Construction of Armenian Identity," in *Politics of Public Memory*, ed. Esra Ozyurek (Syracuse, NY: Syracuse University Press, 2007), 141, 157, 160.

6. U.N. Doc. No. E/CN. 4/Sub. 2/1985/6 and Corr. 1; U.N. Doc. No. E/CN. 4/1995/2, pp. 60 and E/CN. 4/Sub. 2/1994/56, p. 60; Resolution on a Political Solution to the Armenian Question, Doc. A2–33/87, reprinted in *The Encyclopedia of Genocide*, ed. Israel Charny (ABC-CLIO, 1999), 1:80–81; Affirmation of the United States Record on the Armenian Genocide—Resolution, H.R. Rep. No. 111–622, http://thomas.loc.gov/cgi-bin/cpquery/ ?&dbname=cp111&sid=cp1115fDG3&refer=&r_n=hr622.111&item=&&&sel=TOC_8438&.

7. Treaty of Lausanne (Treaty of Peace, signed at Lausanne), 24 July 1923, arts. 38–45, in *The Treaties of Peace 1919–1923*, vol. 2 (Washington, DC: Carnegie Endowment for International Peace, 1924), http://wwi.lib.byu.edu/index.php/Treaty_of_Lausanne; see also Treaty of Sèvres (Treaty of Peace between Allied and Associated Powers and Turkey), arts. 147–150, in *Peace Treaties: Various Treaties and Other Agreements between the Allies and Associated Powers*, ed. Sen. Henry Cabot Lodge (Washington, DC: Government Printing Office, 1921), 360.

8. E.g., Robert Melson, "Revolution and Genocide: On the Causes of the Armenian Genocide and the Holocaust," in *The Armenian Genocide: History, Politics, Ethics*, ed. Richard G. Hovannisian (New York: Palgrave Macmillan, 1982), 96; Stephan Astourian, "Genocidal Process: Reflections on the Armeno-Turkish Polarization," in Hovannisian, *Armenian Genocide*, 58–59.

9. Near East Relief, Report to the Congress of the United States of America for the Year Ending December 31, 1920, S. Doc. No. 5 (1921); Henry Morgenthau, *The Tragedy of Armenia* (London: Spottiswoode, 1918), 13.

10. Henry Elisha Allen, *The Turkish Transformation: A Study in Social and Religious Development* (New York: Greenwood, 1968), 78.

11. Hrayr S. Karagueuzian and Yaïr Auron, *A Perfect Injustice: Genocide and Theft of Armenian Wealth* (New Brunswick, NJ: Transaction, 2009), 17–18, 62; Antranig Chalabian,

"My Answer to Prof. Ronald G. Suny: The Armenian Genocide Began Not in 1915, but in 1514, during the Reign of Sultan Selim I (1512–1520)," *Armenian Reporter International* 33 (April 2000): 3–4.

12. Joannes Gennadios, "Greek Church," in *Chambers's Encyclopædia*, vol. 5, ed. William and Robert Chambers (Philadelphia: J. B. Lippincott, 1890), 401; Marjorie Housepian Dobkin, *Smyrna 1922: The Destruction of a City* (Kent, OH: Kent State University Press, 1988), 22; R. J. Rummel, *Statistics of Democide: Genocide and Mass Murder since 1900* (Münster: LIT Verlag Münster, 1998), 97–98; R. J. Rummel, *Death by Government* (New Brunswick, NJ: Transaction, 2008), 61; Viscount James Bryce, "Preface," in *The Treatment of Armenians in the Ottoman Empire, 1915–1916*, ed. Ara Sarafian (London: Gomidas Institute, 2000), 23; Vahakn Dadrian, *The History of the Armenian Genocide: Ethnic Conflict from the Balkans to Anatolia to the Caucasus* (Oxford: Berghahn, 1995), 12; Richard Davey, *The Sultan and His Subjects* (London: Chatto and Windus, 1907), 342; Thea Halo, *Not Even My Name: From a Death March in Turkey to a New Home in America, a Young Girl's True Story* (New York: Macmillan, 2000), 100; Arman J. Kirakossian, ed., *The Armenian Massacres, 1894–1896: U.S. Media Testimony* (Detroit: Wayne State University Press, 2004), 164, 167.

13. The Greeks, Persians, Arabs, Romans, and Assyrians themselves often referred to "Assyria" and the "Assyrians" as distinct lands and populations. Hannibal Travis, "On the Existence of National Identities before 'Imagined Communities': The Example of the Assyrians of Mesopotamia, Anatolia, and Persia," in *The Assyrian Heritage: Continuity in Rituals, Symbols, and Language*, ed. Sargon Donabed, Aryo Makko, and Onver Cetrez (Uppsala, Sweden: Acta Universitatis Upsaliensis, 2013), 87–131. Texts in the language of the neo-Assyrian Empire (i.e., Aramaic) described the conversion to Christianity of the Assyrians. "The Doctrine of Addaeus," in *Ancient Syriac Documents relative to the Earliest Establishment of Christianity in Edessa and the Neighboring Countries*, trans. William Cureton (Amsterdam: Oriental Press, 1967), 6, 16. The so-called Syrian Orthodox or "Jacobite" Christians of Turkey called themselves "Assyrians" in the United States. Sargon Donabed, "Rethinking Nationalism and an Appellative Conundrum: Historiography and Politics in Iraq," *National Identities* 4, no. 2 (2012): 14, 41, http://papers.ssrn.com/s013/papers.cfm?abstract_id=2089774. After inroads by various missionary groups, the Assyrians became known to Western officials as Chaldeans, Nestorians, Syrian Orthodox, and Syrian Catholics. Hirmis Aboona, *Assyrians, Kurds, and Ottomans: Intercommunal Relations on the Periphery of the Ottoman Empire* (Amherst, NY: Cambria, 2008), ch. 5; S. H. Longrigg and F. Stokes, *Iraq* (London: Ernest Benn, 1958), 63; "Nestorius and Nestorianism," *The Catholic Encyclopedia*, vol. 10, ed. Charles Herbermann et al. (New York: Robert Appleton, 1911), http://www.newadvent.org/cathen/10755a.htm; "Patriarch and Patriarchate," in *The Catholic Encyclopedia*, vol. 11, http://www.newadvent.org/cathen/11549a.htm; Simo Parpola, "National and Ethnic Identity in the Neo-Assyrian Empire and Assyrian Identity in the Post-Empire Times," *Journal of Assyrian Academic Studies* 18 (2004): 5–40; Robin E. Waterfield, *Christians in Persia* (London: George Allen and Unwin, 1973), 23; William Warda, "Assyrian Heritage of the Church of the East, Chaldean Church and the Syrian Orthodox Church," *Christians of Iraq* (2004), http://www.christiansofiraq.com/reply.html; Aboona, *Assyrians, Kurds, and Ottomans*, 36–37; "Massacre of the Nestorian Christians," *Times* (London), 6 September 1843, http://www.atour.com/~history/london-times/20000801b.html; Gabriel Oussani, "The Modern Chaldeans and Nestorians, and the Study of Syriac among Them," *Journal of the American Oriental Society* 22 (1901): 81; K. Kessler, "Nestorians," in *The New Schaff-Herzog Encyclopedia of Religious Knowledge*, ed. Samuel M. Jackson et al. (New York: Funk and Wagnalls, 1910), 123; Emilius Clayton, British vice-consul in Van, "Report on

Reforms in Van," 29 November 1879, in *British Documents on Ottoman Armenians (1856–1880)*, vol. 1, ed. Bilal Şimşir (Ankara: Turkish Historical Society, 1989), 646; Dr. Robert Walsh, "Chaldeans," in *The Christian Spectator*, vol. 8 (New York: J. P. Haven, 1826), 271. See also *L'Action assyro-chaldéenne: L'Assyro-Chaldée devant la Conférence de la Paix*, ed. M. Kyriakos and V. Yonanu (Vicariat Patriarchal Assyro-Chaldéen, 1920), 25 (these figures include Chaldeans and the "Jacobite" or Syrian Orthodox Christians); Travis, "On the Existence of National Identities," 87–110.

14. Israel Charny, "The Psychological Satisfaction of Denials of the Holocaust or Other Genocides by Non-Extremists or Bigots, and Even by Known Scholars," *Idea Journal* 6 (2001), http://www.ideajournal.com/articles.php?id=27; Gerard Libaridian, ed., *A Crime of Silence: The Armenian Genocide* (London: Zed, 1985), 83–84, 244, back cover.

15. Marjorie Housepian Dobkin, "What Genocide? What Holocaust? News from Turkey, 1915–1923: A Case Study," in *The Armenian Genocide in Perspective*, ed. Richard G. Hovannisian (New Brunswick, NJ: Transaction Books, 1987), 97–110, 102; "Turkey Condemns Its War Leaders," *New York Times*, 13 July 1919, http://select.nytimes.com/gst/abstract .html?res=F70B10FC395B11728DDDAA0994DF405B898DF1D3; Vahakn D. Dadrian and Taner Akçam, *Judgment at Istanbul: The Armenian Genocide Trials* (Oxford: Berghahn Books, 2011), 120–121, 325, 327.

16. For example, Dadrian cited the British historian Arnold Toynbee as describing "deportations of 1915," which Dadrian argued were "large-scale massacres" meant to resolve the "Armenian Question," but Toynbee did not identify the deportations as only a solution of such a "Question," but as "atrocities" affecting the "Armenian or Nestorian inhabitants of the Near East," and the volume Toynbee edited identified the Nestorians as Assyrians who are "better known" as Nestorians or Syrians. Ibid., 198. Compare Arnold Toynbee, "Memorandum by the Editor," in *The Treatment of Armenians in the Ottoman Empire, 1915–1916: Documents Presented to the Viscount Grey of Falloden by Viscount Bryce*, ed. Ara Sarafian (Reading, UK: Taderon, 2000), 34; Paul Shimmun, "Hakkiari," in Sarafian, *Treatment of Armenians*, 200.

17. Rouben Paul Adalian, "The Armenian Genocide," in *Century of Genocide: Critical Essays and Eyewitness Accounts*, 2d ed. (New York: Routledge, 2009), 55; Frank Chalk and Kurt Jonassohn, *The History and Sociology of Genocide* (New Haven, CT: Yale University Press, 1992), 282; Vahakn Dadrian, "Documentation of Armenian Genocide in German Sources," in Charny, *Encyclopedia of Genocide*, 1:90–96; Robert Melson, "The Armenian Genocide and the Holocaust Compared," in Charny, *Encyclopedia of Genocide*, 1:69–70; Robert Melson, *Revolution and Genocide: On the Origins of the Armenian Genocide and the Holocaust* (Chicago: University of Chicago Press, 1992); Ara Sarafian, ed. *United States Official Documents on the Armenian Genocide*, vols. 1–4 (Watertown, MA: Armenian Review, 1993–1997); Dadrian, *History of the Armenian Genocide*, xvii–xviii and passim; Vahakn Dadrian, *German Responsibility in the Armenian Genocide: A Review of the Historical Evidence of German Complicity* (Watertown, MA: Blue Crane Books, 1996), 230; Mark Levene, *Genocide in the Age of the Nation-State: The Rise of the West and the Coming of Genocide* (London: I. B. Tauris, 2005), 203; Katherine Derderian, "Common Fate, Different Experience: Gender-Specific Aspects of the Armenian Genocide, 1915–1917," *Holocaust and Genocide Studies* 19 (2005): 1–25; Ronald Grigor Suny, "Writing Genocide: The Fate of the Ottoman Armenians," in *A Question of Genocide: Armenians and Turks at the End of the Ottoman Empire*, ed. Ronald Suny and Fatma Muge Gocek (Oxford: Oxford University Press, 2010), 41.

18. E. W. McDowell, "The Nestorians of the Bohtan District," in Sarafian, *Treatment of Armenians*, 180; Viscount James Bryce, "Preface," in Joseph Naayem, *Shall This Nation*

Die? (New York: Chaldean Rescue, 1921), 10–12; William Walter Rockwell, "The Total of Armenian and Syrian Dead," *New York Times Current History Magazine* 9 (October–December 1916): 337–338; William Walter Rockwell, *The Pitiful Plight of the Assyrian Christians in Persia and Kurdistan* (New York: American Committee for Armenian and Syrian Relief, 1916), 14; Abraham Yohannan, *The Death of a Nation; or, The Ever Persecuted Nestorians or Assyrian Christians* (New York: G. P. Putnam's Sons, 1916), 115, 149. See also Peter Balakian, *The Burning Tigris: The Armenian Genocide and America's Response* (New York: HarperCollins Publishers, 2004), 123.

19. Johannes Lepsius estimated somewhat higher numbers as of 1915 or so, perhaps due to population growth, i.e., 105,000 Armenians and 60,000 Assyrians (Nestorians and Chaldeans). Johannes Lepsius, *Der Todesgang des armenischen Volkes* (Potsdam: Tempel-verlag, 1919), 74.

20. Minister of the Interior Talât to Diyarbakir vilayet, BOA.DH.SFR, nr 54/406, quoted in David Gaunt, *Massacres, Resistance, Protectors: Muslim-Christian Relations in Eastern Anatolia during World War I* (Piscataway, NJ: Gorgias Press, 2006), 73–74; F.O. 424/107, pp. 173–179, no. 104/.3 (table II), *in British Documents on Ottoman Armenians (1880–1890)*, vol. 2, ed. Bilal Şimşir (Ankara: Turkish Historical Society, 1983), 132, 134; Gaunt, *Massacres*, 23; Richard G. Hovannisian, *The Republic of Armenia: The First Year, 1918–1919* (Berkeley: University of California Press, 1971), 330–331; Raymond Kévorkian, *The Armenian Genocide: A Complete History* (London: I. B. Tauris, 2010), 699, 751, 770; Prime Ministry Directorate of State Archives, Osmali Belgelerinde Ermeniler (1915–1920) [Ottoman Documents on Armenians, 1915–1920], 69 (Record 71), cited in Taner Akçam, "Deportation and Massacres in the Cipher Telegrams of the Interior Ministry in the Prime Ministerial Archive (Başbakanlık Arşivi)," *Genocide Studies and Prevention* 1 (2006): 305, 310; Ottoman official quoted in *British Foreign Office Dossiers on Turkish War Criminals*, ed. Vartkes Yeghiayan (Pasadena, CA: American Armenian International College, 1991), 251; Arnold Toynbee, "Azerbaijan and Hakkiari," in Sarafian, *Treatment of Armenians*, 135; Empire du Perse, Vizārat-i Umūr-i Khārijah, *Neutralité Persane: Documents Diplomatiques* (Paris: Imprimerie Georges Cadet, 1919), 10, 17, 132, 137–139, 153, 155; Gaunt, *Massacres*, 63, 82, 111.

21. German Ambassador on Extraordinary Mission in Constantinople, Hohenlohe-Langenburg, to the German Imperial Chancellor, Bethmann Hollweg, DE/PA-AA/R14094, 1916-A-33457, No. 477, sent 08/06/1915 p.m. (31 July 1915); German Vice-Consul in Mosul, Holstein, to the German Ambassador on Extraordinary Mission in Constantinople, Hohenlohe-Langenburg, DE/PA-AA/R14094, 1916-A-33457, No. 11, sent 07/15/1915 07:00 p.m. (15 July 1915); German Vice-Consul in Mosul, Holstein, to the German Ambassador on Extraordinary Mission in Constantinople, Hohenlohe-Langenburg, DE/PA-AA/R14094, 1916-A-33457, No. 14, sent 07/21/1915 03:00 p.m. (21 July 1915); German Consul in Aleppo, Rößler to the German Ambassador on Extraordinary Mission in Constantinople, Hohenlohe-Langenburg, DE/PA-AA/R14094, 1916-A-33457, No. A53a/1915/5779, A-30049, sent 10/17/1915 a.m. (27 September 1915); German Consul in Mosul, Rößler, to the German Imperial Chancellor, Bethmann Hollweg, DE/PA-AA/R14094, 1916-A-33457, No. 90/B. No. 1950, sent 09/26/1915 p.m. (3 September 1915). Austro-Hungarian report quoted in Vahakn Dadrian, "Documentation of the Armenian Genocide in German and Austrian Sources," in *The Widening Circle of Genocide: Genocide: A Critical Bibliographic Review*, vol. 3, ed. Israel Charny (New Brunswick, NJ: Transaction, 1994), 109.

22. Taner Akçam, *A Shameful Act: The Armenian Genocide and the Question of Turkish Responsibility* (New York: Metropolitan Books, 2006), 121; Wien HHStA, PA, Türkei XII, Liasse

467 LIV, Griechenverfolgungen in der Türkei 1916–1918, No. 97/pol., Konstantinopel (19 January 1916), (2 January 1917), http://www.greek-genocide.org/quotes.html#bkmk5t; Wien HHStA, PA, Türkei XII, Liasse 467 LIV, No 6/P., Konstantinopel (20 January 1917); Austrian Consul for Trebizond, Ernst von Kwiatkowski, to the Minister of the Imperial and Royal House and for Foreign Affairs, Ottokar Grafen Czernin von und zu Chude-nitz, ZI. 45/pol. Samsoun, 12 November 1917, Persecution of the Greeks in Bafra, (vgl. ZI. 206/A von heute), http://www.greek-genocide.org/docs/adp/kwiatkowski_12 _november_1917.pdf; Speros Vryonis, "Greek Labor Battalions in Asia Minor," in *The Armenian Genocide: Cultural and Ethical Legacies*, ed. Richard Hovannisian (New Brunswick, NJ: Transaction, 2007), 287.

23. The British referred to the Nestorian or Syrian Christians as "Nestorians, Syro-Chaldeans, or Assyrians." George Walter Prothero, ed., *Peace Handbooks: Turkey in Asia (II)*, nos. 61–66 (London: Foreign Office, 1920), 5.

24. Viscount James Bryce, "Preface," in Naayem, *Shall This Nation Die?*, http://www.lulu .com/items/volume_2/140000/140495/2/preview/Naayem_Preview.pdf; Prothero, *Peace Handbooks*, 26; A. S. Safrastian, "Bitlis, Moush and Sassoun," in Sarafian, *The Treatment of Armenians*, 120. See also E. W. McDowell, "The Nestorians of the Bohtan District," in Sarafian, *Treatment of Armenians*, 211; Paul Shimmon, "Urmia, Salmas and Hakkiari," in Sarafian, *Treatment of Armenians*, 198; Dr. William Shedd, "Urmia," in Sarafian, *Treatment of Armenians*, 137–140; Jacob Sargis, "Urmia," in Sarafian, *Treatment of Armenians*, 189–191; Edwin Montagu, Secretary of State for India, to the Foreign Office, C.P. 2073, 4 November 1920, app., encl., High Commissioner for Mesopotamia to George Curzon, Foreign Secretary, 27 October 1920; Maj. E. Noel, *Diary of Maj. E. Noel on Special Duty* (n.p., 1919), 1; Maj. E. Noel, *Christian Massacres of 1915 in Diarbekir Vilayet* (n.p., 1919); Yeghiayan, *British Foreign Office Dossiers*, 5–19; "Question of the Frontier between Turkey and Iraq," *League of Nations Official Journal* 5 (1924): 1649; Lt. Col. Ronald S. Stafford, *The Tragedy of the Assyrians* (1935; rpt. New York: Columbia University Press, 2003), ch. 2.

25. Henry I. Morgenthau, *Ambassador Morgenthau's Story* (1918; rpt. Taderon Press, 2000), 214; "Morgenthau Urges Carving of Turkey," *Los Angeles Times*, 12 December 1918, I-1; Sarafian, *United States Official Documents*, 1:48–49; Leslie A. Davis, *The Slaughterhouse Province: An American Diplomat's Report on the Armenian Genocide* (Athens: Caratzas, 1990), 144–145; "More Violence by Turks," *Los Angeles Times*, 8 March 1915, II-1; "Uru-mia Station," in *Reports of the Missionary and Benevolent Boards and Committees to the General Assembly of the Presbyterian Church in the U.S.A.* (New York: Office of the General Assembly, 1917), 307; Suzanne E. Moranian, "A Legacy of Paradox: U.S. Foreign Policy and the Armenian Genocide," in Hovannisian, *Armenian Genocide*, 322; Simon Payas-lian, "The United States Response to the Armenian Genocide," in *Looking Backward, Moving Forward: Confronting the Armenian Genocide*, ed. Richard G. Hovannisian (New Brunswick, NJ: Transaction, 2003), 52–53, 64–71; "Senator King Urges Action against Turks," *New York Times*, 3 February 1922, 2; George Horton, *The Blight of Asia: An Account of the Systematic Extermination of Christian Populations by Mohammedans and the Culpa-bility of Certain Great Powers; With the True Story of the Burning of Smyrna* (Indianapolis: Bobbs-Merrill, 1926), 220; Constantine G. Hatzidimitriou, *American Accounts Docu-menting the Destruction of Smyrna by the Kemalist Turkish Forces: September 1922* (Athens: Caratzas, 2003), 110.

26. Ignatius Elias III, Ancient Syrian Patriarch of Antioch, to the British Foreign Secretary, Lord Curzon, F.O. 371/6356, XC 4360, E 2540, 16 February 1921; Severius Barsoum, delegate of Patriarch of Antioch, to Lloyd George, F.O. 371, E1242/16/118, 8 March 1920; Severius Barsoum, delegate of Patriarch of Antioch, to Lloyd George,

F.O. 371, E1221/[illegible]/108, 6 March 1920; "Chaldean Victims of the Turks," *Times* (London), 22 November 1919, 11; "The League and Mosul," *New York Times*, 29 October 1924, 20; Near East Relief, *1920 Report*, available online at http://books.google .com/books?id=nz9orQwe5UsC&pg=PT6; "Assyrian Genocide," in *Dictionary of Genocide: A–L*, ed. Samuel Totten, Paul Robert Bartrop, and Steven L. Jacobs (Santa Barbara, CA: ABC-CLIO, 2008), 25–26; Gaunt, *Massacres*, 300–304; Tessa Hofmann, "Mit einer Stimme sprechen—gegen Volkermord," in *Verfolgung, Vertreibung und Vernichtung der Christen im Osmanischen Reich*, ed. Tessa Hofmann (Münster: LIT Verlag Münster, 2004), 111; Adam Jones, *Genocide: A Comprehensive Introduction*, 2nd ed. (London: Routledge, 2010), 151; Martin Tamcke, "Der Genozid an den Assyrern/Nestorianern (Ostsyrische Christen)," in Hofmann, *Verfolgung*, 111. Ambassador Morgenthau's estimate did not break out Assyrians, but deducting 250,000 Greeks and 1.5 million Assyrians leaves 250,000 Assyrians. "Morgenthau Urges," 1-1.

27. Henry I. Morgenthau, "The Greatest Horror in History," *Red Cross Magazine* 13 (1917): 15; "Morgenthau Calls for Check on Turks," *New York Times*, 5 September 1922, 3; Henry I. Morgenthau, *Ambassador Morgenthau's Story* (New York: Doubleday, Page, 1918/1919), 324–325; Horton, *Blight of Asia*, 115; Turkish nationalist policy quoted in Hatzidimitriou, *Destruction of Smyrna*, 110; high commissioner quoted in ibid., 51; Rummel, *Statistics of Democide*, 95.

28. Western estimate in, e.g., William Pember Reeves, "Turkish Rule over Christian Peoples," *Christian Science Monitor*, 1 February 1919, in *Before the Silence Subtitle: Archival News Reports of the Christian Holocaust That Begs to Be Remembered*, ed. Sofia Kontogeorge Kostos (Piscataway, NJ: Gorgias Press, 2011), 32; Horton, *Blight of Asia*, 72; Ryan Gingeras, *Sorrowful Shores: Violence, Ethnicity, and the End of the Ottoman Empire* (Oxford: Oxford University Press, 2009), 74–75; the Marquess Curzon of Kedleston to Lord Hardinge (Paris) and to Mr. Kennard (Rome), No. 454 Telegraphic [E 8784/143/44], 4 August 1921, in *Documents on British Foreign Policy, 1919–1939*, series 1, vol. 17: *Greece and Turkey*, ed. William Mendicott et al. (London: HMSO, 1970), 344; Sir H. Rumbold (Constantinople) to the Marquess Curzon of Kedleston, No. 949 [E 11678/143/44], 15 October 1921, *in Documents on British Foreign Policy*, 17:439–442; the Marquess Curzon of Kedleston to Lord Hardinge (Paris), No. 344 [F 1248/5/44], 2 February 1922, *in Documents on British Foreign Policy*, 17:595–598; British ambassador quoted in *Documents on British Foreign Policy*, 17:817n1; Mr. Bentinck (Athens) to the Earl of Balfour, No. 262 Telegraphic [E 7471/5/44], 27 July 1922 (received 28 July, 8.30 a.m.), *in Documents on British Foreign Policy*, 17: 894–895.

29. "Turks Slaughter Christian Greeks," *Lincoln Daily Star*, 19 October 1917, 7; Stanley E. Hopkins, "Report on Conditions in the Interior of Anatolia under the Turkish Nationalist Government" (16 November 1921), http://www.greek-genocide.org/doc_usfo _rcia_1.html; Maj. F. D. Yowell, "Turkish Atrocities," *New Armenia* 14 (1922): 123; Jones, *Genocide*, 166; Adam Jones, "Notes on the Genocides of Christian Populations of the Ottoman Empire," Genocide Text (blog), 2007, http://www.genocidetext.net/iags_resolution _supporting_documentation.htm; Near East Relief representative Hatzidimitriou, *Destruction of Smyrna*, 80–81; American report quoted in ibid., 70–71.

30. Vahakn Dadrian, "Towards a Theory of Genocide," *Holocaust and Genocide Studies* 5 (1990): 129–143, 138–139; Vahakn Dadrian, "The Convergent Aspects of the Armenian and Jewish Cases of Genocide: A Reinterpretation of the Concept of 'Holocaust,'" *Holocaust and Genocide Studies* 5 (1988): 151–169, 163.

31. Marjorie Housepian Dobkin, "The Unremembered Genocide," *Commentary* 42 (1966): 55–61; Marjorie Housepian, "The Unremembered Genocide," in *Genocide and Human*

Rights: A Global Anthology (Lanham, MD: University Press of America, 1982), 99–115; Dadrian, *History of the Armenian Genocide*, xviii; Rouben Paul Adalian, "The Armenian Genocide," in *Century of Genocide: Critical Essays and Eyewitness Accounts*, ed. Samuel Totten and William Parsons (London: Routledge, 2009), 55, 71; Rouben Paul Adalian, "Ataturk, Mustafa Kemal," in *Encyclopedia of Genocide*, 1:110–111; Vahakn Dadrian, "Documentation," in *Encyclopedia of Genocide*, 1:90–92; Derderian, "Common Fate," 1–25.

32. Estimates of Armenian survivors as of 1927 stand at 77,000, while there were between 31,000 and 120,000 Greeks, depending on whether one counts those who spoke mostly Greek or those who reported being Greek Orthodox, and depending on how many Assyrians one assumes remained in Turkey (so as to make up a total of 71,000 Assyrians and Greeks by religion in 1927). Allen, *Turkish Transformation*, 78; W. C. Brice, "The Population of Turkey in 1950," *Geographical Journal* 120 (1954): 347, 350. Although both Armenians and Greeks were probably undercounted because Christians might have evaded registration so as to avoid being drafted or paying taxes, the Ottoman censuses logged 1.16 million Greeks and 1.1 million Armenians in 1906–1907, and 1.29 million Greeks and 1.25 million Armenians in 1914. Servet Mutlu, "Late Ottoman Population and Its Ethnic Distribution," *Nüfusbilim Dergisi: Turkish Journal of Population Studies* 25 (2003): 9, 11. As noted above, other estimates of Greeks reached seven million.

33. U.S. Department of State, *Country Reports on Human Rights Practices for 1992* (Washington, DC: Government Printing Office, 1993), 940–41, http://www.archive.org/stream/countryreportson1992unit/countryreportson1992unit_djvu.txt; Ervand Abrahamian, *Iran between Two Revolutions* (Princeton, NJ: Princeton University Press, 1982), 12.

34. "Why the Greeks Fled," *Manchester Guardian*, 29 June 1914; "Massacre of Greeks Charged to the Turks," *Atlanta Constitution*, 17 June 1914; Talcott Williams, "Greek Deportations," *New York Times*, 8 October 1917, all quoted in Sofia Kontogeorge Kostos, *Before the Silence: Archival News Reports of the Christian Holocaust That Begs to Be Remembered* (Piscataway, NJ: Gorgias Press, 2010), 79, 78, 91; Taner Akçam, *From Empire to Republic: Turkish Nationalism and the Armenian Genocide* (New York: Zed Books, 2004), 147; Hannibal Travis, *Genocide in the Middle East: The Ottoman Empire, Iraq, and Sudan* (Durham, NC: Carolina Academic Press, 2010), 286; His Grace Germanos, Archbishop of Amassia and Samsoun, *The Turkish Atrocities in the Black Sea Territories* (Manchester: Norbury, Natzio, 1919), 6; Williams, "Greek Deportations," 10; Shanon Lawson, "Talcott Williams Papers: 1894–1925," last modified November 1997, http://www.lib.udel.edu/ud/spec/findaids/wllms_ta.htm; Akçam, *A Shameful Act*, 106–107; Akçam, *From Empire to Republic*, 147–148.

35. Rummel, *Death by Government*, 224, 229–231, 234; Rummel, *Statistics of Democide*, 91–101; Arthur Lincoln Frothingham, Thomas Churchill, Arthur Lovejoy, R. M. McElroy, C. C. Pearson, Henry Thompson, C. H. Van Tyne, and Talcott Williams, *Handbook of War Facts and Peace Problems* (New York: National Security League, 1919), 238.

36. Rockwell, "Total of Armenian and Syrian Dead," 337. The U.S. consul in Aleppo, Syria, broke down the 486,000 in Syria in more detail. State Dep't. Record Group 59,867.48/271 (8 February 1916), in Sarafian, *United States Official Documents*, vol. 1.

37. "Armenians Here Seek Freedom for 3,500,000 Kindred," *New York Tribune*, 30 December 1918, 2, http://chroniclingamerica.loc.gov/lccn/sn83030214/1918–12–30/ed-1/seq-2/;words=Boghos+Nuber; Fuat Dündar, *Crime of Numbers: The Role of Statistics in the Armenian Question (1878–1918)* (New Brunswick, NJ: Transaction, 2010), 154–155; George Montgomery, "The Non-Arab Portion of the Ottoman Empire, Library of Congress Manuscript Division," box 21, January–February 1920 (New York: Armenia-America Society, 1919); Steven T. Katz, "Uniqueness: The Historical Dimension," in *Is*

the Holocaust Unique? Perspectives on Comparative Genocide, ed. Alan Rosenbloom (Boulder, CO: Westview, 2009), 71–73 (citing Johannes Lepsius, *Deutschland und Armenien 1914–1918* [Potsdam, Ger.: Tempelverlag, 1919], lxv, 160, 283; Richard Hovannisian, "Ebb and Flow of the Armenian Minority in the Middle East," *Middle East Journal* 1 [1974]: 19–32, 20; Arnold Toynbee and Viscount James Bryce, *The Treatment of Armenians in the Ottoman Empire, 1915–1916* [London: HMSO, 1916], 650); Katz, "Uniqueness," 71–73; Libaridian, *Crime of Silence*, 54, 158; Arnold Toynbee, *The Western Question in Greece and Turkey* (London: Howard Fertig, 1970), 342. See also Akçam, *A Shameful Act*, 183.

38. Donald Bloxham, *The Great Game of Genocide: Imperialism, Nationalism, and the Destruction of the Ottoman Armenians* (Oxford: Oxford University Press, 2005), 89, 98; Dadrian, *History of the Armenian Genocide*, xviii; Dündar, *Crime of Numbers*, 145–149; Guenter Lewy, *The Armenian Massacres in Ottoman Turkey: A Disputed Genocide* (Salt Lake City: University of Utah Press, 2005), 238–241; Lucy S. Dawidowicz, *The War against the Jews, 1933–1945* (New York: Penguin, 1987), 472–479; Raul Hilberg, *The Destruction of the European Jews*, vol. 1 (New Haven, CT: Yale University Press, 2003), 1302; Hilberg, *Destruction of the European Jews*, 1307; Rummel, *Death by Government*, 228–229.

39. Israel Charny, "The Psychological Satisfaction of Denials of the Holocaust or Other Genocides by Non-Extremists or Bigots, and Even by Known Scholars," *Idea* 6 (2001), http://www.ideajournal.com/articles.php?id=27; Steven T. Katz, *The Holocaust in Historical Context*, vol. 1 (Oxford: Oxford University Press, 1994), 24; Steven T. Katz, "The 'Unique' Intentionality of the Holocaust," *Modern Judaism* 1 (1981), 167, 174–176; Katz, "Uniqueness," 69; Lewy, *Armenian Massacres*, ix, 43, 53, 57, 62, 90, 150, 235–241, 245, 248, 251–253, 268; Guenter Lewy, *The Nazi Persecution of the Gypsies* (Oxford: Oxford University Press, 2000), 225–226; Guenter Lewy, "The First Genocide of the 20th Century? (Armenian Massacres, 1915–1916)," *Commentary* 120 (2005): 47–52; Guenter Lewy, "Revisiting the Armenian Genocide," *Middle East Quarterly* 12 (2005): 3; "A Black Friday," *New York Times*, 3 December 1922, http://select.nytimes.com/gst/abstract.html?res=FA0716F73E5 E1A738DDDAA0894DA415B828EF1D3; W. C. Brice, "The Population of Turkey in 1950," *Geographical Journal* 120 (1954): 347, 350; Ferydoon Firoozi, "Tehran: A Demographic and Economic Analysis," *Middle Eastern Studies* 10 (1974): 64; League of Nations, *Question of the Frontier between Turkey and Iraq* (Paris: Imprimeries Réunies, 1925), 51–52, 79, 82–88.

40. Yehuda Bauer, *They Chose Life: Jewish Resistance in the Holocaust* (New York: American Jewish Committee Institute of Human Relations, 1973), 21; Yehuda Bauer, *Remembering for the Future: Working Papers and Addenda* (Oxford: Pergamon, 1989), 3, 166; Lucy S. Dawidowicz, *A Holocaust Reader* (West Orange, NJ: Behrman House, 1976), 381; Lucy Dawidowicz, "Statement," in *Investigation into Certain Past Instances of Genocide and Exploration of Policy Options for the Future* (Washington, DC: Government Printing Office, 1976), 115; Hilberg, *Destruction of the European Jews*, 1128; Yosef Eisen, *Miraculous Journey: A Complete History of the Jewish People from Creation to the Present* (Jerusalem: Targum, 2004), 473; Marc Dollinger, *Quest for Inclusion: Jews and Liberalism in Modern America* (Princeton, NJ: Princeton University Press, 2000), 17.

41. Norman M. Naimark, *Fires of Hatred: Ethnic Cleansing in Twentieth-Century Europe* (Cambridge, MA: Harvard University Press, 2002), 54; Timothy Snyder, *Bloodlands: Europe between Hitler and Stalin* (New York: Basic Books, 2010), 1. Hilmar Kaiser refers to an anti-Armenian "genocide" but to anti-Greek and anti-Nestorian/Syrian "demographic policies," as if the mass killings of Greeks and Assyrians had been either unplanned or part of ordinary demographic planning. Hilmar Kaiser, "Genocide at the Twilight of the Ottoman Empire," in *The Oxford Handbook of Genocide Studies*, ed. Donald Bloxham and A. Dirk Moses (Oxford: Oxford University Press, 2010), 365–384.

42. E.g., Claire Andrieu, Jacques Semelin, and Sarah Gensburger, eds., *Resisting Genocide: The Multiple Forms of Rescue* (New York: Columbia University Press, 2011); Abram L. Sachar, *The Redemption of the Unwanted: From the Liberation of the Death Camps to the Founding of Israel* (New York: St. Martin's, 1983), 47–48.

43. Hannibal Travis, "The Assyrian Genocide: A Tale of Oblivion and Denial," in *Forgotten Genocides: Oblivion, Denial, and Memory*, ed. Rene Lemarchand (Philadelphia: University of Pennsylvania Press, 2011), 135; "Turkey's Progress Towards Accession," EU Res. A6–0269/2006, T6–0381/2006, P6_TA(2006)0381, http://www.europarl.europa.eu/sides/getDoc.do?type=TA&reference=P6-TA-2006–0381&language=EN (accessed 1 October 2007); Law Library of Congress, "Sweden: Parliament Approves Resolution on Armenian Genocide," *Global Legal Monitor*, 16 March 2010, http://www.loc.gov/lawweb/servlet/lloc_news?disp3_1205401871_text (accessed 1 September 2012).

44. Raphael Lemkin, "Genocide as a Crime against International Law," *United Nations Bulletin* 4 (1948): 70; Raphael Lemkin, "War against Genocide," *Christian Science Monitor*, 31 January 1948, 2; Travis, *Genocide in the Middle East*, 29–33.

45. E.g., Raphael Lemkin, *Raphael Lemkin's Dossier on the Armenian Genocide* (Glendale, CA: Center for Armenian Remembrance, 2008). Lemkin's work on the Assyrians of independent Iraq, subjected to a partial genocide in 1933, is available on the website of the Center for Jewish History at http://digital.cjh.org/R/?func=collections-result&collection_id=1661.

10

"The Law Is Such as It Is"

Reparations, "Historical Reality," and
the Legal Order in the Czech Republic

KRISTA HEGBURG

In this chapter, I examine how reparations, a phenomenon often theorized as a liberal tool for victims of historical injustice to attain a voice and call to account the state that perpetrated the violence against them, can function to sublimate the very voices they solicit. Using ethnographic research undertaken in 2004–2005 in the Czech Republic,[1] I focus on the mechanisms through which such an elision of testimony by claimants took place within a Holocaust reparations program geared for Czech Roma, even as the program sought to solicit, and value, Romani testimony. I then turn to a series of Czech court cases in the postsocialist liberal period that challenged the legal categories of reparability, and thus the bounds of whose accounts of persecution would be accorded historicity and whom the law could recognize as a victim of Nazi persecution.

As the editors of this volume note, the Holocaust is not only at the core of twentieth-century genocides but is also the prototype of what Alexander Hinton calls the Genocide Studies Canon. As such, it is the least hidden of the genocides in question in this volume. A series of recent studies by historians and legal theorists in Holocaust studies has asked how this has come to be the case, tracing the evolution of our collective consciousness of the Holocaust to metamorphoses in the domains of law and justice. As perpetrators were called to account in the courtroom—from the trials of the so-called major war criminals in Nuremburg in the 1940s via the Eichmann trial in 1961 on to the recent conviction of one of their many low-level collaborators, John Demjanjuk—the event in question has been transformed, as one observer notes, from the Final Solution into the Holocaust.[2]

Nor has this shift been limited to the courtroom. The efflorescence of Holocaust reparations programs since the end of the cold war testifies to a demand for redress for previously unacknowledged aspects of the Holocaust that emanates from other juridified domains. Reparations programs have centered on the exploitation of slave labor, the looting of cultural property, the refusal of insurance companies to pay on policies taken out by victims of the Nazis, or the refusal of banks to return funds to the heirs of their depositors.[3] These programs, and the longer history of post-Holocaust reparations that began in earnest in the early 1950s, are often the cited as a model in the raft of reparations claims designed to bring some measure of recognition to other atrocities in the past twenty years: claims pressed on behalf of women forced into sexual slavery by the Japanese army in World War II, of the descendents of enslaved African Americans, of the victims of apartheid in South Africa and the Armenian genocide, of survivors of human rights abuses in Latin America, or of the Herero genocide in German Southwest Africa.

The proliferation of claims for reparations in this period has led some observers to theorize them as one of the hallmarks of a post–cold war geopolitical configuration in which citizens have acquired a voice that the states that have wronged them must acknowledge and compensate. Elazar Barkan, for example, sees reparations as the "novel phenomenon . . . [of] nations [acting] morally [to] acknowledge their own gross historical injustices."[4] Theorized in a dialogic vein, reparations become a forum in which victim and perpetrator become important political actors in their negotiations over the proper form of recognition of past wrongs. In these negotiations, previously unacknowledged historical injustices are to be made known, atrocities uncovered, hidden genocides revealed. History, in these formulations, is plural, submerged, mutable, unmoored, and thus subject to political contestation; it is figured as surfeit, as excess, and reparations in turn as the means through which its antinomies reconciled. That is to say, reparations programs generally imply twinned acts of recognition: recognition of claimants' status as victims and of the historicity of the historical injustice through which they became victims.

Yet as legal domains have become a space in which victims narrate both the implementation and the effects of the Holocaust, the process of becoming unhidden has also been fraught by questions of veracity and historicity. In the context of my fieldwork in the Czech Republic, the historicity of the injustice in question in reparations programs obtained only within a particular legal matrix, one that imposed specific chronological and conceptual limits on the history in question. This legal matrix, which underpinned the reestablishment of the Czechoslovak state in the wake of Nazi occupation, lurks in contemporary Czech reparations law and emerges, I argue, when claimants' experiences of persecution exceed the temporal and territorial bounds through which postwar Czechoslovak law sought to contain, and expunge, the fascist past. Thus the possibility that reparations hold out—the revelation and acknowledgment of previously marginalized histories of the Holocaust—found its limit when it approached the legal bulwark of (Czech) sovereignty.

The issue of sovereignty was, as Lawrence Douglas points out, front and center in the initial legal response to what we now call the Holocaust. In his work on the shift in jurisprudential paradigm from the International Military Tribunal (IMT) at Nuremberg in the immediate aftermath of World War II through the Eichmann trial in 1961 to the various international tribunals set up in the wake of more recent genocides, Douglas notes that the original premise of the prosecution in Nuremburg was the violation of sovereignty.[5] The IMT proceedings, he argues, were characterized by an "aggressive war paradigm" designed to address violations of sovereignty, for which the prosecutors had copious documentation from the Nazi state itself. In this paradigm, the charge of genocide was subordinate to the charges of war crimes and crimes against humanity, themselves subordinate to violations of sovereignty, manifest in the charge of crimes against peace.[6] Though not per se hidden, what we now call the Holocaust was eclipsed in a jurisprudence struggling to encompass perpetrators of events for which it had had no prior prohibition or deterrent.[7]

The dearth of victims of Nazi genocide in the witness pool in Nuremberg, a reflection of this state of affairs, is often read as a silencing of the Holocaust.[8] As Annette Wieviorka notes, the Yiddish-speaking poet Abraham Sutzkever, the only witness to give testimony specifically on the destruction of the European Jewry at the IMT, is usually taken as the figure of the elision of victims in Nuremberg. His desire to testify in Yiddish—"I want to speak in Yiddish, any other language is out of the question," he wrote in his diary—was thwarted; no translator was made available, and he gave his account of the mass execution of the Jewish population of Vilnius in halting Russian.[9]

By contrast, the Jerusalem trial of Adolf Eichmann, the SS officer in charge of coordinating the transportation of European Jews to killing centers, featured almost one hundred former camp internees, as well as the charge of "crimes against the Jewish people." The trial was foundational in establishing a discrete narrative of events that we now call the Holocaust as well as the authority of their eyewitnesses and intended victims in recounting how these events unfolded. Wieviorka argues that the trial, which was widely broadcast on the television and radio, inaugurated an "era of the witness" characterized by an "explosion of testimony" about the Nazi genocide, and the concomitant emergence of the witness as a social figure in Western public spheres.[10] Douglas, in turn, argues that the Eichmann trial marked a shift from the aggressive war paradigm to a "jurisprudence of atrocity," focused on genocide, reliant on witness and victim testimony, and still regnant in war crimes prosecutions today. The question of sovereignty, he contends, has become "dead letter."[11]

We can discern a similar set of dynamics in reparations, which, before World War II, were enacted between nation-states. The shift to reparations for individuals, a novelty conceived of by the German-Jewish jurist Nehemiah

Robinson during the Holocaust, mirrors in the shift in war-crimes trials to a victim-centered mode of justice that eschews, at least in part, the traditional concerns of sovereignty.[12] If the atrocity paradigm represents a legal innovation, so too did Holocaust reparations. Yet the Czech case suggests that the subordination of genocide—and thus of a full accounting of victims' experiences—to the prerequisites of sovereignty endures in the subtle mechanics of reparations. In the pages that follow, I trace the issues of veracity, historicity, and the legal bounds of what can be negotiated within reparations programs back to the postwar instauration of the Czechoslovak state in the 1940s. As the Czechoslovak legal order came back into force, it simultaneously cleansed the polity it governed through the production of new categories of citizens and noncitizens. As reparations law imbricates contemporary attempts to redress the atrocities perpetrated by the Nazi state with this period, the specter of a sovereignty anchored in exclusionary logics at odds with the inclusionary redress that reparations seek disrupts, I contend, the efficacy of reparations in revealing hidden histories of genocide.

"Before the Results of the Holocaust"

In 1944, following the Slovak National Uprising in August, German troops invaded Slovakia and crushed the partisan movement that had instigated the rebellion. The Wehrmacht cut a swath through central Slovakia—a mountainous, forested region—an Einsatzgruppe unit and Slovak Hlinka Guards trailing in its wake.[13] As they advanced, partisans, Jews, and Roma scattered. They hid where they could, in the woods in huts or dugouts, foraging for food, as conditions deteriorated with the onset of winter. The invaders and their local collaborators "unleashed unprecedented terror," wrote one eyewitness: they "combed through the woods, meadows, and pastures. If they caught someone suspicious, they often shot him on the spot."[14] In these treacherous conditions, soldiers came across a Slovak Romani teenager in hiding. One of them—or perhaps more than one—raped her, and then left her where she had been found.

Sixty years later, along with thousands of others who had lived through this event, the teenager—by then an elderly woman—filed a claim for compensation in a Czech reparations program. The program offered payouts (*jednorazovky*) to Roma who had gone into hiding (as the official phraseology translates only awkwardly from Czech) "before the results of the Holocaust" (*před důsledky Holocaustu*).[15] And like most of the thousands of other claimants, the woman was turned down, failing at the first step in the program, which required qualifying as a "political prisoner" by terms laid down in 1946 by Law Number 255 on Members of the Czechoslovak Army Abroad and Other Participants in the National Struggle for Liberation.

In the case of the Romani Holocaust, which in a peculiar epistemic lacuna has become known as unknown, the possibility reparations held out—that the victims' accounts of the event might be accorded veracity, valued for their historicity—was doubly important. The unknownness of the event has been attributed over time to a putative Romani forgetting, often at the expense of an examination of the manifold ways the persecution of Roma has been obscured and elided in archival, legal, and historiographic precincts.[16] Restoring Romani voices to the narrative of the Holocaust, thus, would constitute not just an act of acknowledging the persecution of Roma but also an admission that Romani accounts of what happened had been overlooked, gone unheard, or were just ignored.

Over the course of the program, close to 6,500 Roma applied to the office at the Ministry of Defense charged with issuing 255s, as the certificates designating their bearers to be former political prisoners are commonly called. The hurdles in qualifying for a 255 were many: claims forms requested archival documentation, supporting witness testimony, calendrical exactitude on the period of hiding, a retelling of events conforming to a narrative of persecution that lurks in the lapidary terminology of Law 255. With a 255 in hand, a claimant would be entitled to the payout, which would be added to his or her social security benefits. When the process wrapped up about a year and a half later, approximately 250 of the 6,500 applicants had been deemed eligible for the program.[17] In other words, only 3 percent of the accounts entered into a register the state—which specifically sought to recognize and hear Romani claims—considered audible.

I first heard the story of the rape, the kernel of which never went beyond the sketchy details above, in 2004 in a training session for social workers tasked with assisting Romani survivors of the invasion and occupation of Slovakia who were making reparations claims. Social workers from around the country had assembled for this day-long forum at the Ministry of Defense for instruction on the first step in the program—qualifying for Ministry certification as a political prisoner. As rejections for 255s mounted, Romani field social workers (*terénní sociální pracovníci*) were brought in to assist the often illiterate survivors in filing their paperwork.

These social workers—nicknamed *tere áci*, emphasizing the importance of the *terén*, or *terrain*, in their work—ply a field that is ever more a world apart, as the intensifying ghettoization of the increasingly impoverished Romani population undermines attempts to remedy their social exclusion. Employed in a program launched by the government's Office of Romani Community Affairs to place cadres of social workers, themselves usually Romani, in municipalities around the country, the existence of Romani social workers marks a shift in postsocialist state policy toward the assimilation of Roma into what is known as the "majority society" (*majoritní společnost*).

Roma are the most visible minority in the contemporary Czech Republic and, since 1989, the most marginalized. This state of affairs has called forth a welter of governmental initiatives that seek to remedy their exclusion, from social work programs and cultural festivals to school desegregation. All of these are structured by one commonality, namely, that recognizing Romani difference might allow for plural identities to inhabit the category of Czech citizen. This turn to a politics of recognition is a marked shift away from state policy following the breakup of Czechoslovakia in the early 1990s, when many of the Roma residing in the Czech Republic found themselves in a legal limbo, deemed by the Czech state to be Slovak citizens, yet not in possession of Slovak documents necessary to establish their eligibility for Czech citizenship.[18] Today, as liberalism reconsolidates, the state holds out the promise that Roma—most of whom eventually applied for and were granted Czech citizenship—can avail themselves of the full range of rights and privileges this status implies. And this reparations program, which promised the assimilation of experiences of Romani suffering at the hands of Slovaks and Germans into a form of Czech political justice, was clearly received among the Roma with whom I worked as a gesture toward this possibility.

On paper, the program was oddly generous, given that its target demographic had been persecuted by nationals of other countries: the Czech state was extending reparations to Slovak Roma with Czech citizenship for their persecution at the hands of the Germans and Slovaks. The existence of this particular program recognized the generic status of Roma as victims of a historical injustice—they were targets of "the results of the Holocaust"—as well as their contemporary status as Czech citizens, the basis of the state's invitation to bring their stories into a relationship of reparation.

But as is typical in reparations programs, generic status as victim (or citizen) was insufficient to receive the compensation on offer. Status as a claimant required particularity, which here had to fit the definitions laid out in the Czechoslovak legal code from the immediate aftermath of the war. The 1946 law that set the parameters for claims to political prisoner status defined the category as a subject of Nazi persecution who had been "restricted in personal freedom (*omezen na osobní svobodě*) through imprisonment, internment, deportation, or otherwise for the antifascist struggle or political activity aimed directly against Nazi or fascist occupiers, their helpers, or traitors to the Czech or Slovak nation." The reasons for internment could include "political, national, racial, or religious persecution," as long as "the restriction [of personal freedom] . . . lasted at least three months," with exceptions only in the case that the person in question "suffered damage to health or the body of a serious nature or died as a result of [that] restriction [of personal freedom]."[19] If an applicant for status as a Czech political prisoner could prove his or her experiences during the period of occupation known as "unfreedom" (*nesvoboda*) fulfilled these conditions, he or she would receive a certificate known as a 255 from the Ministry of Defense.

In a gesture that replicated the awkward inclusion of Roma into the postsocialist Czech body politic, the lawyer running the training (as well as the reparations program), noted that, "A Rom, like any citizen, can fulfill the conditions of [Law 255]." Most, however, had not, and the story of the rape, or rather the story of the story's reception in this program, had come to exemplify the failures of the program. At the training session, the story of the rape was held up by the *tere áci* as evidence of the problems Roma had in "fulfilling the conditions" of the law. Its brief arc—hiding, capture, violation—was nested, as analepsis, in a longer account whose culmination prompted no dénouement. The teenager, by then an elderly woman, had recounted her rape in her 255 claim with the assistance of a social worker and submitted it to the Ministry of Defense. Ministry officials assessed it in relation to the narrative of events that lurks in Law 255—persecution, restriction, recognition—and found it did not match: the woman, by her own account, had been found. Having been found, her hiding had not lasted a full three months, and that being the case, she was ineligible for reparations.

Later I would hear the story—the arc by then was an initial interpellation as victim, the excursus of persecution, the almost inevitable refusal—from resigned social workers to buttress their explanations of the futility of making claims at all. In the training session, though, it was inflected by the mounting discontent of the people who noted that, for Roma, the embrace Law 255 offered was one that simultaneously held them at arm's length. Much of the morning had been given over to a historian's account of the broad historical sweep of the war and the persecutions that accompanied it. The recitation that followed of the intricacies of Law 255 by the Ministry lawyer who had inherited the job of administering its provisos, though, highlighted the disjuncture between the law and the history it was meant to redress. The historian had choked up as he recounted how Roma and Jews were deported to concentration camps. The lawyer, however, had what he described as an "administrative" (*úřední*) task, and the frustration level of the social workers rose in inverse proportion to his legalistic explanations of the serpentine provisions of Law 255.

"The law," declared the Ministry lawyer, "is such as it is" (*ten zákon je takový, jaký je*), and that, he pointed out, was a mandate for a set of administrative decisions regarding the categorization of citizens. What the law did not address, he noted, was suffering (*utrpení*). Nor did possession of a 255 make a person a political prisoner. "A person is not [a political prisoner] because he has an official paper, but because he fulfilled the conditions of the law," explained the lawyer. Nor did the Ministry automatically know who was (or was not) a political prisoner. It could only accord recognition (*uznání*) to those who had transformed an articulation of suffering into an act that fulfilled legal conditions. This, of course, was the failure of the woman who had detailed her rape as part of her suffering—in the act of telling that story she contravened the conditions of the law.

In the coda to the story of the claim, the social worker for the claimant refiled her paperwork, pointing out the exception in Law 255 to the three-month minimum of the restriction of personal freedom if the claimant has suffered damage to her body. Her client, the social worker argued, should qualify on the grounds of the damage to her health as a result of the rape. The response: absent documentation of the rape or of the consequent medical complications, there could be no exception.

And yet from the perspective of what can be taken a true, this is a paradoxical logic: the testimony of the claimant could not serve as documentation of a rape—simply saying that it had happened does not make it so. But this logic did not extend in reverse; the claimant's testimony of the rape could serve as documentation of the interruption of hiding, ratifying for the purposes of the law the claimant's exclusion from the category of political prisoner.

The disjuncture in this failed attempt to present the testimony of a historical injustice is law. And the self-referentiality of the lawyer's formulation of the stumbling block—"The law is such as it is"—is worth considering further, since it regulates the historicity of events that reparations are meant to bring to light. To do so, I first examine the history of Law 255 and how it came into effect as part of a larger restructuring of the Czechoslovak legal order in the mid-1940s, one fraught with an exclusionary notion of citizenship ratified in part by the categories codified in Law 255. I then turn to a series of court cases arising from reparations programs from the 1990s that challenged the 1946 law and the strictures it placed around the category of political prisoner.

Legal Order

On May 4, 1945, Czechoslovak legal order was restored by executive decree. More accurately, it was decreed on July 27, 1945, to have been restored by an announcement by the Ministry of the Interior that the August 1944 decree by the Czech government in exile regarding the future restoration of legal order was in fact in effect, starting almost three months earlier on May 4.[20] The labyrinthine and self-referential circuitry of executive decrees through which the Czechoslovak government ruled in exile in London—and then as the National Front government back on liberated Czechoslovak territory, which continued until a parliament was constituted in October of 1945—formed a body of law which acts to this day a whole, often proleptic, temporal exoskeleton for the rather chaotic end of the Nazi occupation of the Czech Lands. (Colloquially, these are known as the Beneš Decrees.) This restoration (or renewal) of legal order (*obnovení právního pořádku*) ended what is referred to in Czech law as the "period of unfreedom" (*doba nesvobody*), which began with the occupation of the Czech part of Czechoslovakia in 1939, spanned the period of during which what is today the Czech Republic was the occupied Protectorate of Bohemia and Moravia, and stretched to the Prague Uprising of May 5, 1945.

The idea of decreeing legal order anticipated and warded off the possibility of a legal chaos mirroring events on the ground, as the Nazi state, and the occupation, began to disintegrate. Allied troops were converging on the Nazi-occupied Protectorate of Bohemia and Moravia—the Americans from the West, the Red Army from the East. Death marches from concentration camps had begun crisscrossing the territory in early 1945, leaving a trail of bodies and graves in their wake and bringing the evidence of the mass death of the concentrationary universe into plain view for the Czech public.[21] Slovakia, which had been a fascist Axis-aligned state for most of the war, had been occupied by Germany since the Slovak National Uprising in August of 1944, and the Wehrmacht, along with Einsatzgruppe unit H and Slovak Hlinka Guards, had swept through central Slovakia to quell the uprising, massacring Jews, Roma, and partisans.

Legal order, in this context, brings Czechoslovak sovereignty back into its efficacy over the fragmented territory of prewar Czechoslovakia. Specifically, it brought back the liberal-democratic Czechoslovak state, establishing the continuity of the postwar and interwar states. Legal order also, it becomes clear as the decrees continue, reflects a preoccupation with a new categorical order, with the production of new, and national, taxonomies of citizens of that state. In the new order, some of those citizens—namely, German-speaking Czechoslovak citizens—were stripped of their citizenship, and with a limited exemption for those who could prove their antifascist credentials, their property was expropriated and over the course of the next few years, they were expelled from the country.[22] This process, referred to as a "transfer" (*odsun*) or "resettlement" (*vysídlení*) (a nomenclature still in dispute today), is one of the main and defining political projects of the immediate postwar. Undertaken on the premise of a collective German guilt, the expulsion (*vyhnání*) radically transformed the demographics of Czechoslovakia. Almost three million people, one third of the prewar population, were deported to U.S.- and Soviet-occupied Germany. Following on the heels of the murder in the Holocaust of the vast majority of Czech Jews and Roma, the near-complete expulsion of the German minority ensured that the Czech lands were populated almost exclusively by Czechs.

At the same time, legal order imagined another taxonomy of people who were persecuted by the Nazi state in particular ways, and who become privileged citizens through a particular and slightly obscure piece of Czechoslovak legal code that established the attributes of those whose experiences of persecution would be taken as factual accounts of the Nazi period. This 1946 law, the afore-mentioned Law Number 255, reaches through years of social security statutes and rules that grant its subjects—Czechoslovak political prisoners—a variety of privileges, from a lowered retirement age to free passes on public transportation, benefits that constituted reparations via social security, as Constantin Goschler notes in the East German context.[23]

In addition to these privileges, Law 255 also endowed former political prisoners with rights, particularly to play a part in defining *who* would form part of the polity that this legal order would govern—in essence, who would be recognized as Czechoslovak citizen and who would have that recognition revoked. As the expulsions gained momentum, former political prisoners were increasingly pulled into determining who would be exempt, who among these Germans possessed "antifascist" credentials, who would be allowed to retain Czechoslovak citizenship.[24] In other words, those designated political prisoners played a role in determining whom the law would protect, and whom it would expel: who, in Carl Schmitt's classic formulation of the location of sovereign power, would be placed in the state of exception beyond the protections of the legal order.[25] They did so by testifying at administrative tribunals and in court cases for or against their German "fellow citizens," their version of events accorded facticity thanks to their prior classification as Czechoslovak political prisoner under Law 255.

The importance of Law 255 faded from prominence over time; the expulsions came to a close in the late 1940s, and Eastern European citizens were generally excluded from the waves of reparations programs that began in earnest the 1950s in the West. But following the Velvet Revolution of 1989 and the return to liberal democracy in Czechoslovakia, attempts to extend reparations to new groups of previously marginalized citizens reinstated the importance of the category of political prisoner.

The main reparations law passed in the Czech Republic in 1994, Law Number 217 on the Provision of One-Time Financial Sums to Certain Victims of Nazi Persecution,[26] recognized the excess of history in its preamble, which stated the impossibility of fully addressing all of the past suffering it was meant to cover. This point was brought most tangibly to the fore when applicants for reparations under Law 217 found that they had to establish their eligibility via Law 255. The discrepancies between the benefits Law 217 held out, and the restrictions Law 255 imposed produced a series of court cases pursued by disaffected claimants whose status as victims of Nazism did not, as in the case I examined previously of the Romani woman who had been raped, quite fit into the parameters laid out in 1946.

In these cases, the Czech Constitutional Court found itself adjudicating a range of issues, from how to define *concentration camp* to how to interpret the intent of the Nazi regime to persecute someone, all within the confines of a question about the definition of a political prisoner. Some of the cases echoed the debates from the immediate postwar about the nature of the activity or reason for which someone was interned, and whether certain categories of offenses could qualify as antifascist struggle or anti-Nazi political activity. In one case, a woman argued before the court that she should receive reparations under Law 217 for her father's imprisonment, for which he had never received reparations because he had been arrested by the Criminal Police for black-market profiteering and deemed a "career criminal." The complainant held that the charge of profiteering against her father was a pretext for his persecution, which in reality took place because of his resistance activities. The court ruled against her claim, pointing out that the only evidence available concretely pointed to her father's arrest for overpricing fruit and butter and for dealing bicycles and cigarettes on the black market. Absent any countervailing evidence that her father had in fact been involved in resistance activities, she was deemed ineligible for reparations.[27]

In another case, a complainant requested reparations for the time she spent in hiding to elude deportation for racial reasons to a concentration camp. Her father, she stated, was Jewish and had been interned in Theresienstadt ghetto, where she was to be sent once she reached the age of three. The family with which her parents hid her could not let her out of the house, since she was subject to all the restrictions affecting Jews at the time, and could not get ration coupons for her. She could not see other children. Thus even given the care the family hiding her provided, she argued, she was "hidden in humanly completely undignified conditions." She also contracted meningitis, which she barely survived and suffers the effects of to the present. In making her claim to the Social Security Administration, she appended proof from the Council of the Prague Jewish Community that her father had been imprisoned in Theresienstadt as a Jew, as well as a copy of her request to the Ministry of Defense for a 255 certificate.

She was subsequently turned down by the Ministry for a 255 on the grounds that hiding could not be "qualitatively or quantitatively comparable" to the intent of Law 255, which understood the restriction of personal freedom to be caused by the "Nazi persecutory apparatus" through imprisonment or internment. The issue at stake with the 255, the court agreed, was whether the restriction of personal freedom was result of "fundamental intervention in personal freedom related to the exercise of the Nazi and fascist regime's despotism." The claimant countered that her hiding had been actuated by the Nazi persecutory apparatus, and that as the daughter of a Jewish victim, she too would have been interned had she not hidden. Though sympathetic to the claimant, the court denied her claim, noting that "even if it is led by the effort to temper the impact of the law on cases that are worthy cases, it cannot exceed the limits fixed by law, without the law conceding such a possibility."[28]

In the most detailed decision the court wrote on the question of the limits of the category of political prisoner, the question of the category's relation to history, and historicity—the very thing meant to be negotiable in reparations— emerges most plainly. The suit, filed by Ladislav Doležal, went to the Constitutional Court in 1999, which ruled against him. Doležal had applied to an earlier reparations program, one that compensated surviving relatives of Nazi victims. He was the son of a man who had been captured by a retreating SS unit on May 5, 1945, shortly before liberation but after the date the Czechoslovak legal order was officially restored. The elder Doležal was executed when his captors discovered his partisan identity card; his body was found later, dispersed among several mass graves. But to qualify him for reparations, Doležal's father had to fit the definition of the Czechoslovak political prisoner laid down in Law 255, and this, he did not—the persecution of the Czechoslovak political prisoner had to have occurred during the legally defined Nazi period, but the elder Doležal had been killed on the first day of the "restored legal order." The Nazi period had come to an end, and thus Doležal's father could not legally be a Czechoslovak political prisoner, nor could his son receive a payout for his father's persecution and killing.

The suit Doležal subsequently filed pitted the precepts of the postsocialist rule of law against the governmental decrees that dictated the postwar restoration of legal order. He and his lawyer argued that the time limit should be put aside on the grounds that it generated a conflict with the principles of equality (*rovnost*) and commensurability (*přiměřenost*)—akin to the notion of equal protection in the U.S. Constitution—guaranteed by the Charter of Fundamental Rights and Basic Freedoms (*Listina základních práv a svobod*) in 1991.[29] Furthermore, Doležal's suit asserted, "intrinsic historical reality" had given the legislators of the 1946 law no reason for the assignation of the dates in question. The court's decision notes that Doležal "emphasized . . . that though the so-called Third Reich was in its death throes (*prožívala svoji agonii*) in the beginning days of May 1945, that in the case of murdered victims of Nazism (*zavražděných obětí nacizmu*) in the days after May 4, 1945, up to liberation, it was not a question of the initiative of some fanatical individual (*nejáký fanatický jednotlivec*), but rather of the act of an armed component (*čin ozbrojené složky*) of the Nazi state."

In its making its decision, the court considered briefs from several interested parties. Some of the arguments emanating from administrative quarters were rather prosaic, anticipating a disruptive domino effect through the body of social-welfare law: since political prisoner status conferred particular retirement benefits, for example, the number of pensioners and the amounts of their pension would have to be recalculated. The Ministry of Defense also pointed out that it was "far from prepared" to review and revise the some 300,000 255 certificates they had already issued since 1946, in the event that a court judgment annul part of the original definition used to evaluate eligibility.

But the Ministry was equally concerned with preserving the historico-legal sanctity of Law 255, extending this concern to the intent of its legislators. It pointed out that not everyone who was a victim of Nazi occupation is entitled (*má nárok*) to certification as a Czechoslovak political prisoner, a "fact" that Law 217 "does not recall" (*nepamatuje*), and that the 255 certificate was mainly intended for those "citizens who went through Nazi concentration camps and were imprisoned on the grounds of their resistance activities, national, political, racial, or religious persecution." Opening up the temporal horizons of the law would produce new groups of people who could qualify as political prisoners, and thus for reparations, even though the original law did not have them "in mind" (*na mysli*). These were not the only problems the Ministry anticipated. The danger in contravening the original intent of the legislators was the disruption it would effect among those who had already been established as political prisoners according to law. Changing the terms of the 255 to produce newly entitled groups of persecutees, the Ministry predicted, would provoke not only "incomprehension" but also "quarrelsomeness" among living Czechoslovak political prisoners.

The court also consulted Václav Klaus, then president of the parliament and later president of the country from 2003 to 2013. Klaus argued that Doležal was ineligible for political prisoner status and staked his case on the indefeasibility of the presidential decrees. Law 255's chronological dictate derived, Klaus noted, from the period of "unfreedom" established by presidential decree for the purpose renewing the legal order. This "temporal division of dates"—which begins on the date German troops occupied Bohemia and Moravia on March 15, 1939, and ends the day before the Prague Uprising began—"is a historical fact" (*historickou skutečností*), wrote Klaus, and as such, he continues, "possesses its own logic and from this perspective is invariable (*neměnný*)."[30] In other words, the legal right to have one's experience taken as a factual, and reparable, account of history depends, in turn, on a historical fact instituted as such by its inscription in the legal order of the Czechoslovak state. Klaus's interpretation reiterated the Ministry of Defense lawyer's formulation of Law 255—"the law is such as it is"—and underscores that law is the condition of possibility of historicity.

Thus the court's argument was twofold: changing the law would disrupt both a mutually instituting relationship between law and history that obtains in the period of the "renewal of legal order" (and Czechoslovak sovereignty) in the immediate aftermath of the war, and the social and political order that arose in relation to the legal category of the political prisoner. And if this sovereignty is the limit for—and limitation of—the inclusion of others, particularly minorities, in the pool of people whose accounts of the Holocaust were taken as truthful and reparable, reparations inadvertently reinstantiate the exclusionary logic animating the exercise of postwar sovereign power, locating at the heart of liberal attempts to recognize and tolerate the presence of minorities in the contemporary Czech state. The explosion of testimony in the era of witness that has rendered the Holocaust the most known genocide of the twentieth century, in other words, has not ensured that all Holocaust testimony is heard equally. The elision with which I started—the rape of a Slovak-Romani teenager hiding in the forest by unidentified soldiers—requires us to turn our scholarly gaze, as the editors point out, to the forms of justice (victor's or otherwise) "whereby the people on the underside of power are removed from the story."

ACKNOWLEDGMENTS

I thank the participants in the United States Holocaust Museum's Summer Research Workshop, "Jews and the Law in Modern Europe: Emancipation, Destruction, Reconstruction," held at the Museum August 1–12, 2011, for sharing their expertise, which has informed my argument here. The views expressed here are mine alone and do not necessarily represent those of the United States Holocaust Memorial Museum.

NOTES

1. The fieldwork on which this article is based was made possible by a Fulbright-Hays Doctoral Dissertation Research Award.
2. Lawrence Douglas, "From IMT to Eichmann: The Emergence of a Jurisprudence of Atrocity" (lecture presented at the "The Eichmann Trial in International Perspective" conference sponsored by the United States Holocaust Memorial Museum and the Topography of Terror Foundation, Berlin, Germany, 25 May 2011).
3. See Michael Bayzler and Roger P. Alford, eds., *Holocaust Restitution: Perspectives on the Litigation and Its Legacy* (New York: New York University Press, 2006).
4. Elazar Barkan, *The Guilt of Nations: Restitution and Negotiating Historical Injustices* (Baltimore: Johns Hopkins University Press, 2001), xvi, xviii.
5. Douglas, "From IMT to Eichmann"; and Lawrence Douglas, "Demjanjuk in Munich: War Crimes Trials in Historical Perspective" (Joseph and Rebecca Meyerhoff Annual Lecture at the United States Holocaust Memorial Museum, Washington, DC, 25 October 2011).
6. Douglas, "From IMT to Eichmann."
7. See Lawrence Douglas, *The Memory of Judgment: Making Law and History in the Trials of the Holocaust* (New Haven, CT: Yale University Press, 2001), especially ch. 2, "The Idiom of Judgment."
8. For an accounting of Jewish involvement in postwar justice projects, see Laura Jockusch, "Justice at Nuremberg? Jewish Responses to Allied War Crimes Trials in Postwar Germany," *Jewish Social Studies* (forthcoming); and Gabriel Finder and Laura Jockusch,

eds., *Jewish Honor Courts: Revenge, Retribution and Reconciliation in Europe and Israel after the Holocaust* (Detroit: Wayne State University Press, forthcoming 2014).

9. Annette Wieviorka, *The Era of the Witness*, trans. Jared Stark (Ithaca, NY: Cornell University Press, 2006), 31–32; and "Abraham Sutzkever, Yiddish writer & partisan, & Polish underground members testify at Nuremberg Trial," US Army Signal Corps, Nuremberg, Germany, 02/27/1946, Story RG-60.2842, Tape 2351, U.S. Holocaust Memorial Museum Steven Spielberg Film and Video Archive, accessed 15 September 2012, http://resources.ushmm.org/film/display/detail.php?file_num=2998. I thank Laura Jockusch for bringing this footage to my attention.

10. Wieviorka, *Era of the Witness*, 140 and passim.

11. Douglas, "From IMT to Eichmann."

12. Nehemiah Robinson, *Indemnification and Reparations* (New York: Institute of Jewish Affairs, 1949). See also Ariel Colonomos and Andrea Armstrong, "German Reparations to the Jews after World War II: A Turning Point in the History of Reparations," in *The Handbook of Reparations*, ed. Pablo de Grieff (New York: Oxford University Press, 2006), 390–419.

13. Tatjana Tönsmeyer, "Die Einsatzgruppe H," in *Finis Mundi: Festschrift für Hans Lemberg zum 65. Geburtstag* (Stuttgart: Joachim Hösler u. Wolfgang Kessler, 1998), 167–188; Ján Stanislav, "Poznámky k represáliám na Slovensku koncom druhej svetovej vojny" [Notes on the reprisals in Slovakia at the end of the Second World War], in *Slovensko na konci druhej svetovej vojny (stav, východiska a perspektívy)* [Slovakia at the end of the Second World War (status, starting points, and perspectives)], ed. Valerián Bystrický and Štefan Fano (Bratislava: Historický ústav SAV, 1994), 207–220; Ján Stanislav and Stanislav Mičev, "The Anti-Jewish Reprisals in the Slovakia from September 1944 to April 1945," in *The Tragedy of Slovak Jews*, ed. Dezider Tóth (Banská Bystrica: Datei, 1992), 205–245. For firsthand accounts, see Henry Amin Herzog, . . . *And Heaven Shed No Tears* (Madison: University of Wisconsin Press, 1998), 213–248; interview with Paul Kovak, 23 March 1990, RG-50.030*0117, U.S. Holocaust Memorial Museum Oral History Archives, transcript available at http://collections.ushmm.org/artifact/image/h00/00/h0000124 .pdf. See also Bedřich Róna, *Osudy z temných časů* [Fates from dark times] (Prague: G + G, 2003), ch. 4. I thank James Mace Ward for sharing his expertise on this subject.

14. Róna, *Osudy z temných časů*, 27.

15. The term *před* [before] in Czech has both a temporal and spatial sense.

16. See, for example, Jerzy Ficowski, "The Polish Gypsies of To-day," *Journal of the Gypsy Lore Society*, 3rd ser. 29 (1950): 92–102; Isabel Fonseca, *Bury Me Standing: The Gypsies and Their Journey* (New York: Vintage, 1995), 275–276; Inga Clendinnen, *Reading the Holocaust* (New York: Canto, 1999), 8; István Pogány, *The Roma Café: Human Rights and the Plight of the Romani People* (London: Pluto, 1994). See also Michael Stewart, "Remembering without Commemoration: The Mnemonics and Politics of Holocaust Memories among European Roma," *Journal of the Royal Anthropological Institute* 10 (2004): 561–582; Alaina Lemon, *Between Two Fires* (Durham, NC: Duke University Press, 2000); Krista Hegburg and Yasar Abu Ghosh, "Guest Editors' Introduction: Roma and Gadje," *Anthropology of East Europe Review* 25 (2007): 5–11.

17. ČTK, "Prezident pobouřil Romy" [President outraged Roma], *Lidové noviny*, 16 May 2005.

18. Jiřina Šiklová and Marta Miklusaková, "Law as an Instrument of Discrimination," *East European Constitutional Review* 7 (1998), accessed 10 October 2012, http://www1.law.nyu .edu/eecr/vol7num2/special/denyingcitizenship.html.

19. Zákon č. 255 ze dne 19. prosince 1946 Sb. o příslušnících československé armády v zahraničí a o některých jiných účastnících národního boje za osvobození [Law No. 255 on Members of the Czechoslovak Army Abroad and Other Participants in the National Struggle for Liberation], in Sbírka zákonů a nařízení republiky Československé, 1946, part 107, 1677–1685, available at http://www.abscr.cz/data/pdf/normy/zakon255-1946 .pdf.

20. Vyhláška o platnosti ústavního dekretu prezidenta republiky ze dne 3. srpna 1944, č. 11 Úř. věstníku čs., o obnovení právního pořádku, and Nařízení, jímž se stanoví konec doby nesvobody pro obor předpisů o obnovení právního pořádku, in Sbírka zákonů a nařízení republiky Československé, 1945, č. 30–31, part 15, 51–54, available at http://aplikace.mvcr.cz/archiv2008/sbirka/1945/sb15-45.pdf.

21. Vladimír Třeštík, "Pochody smrti a hromadné hroby jejich obětí v Čechách" (Death marches and the mass graves of their victims in the Czech lands), in *Památná místa boje československého lidu proti fašismu* (The memorial places of the struggle of the Czechoslovak people against fascism), ed. Jaromír Hořec (Prague: Naše vojsko, 1955), 353.

22. Tomáš Staněk, *Odsun Němců z Československa 1945–1947* (The transfer of Germans from Czechoslovakia 1945–1947) (Prague: Československá akademie věd and Naše vojsko, 1991).

23. Constantin Goschler, "German Compensation to Jewish Nazi Victims," in *Lessons and Legacies VI: New Currents in Holocaust Research*, ed. Jeffry M. Diefendorf (Evanston, IL: Northwestern University Press, 2004), 388–389.

24. For Czechoslovaks identified as German, designation as "antifascist" meant exemption from the set of rules that applied to the German-speaking population. German antifascists could receive the same level of rations as Czechs, did not have to perform forced labor, could keep their citizenship, and were protected from property expropriation and ultimate expulsion. Imprisonment in the Nazi camp system was not enough to establish antifascist credentials for Germans, even initially those who were Jewish; they had to be verified by their fellow Czech inmates as having "actively participated in the struggle for [Czechoslovakia's] liberation" (*aktivně se zúčastnili boje za její osvobození*) to be deemed antifascist. Staněk, *Odsun Němců z Československa*, 140–144.

25. Carl Schmitt, *The Concept of the Political*, trans. George D. Schwab (Chicago: University of Chicago Press, 2007).

26. Zákon č. 217 ze dne 2. listopadu 1994 o poskytnutí jednorázové peněžní částky některým obětem nacistické perzekuce, in Sbírka zákonů České republiky, 1994, part 67, 2112–2113, available at http://aplikace.mvcr.cz/archiv2008/sbirka/1994/sb67-94.pdf.

27. I.ÚS 438/01, Vojen Güttler (Ústavní soud 2001), available online at http://nalus.usoud .cz, accessed 3 May 2011.

28. II.ÚS 209/2000, Vojtěch Cepl (Ústavní soud 2001), available online at http://nalus .usoud.cz, accessed 3 May 2011.

29. The full text of the Charter, enacted as part of the constitutional order (*ústavní pořádek*) of Czechoslovakia (and thus of its successor states), can be found online in Czech at http://www.psp.cz/docs/laws/listina.html, and in its official English translation at http://angl.concourt.cz/angl_verze/rights.php, accessed 24 January 2009. As it stakes its authority on the theory of natural law, the tenets of the Charter are considered inviolable by lawmaking.

30. Princip rovnosti—vyloučení některých osob z kategorie čsl. politického vězně, Pl.ÚS 10/99, Vladimír Jurka (Ústavní soud 1999), available online at http://nalus.usoud.cz, accessed 3 May 2011.

CONTRIBUTORS

DANIEL FEIERSTEIN holds a PhD in Social Sciences from the University of Buenos Aires, Argentina, where he founded and is the chair of Genocide Studies. He is also the director of the Centre for Genocide Studies at the National University of Tres de Febrero, Argentina, and researcher at CONICET (Consejo Nacional de Investigaciones Científicas y Técnicas, Argentine National Council of Scientific and Technical Research). He is the current second vice president of IAGS (International Association for Genocide Scholars) and was a consultant to the United Nations, helping to prepare Argentina's National Plan to Combat Discrimination (2004–2006) and National Human Rights Plan (2007–2008). His recent books include *Genocidio como práctica social: Entre el nazismo y la experiencia argentina* (Genocide as a social practice: Between Nazism and the experience of Argentina, 2007); *Terrorismo de estado y genocidio en América Latina* (State terrorism and genocide in Latin America, 2009); and, in collaboration with Marcia Esparza and Henry Huttenbach, *State Violence and Genocide in Latin America* (2010). He has published several articles and chapters in specialized journals in English (*Journal of Genocide Research, Journal of Genocide Studies and Prevention, Oxford Handbook on Genocide Studies, Yad Vashem Studies*, among others), Spanish, and Hebrew. His e-mail is dfeierstein@genocidescholars.org.

DONNA-LEE FRIEZE has published widely on genocide, film, and philosophy and is a Prins senior fellow at the Center for Jewish History in New York City and a visiting fellow at the Alfred Deakin Research Institute in Melbourne. Her teaching and research areas include genocide studies, film, and philosophy. She is the editor of Raphael Lemkin's autobiography, *Totally Unofficial* (2013).

KRISTA HEGBURG is a program officer and staff scholar at the Center for Advanced Holocaust Studies at the United States Holocaust Memorial Museum. She has a PhD in Anthropology from Columbia University. She has taught in the Department of Anthropology at Rutgers, the State University of New Jersey, and at the University of Lower Silesia in Wroclaw, Poland, where she was a cofounder of the International Institute for the Study of Culture and Education.

ALEXANDER LABAN HINTON is the founder and director of the Center for the Study of Genocide, Conflict Resolution, and Human Rights and a professor of anthropology at Rutgers University. He is the author of the award-winning *Why Did They Kill? Cambodia in the Shadow of Genocide* (2005) and has edited or co-edited six collections. In recognition of his work on genocide, the American Anthropological Association selected Hinton as the recipient of the 2009 Robert B. Textor and Family Prize for Excellence in Anticipatory Anthropology. He is also currently president of the International Association of Genocide Scholars and a visitor at the Institute for Advanced Study in Princeton.

DOUGLAS IRVIN-ERICKSON is a doctoral candidate in the Division of Global Affairs and a graduate student associate of the Center for the Study of Genocide, Conflict Resolution, and Human Rights at Rutgers University, Newark. He is currently completing his dissertation on the life and works of Raphael Lemkin.

ELISA VON JOEDEN-FORGEY is a visiting scholar in the Department of History at the University of Pennsylvania, where she also teaches courses on genocide, human rights, war, and imperialism. Her work on German imperial history has been published in several journals and collected volumes. Her current research on gender and genocide has appeared in the *Journal of Genocide Studies and Prevention*, *The Oxford Handbook on Genocide*, the collected volume *New Directions in Genocide Research*, and the forthcoming *Hidden Genocide: Power, Knowledge, and Memory*. She is currently completing a book on gender and the prevention of genocide, which will be published by the University of Pennsylvania Press.

ADAM JONES is an associate professor of political science at the University of British Columbia in Kelowna, Canada. He is the author of *Genocide: A Comprehensive Introduction* (2nd ed. 2011) and the author or editor of over a dozen other books, including *The Scourge of Genocide* (2013) and *Gender Inclusive: Essays on Violence, Men, and Feminist International Relations* (2009). He is also a widely published photojournalist whose work was highlighted recently in an e-book, *In Iran: Text & Photos* (2013).

THOMAS LA POINTE is a co-director of the Center for Peace, Justice and Reconciliation and an assistant professor of literature and composition at Bergen Community College. His research interests include the representation of political and ethnic violence in fictional narratives and visual art. He has served as a visiting professor at the Shanghai International Studies University, China, and as a journalist and researcher at the Institute for Central American Studies, Costa Rica.

CHRIS MATO NUNPA, PhD, is a Wahpetunwan ("Dwellers in the Leaves") Dakota from the Pezihuta Zizi Otunwe ("Yellow Medicine Community") in southwestern Minnesota. He is now retired, having served as an associate professor of Indigenous Nations and Dakota Studies at Southwest Minnesota State University, Marshall, for sixteen years. His special research interest is genocide of the indigenous peoples of the United States, in general, and genocide of the Dakota people of Minnesota, specifically. He is currently working on a book titled *A Sweet-Smelling Savour: Genocide, the Bible, and the Indigenous Peoples of the U.S.* Dr. Mato Nunpa has been invited to speak around the world about his work. Presently, he is serving as chairman of the board of directors for the educational nonprofit corporation Oceti Sakowin Omniciye ("Seven Fires Summit"), which has been working on events and conferences related to the Sesquicentennial of the Dakota-U.S. War of 1862.

A. DIRK MOSES is a professor of global and colonial history at the European University Institute, Florence, and an associate professor of history at the University of Sydney. He is the author of *German Intellectuals and the Nazi Past* (2007) and the editor of several anthologies on genocide, including *Empire, Colony, Genocide: Conquest, Occupation, and Subaltern Resistance in World History* (2008) and, with Donald Bloxham, *The Oxford Handbook of Genocide Studies* (2010). He is the senior editor of the *Journal of Genocide Research.*

WALTER RICHMOND is an assistant professor and director of the Russian Studies Program at Occidental College. His area of specialization is the history of the peoples of the Caucasus. His first book, *The Northwest Caucasus: Past, Present, Future* (2008), is the first comprehensive history of the region in English. His new book, *The Circassian Genocide* (2013), employs rare archival and other materials to paint the first complete picture of Russia's 1864 destruction of the Circassian nation and its aftermath. He has also published several articles on Stalin's ethnic cleansing of Caucasus peoples during the Second World War.

HANNIBAL TRAVIS, JD Harvard, 1999, is associate professor of law, Florida International University College of Law. He is the author of *Genocide, Ethnonationalism, and the United Nations: Exploring the Causes of Mass Killing Since 1945* (2012) and *Genocide in the Middle East: The Ottoman Empire, Iraq, and Sudan* (2010); has contributed to the edited collections *Impediments to the Prevention and Intervention of Genocide* (2012) and *Forgotten Genocides* (2011); and has published articles in such journals as *Genocide Studies and Prevention* and the *Journal of Assyrian Academic Studies.*

INDEX

Afghanistan, 110
Alexander II, emperor of Russia, 114–117
Alsace-Lorraine, 54–55
American Indians, *see* indigenous peoples
anchoring genocide, 12, 131, 141–146
annihilation, 68, 71, 74, 77–78, 111, 120, 157, 176
anti-Semitism, 22–23, 25, 27, 29
Argentina, 68–72, 78
Argentine National Courts, 78; Federal Oral Criminal Tribunal no. 1 for La Plata, 71
Armenian genocide, 1, 4–6, 11–13, 22–23, 31, 36, 46, 69, 72, 121, 142, 145, 194; constructing, 170–183; victims of, 85, 97
Assyrians, 1, 4, 11; victims of genocide, 171–183
Auschwitz, 41. *See also* concentration camps
Australia, 1, 10, 39, 44, 88–92; culture of, 83, 91; federal government, 83, 91; and the Stolen Generations, 1, 84, 87, 88, 90, 91; and U.N. Genocide Convention, 85, 86
Australian Aborigines, *see* indigenous peoples
Austro-Hungarian Empire, 25, 176
authoritarianism, *see* totalitarianism

Balkans, 73, 142, 171, 183
Bangladeshi genocide, 6
Bauman, Zygmunt, 16n19, 75, 77, 89, 90
Benjamin, Walter, 5–6
binary thinking: "barbaric (savage)/civilized," 3, 7, 9, 24–25, 39, 44; and critical genocide studies, 78, 142, 170; "good guys/bad guys," 68–69, 70, 76, 78; and hidden genocides, 72, 78; in the Rome Statute and Genocide Convention, 70–71; "us/them," 75. *See also* Christianity: Christian-Muslim conflict
Bismarck, Otto von, 53–55
Bosnia-Herzegovina, 5–6, 22, 43, 72–73, 109, 171
bounties, 97, 101, 106
Britain, *see* United Kingdom
Buddhism, 149–150, 153, 163–166
Bureau of Indian Affairs (BIA) (U.S.), 102

Burundi, 6, 130–136, 141, 143–144, 147. *See also* Great Lakes genocides
Butler, Judith, 23–24, 41

Cambodia, *see* Democratic Kampuchea (DK); People's Republic of Kampuchea
Cambodian genocide, 5–6, 30, 72–73, 149–167, 171. *See also* Khmer Rouge
Cameroon, 53, 55, 57, 59, 62
Canada, 10, 22, 27; and conquest and massacres, 24; and First Nations, 39–43; and Jewish refugees, 25; and memorials, 37, 38; and multiculturalism, 23, 37; and Nazi war criminals, 27–28; and Ukrainian genocide survivors, 34
Canadian Arab Federation, 30
Canadian Islamic Congress, 30
Canadian Museum for Human Rights, 5, 10, 21–25, 30, 33–39, 42–45
capitalism, 149
Carthaginian genocide, 6
Cheyenne, 99–100
Christianity, 14–15, 29, 56, 69, 73, 185n13; anti-Christian ideology, 11; Assyro-Chaldean Church, 177, 180; Christian-Muslim conflict, 69, 73; and colonial missionary genocide, 102; and early Turkish republic, 170, 172; East Orthodox Church, 180; and military conquest of North America, 96, 102; Nestorian Church, 177, 180; Ottoman Christian genocide, 175–181, 183; and Ottoman Empire, 121, 143, 170, 171, 175; and production of modern national identity, 75; relationship of Church and State, 32, 102, 104; Syrian Church, 178, 180; and Western juridical models based on Christian forgiveness, 166; and Young Turk Ittihadist party, 69
Circassia, 1, 9–10, 13, 109; and the Bolshevik Revolution, 119; British interests in, 119; and critical genocide studies, 121; destruction of, by Russian empire, 113–117; hidden genocide in, 110, 112–113, 119; religion of, 109
citizenship, 15, 52, 54, 58, 63, 75, 198, 200–202

213

CPSIA information can be obtained at www.ICGtesting.com
Printed in the USA
BVOW08s1023061113

335482BV00002B/4/P